DATE			

DIXIECRATS AND DEMOCRATS:
Alabama Politics
1942-1950

DIXIECRATS AND DEMOCRATS

Alabama Politics 1942-1950

WILLIAM D. BARNARD

THE UNIVERSITY OF ALABAMA PRESS
UNIVERSITY, ALABAMA

For my mother and father who, by their
example, instilled in their children a
respect for the dignity of all human
kind, and for Will, Meg, and Josh,
who are fortunate enough to be
numbered among their grandchildren.

CONTENTS

A section of photographs appears following page 58.

ACKNOWLEDGMENTS

The debts, both intellectual and personal, which any individual incurs are numerous. They are often unstated and unrealized. To have the opportunity to acknowledge those debts formally is an infrequent but welcome privilege.

I am indebted to an excellent high school teacher, Maude Thomas, who excited my interest in the history of this nation. I shall long remain grateful to O. Lawrence Burnette, then on the faculty of Birmingham-Southern College, for the example of exemplary teaching and scholarship he provided. Similarly, I am indebted to Edward E. Younger of the University of Virginia for his guidance in the research and writing of this manuscript. He is indeed a gentleman, and the patience and constant encouragement he gave me were as indispensable as his scholarly advice and counsel.

In countless ways over the years of graduate school and since, four friends, William H. Leary, Richard G. Lowe, Robert M. Saunders, and Alfred Y. Wolff, have provided encouragement and the benefit of their criticism. James P. McPherson's shrewd understanding of Alabama politics as well as his friendship have been most valuable to me. Similarly Ralph and Myra Hammond of Arab, Alabama, have seen this project grow from an idea to a completed manuscript and have been unfailing in their hospitality and assistance.

Howard F. Mahan, Chairman of the Department of History of the University of South Alabama, was a source of gentle prodding and encouragement. The faculty in history which he has assembled and of which I was privileged to be a part during the period in which this manuscript was completed were remarkable for the sustenance and support they provided. Mrs. Doris Watt of the clerical staff of the Department was generous in offering both clerical assistance and personal support.

The Research Committee of the University of South Alabama generously made available funds that permitted me, in connection with another research project as well as this one, to use the papers of Aubrey

W. Williams and of the Democratic National Committee in the Franklin D. Roosevelt Library in Hyde Park, N. Y.

The historian's debt to the librarians and archivists of this country is incalculable. I am particularly grateful to the staff of the Birmingham Public Library (especially to George Stewart), of the University of South Alabama Library, and of the Alabama State Department of Archives and History (especially to Milo Howard, Director, and to Virginia Jones of the manuscripts division).

I am indebted to John W. Bloomer, Managing Editor of *The Birmingham News,* for access to the files of photographs at the *News,* and to Charles Brooks, editorial cartoonist of *The Birmingham News,* who began his long association with the *News* in 1948 and who permitted me to include samples of his work. Senator John Sparkman, former governor James E. Folsom, and Mrs. Frank M. Dixon also graciously provided photographs for inclusion.

Finally, it is to my wife, Holly, that I must acknowledge the most profound debt. Without her aid in research, her criticism and encouragement in the writing, her diligence in the typing, and her insistence that a basically indolent husband see the work through to publication, this book would not have appeared.

Despite the magnitude of my indebtedness to others, the burden of responsibility for both fact and interpretation in the text which follows is, of course, my own.

INTRODUCTION

By the late 1930's, the New Deal was in retreat. The sense of crisis that had ensured support for New Deal measures in the early 'thirties had passed, and President Roosevelt had handed his opponents a powerful symbolic issue with his attempt to enlarge the Supreme Court in 1937. Despite his overwhelming victory in 1936, Roosevelt's efforts to purge his party of conservative spokesmen in 1938 collapsed when the homefolks, particularly in the South, rallied against "outside interference," even by so popular a President as Franklin Roosevelt. Anti-New Deal sentiment swelled throughout 1939 and 1940, and the tradition-shattering run for a third term alienated even some supporters of the New Deal. But the coming of the war, while sapping the administration's commitment to domestic reform, also stilled the strident voices of Roosevelt's most vocal critics. Faced with enemies from without, the country joined in a season of patriotic unity.

Yet, beneath the surface, despite the protestations of support for the country and for the President in a time of war, anti-New Deal sentiment ran strong in many circles. The New Deal still carried the stigma of partisan identification, and the changes it had wrought were too recent to be regarded as permanent fixtures of the economic and political life of the nation. Conservative opponents of the New Deal cherished the notion that the New Deal tide could be reversed, and they were determined that the wartime emergency would not be used as an excuse for further "regimentation" and "social experimentation." Throughout the war years, conservatives regarded the war as prolonging unnaturally the reign of Roosevelt and the New Deal. They eagerly awaited the war's end and the passing of "that man" from political power. The conservative resurgence could then begin in earnest.

In the South, the conservative arsenal was stocked with a variety of potent weapons. Sectional pride had been offended by the President's 1938 statement that the South represented "the Nation's No. 1 economic problem." The activities of Mrs. Roosevelt, especially those in behalf of Negroes, offended many Southerners, and the centralizing impact of the New Deal ran counter to the conventional Southern rhetoric of states' rights and limited government. The wartime emphasis on efficiency made the charges of extravagance and waste leveled at the relief effort of the 1930's all the more telling, while the repeal of the two-thirds rule at the Democratic convention of 1936 reminded many Southerners of the lessened role of the South in party affairs. So did the administration's sensitivity to the demands of organized labor and to the racial and ethnic blocs in the industrialized North and East. Moreover, business leadership, in the South as well as in the remainder of the nation, had never fully recovered from the psychological shock of displacement from the seats of power—a shock all the more galling when positions of leadership and power fell to labor leaders, social workers, college professors, and machine politicians.

The ingredients for a conservative counterattack on the New Deal in the South were powerful and ready. But so long as F.D.R. lived they worked to no avail. Despite the grumblings of Southern conservatives and the sporadic outbreaks of revolt in Mississippi, Texas, and Louisiana, Roosevelt swept the South in 1940 and again in 1944. But with F.D.R. gone, with the memory of the depression dulled by postwar prosperity, with the race issue inflamed, and with Harry Truman on the ballot, Roosevelt's party lost five of the states of the old Confederacy in 1948.

Even while F.D.R. lived, Southern supporters of the New Deal— Senators such as Claude Pepper of Florida and Lister Hill of Alabama— were open targets for conservative challengers who hoped to regain control of state politics from the New Deal's adherents and to put the New Deal on the defensive nationally. Such challenges to Southern supporters of the New Deal generally failed before 1948. But during and after that year of the Dixiecrat revolt, Southern liberals were increasingly vulnerable. Many failed to survive.

George B. Tindall has recently written that by 1945 the South's political leaders had retreated in domestic affairs "back within the parapets of the embattled South, where they stood fast against the incursions of social change." [1] Certainly that process was at work in Alabama. Conservative discontent with the New Deal had been building throughout the late 'thirties. In 1942 and 1943, outgoing-Governor Frank Dixon had given voice to the hostility of embittered Southern conservatives. Dixon was a leader of the conservative faction within the Democratic party in Alabama and as governor had fought the further extension of federal power. He realized that the gradual drift of power to the central government had been under way since the nation's founding, but he charged that it was the New Deal that carried the process furthest and fastest.[2]

"In the distress and confusion of the early Thirties there was created out of the ambitions of men a new engine of acceleration . . . ," Dixon wrote. "For the purpose, I think, of obtaining final political control, of striking down the local governments and of bringing home to the people of the states the thought that their allegiance must be to the Washington bureaucracy rather than to their own elected officials," the states were by-passed and New Deal programs and agencies worked directly with individuals and cities.

With the coming of the war, Dixon argued, the process of centralization and social reform, rather than abating, accelerated. "Every fanatic social reformer . . . has remained in Washington, greatly increasing his clamor, insisting that his individual crackpot reform is essential to the winning of the war." The ominous trend of wartime social experimentation was illustrated by "the tragically mistaken efforts . . . now going on, under the pretense of winning the war, to force, by yet another federal action, an organic change in the relationship between the two races in the South."

The position of Southern whites, of Southern Democrats, Dixon argued, "is anomalous in the extreme. It is their own party which is dynamiting their social structure, which is arousing bitterness and recrimination, which is attempting to force crackpot reforms on them in a time of national crisis." There were efforts under way, however, to reverse the trend. "Suggestions are rife," Dixon said, "as to the formation of a Southern Democratic party, the election of unpledged representatives to the electoral college. Ways and means are being discussed daily to break our chains. We will find some way," he vowed, "and find it regardless of the effect on national elections. . . . For the Federal Government, in Democratic hands, is now tampering with the one thing we cannot permit, will not permit, whatever the price to ourselves."

The assault upon the New Deal, linked as it was to a defense of states' rights and white supremacy, took on added dimension in the years following Dixon's speeches. In 1944, Senator Lister Hill, a loyal partisan of the New Deal who had nominated F.D.R. for a third term in 1940 and who then served as Democratic whip in the Senate, was strongly challenged in the Democratic primary. His conservative opponent, James A. Simpson, a corporate lawyer from Birmingham and a veteran state legislator, was closely tied to the business and industrial interests of the state and to the anti-New Deal faction within the Democratic party.[3]

The 1944 primary contest between Hill and Simpson was an important test of anti-New Deal sentiment in the South. Hill repulsed the conservative challenge with slightly over 55% of the vote. His opponent received over 100,000 of the 228,000 votes cast, however.[4] The closeness of the contest and the tone of the opposition's attack upon the national "bureaucracy" and upon the New Deal's spongy position on race were unmistakable signals that the progressive wing of the Democratic party could expect hard challenges in the years ahead. The use of the race issue against Hill in 1944 foreshadowed its importance in future intra-party contests, just as it echoed similar struggles in the past. The effort to roll back the New Deal, to defeat its adherents, and to reinstate conservative dominance in Alabama's political life was clearly under way.

Conservative hopes were high at war's end. The death of former-Governor Bibb Graves in 1942 had removed the most powerful single leader in the pro-New Deal faction of the party and had bouyed conservative prospects considerably. The good showing of Hill's opponent in 1944 seemed a favorable portent. Those of conservative bent undoubtedly looked forward to the gubernatorial election of 1946 with optimism. Little did anyone foresee the emergence of a new political figure in 1946, a man of liberal views who could not only parry the post-war conservative thrust but strike at the institutional basis of conservative strength as well. James E. "Big Jim" Folsom upset expectations of a conservative resurgence and lent seemingly invincible force to the liberal wing of the party.

Unlike his fellow liberals within the state party, Folsom's political roots were embedded not in the New Deal of the 1930's nor in the progressivism of the teens and twenties. Rather they lay deeper in the Populism of the 1890's and deeper still in the social and political outlook of the age of Jackson. Folsom gave political impetus to the liberal impulse in Alabama politics in the 1940's, so much so that in 1947 a writer for the *Nation* described Alabama as "the most liberal state in the South," an oasis of enlightenment wedged between reactionary Georgia and Mississippi.[5]

The liberal establishment in the state was almost as surprised at Folsom's emergence as the state's conservatives were. But, led by Lister Hill, they quickly appropriated Folsom for their own. Later in 1946, John Sparkman was elected to join Hill in the United States Senate. The liberal wing of the party seemed securely entrenched. Alabama, of all Southern states, semed most likely to avoid a postwar reaction to New Deal advances.

But that was not to be. By 1948, the strength of the conservative challenge and the potency of the race issue had shattered the liberal ascendency of 1946. Before that could be accomplished, however, the political effectiveness of James E. (Big Jim) Folsom had to be countered.

Folsom had emerged as the most powerful political figure in the state in 1946 and had turned back the conservative challenge to liberal dominance of the state's political life. He added immensely to the strength of the progressive wing of the party in the first years of his first administration—and to its problems in the years following. Any history of the intra-party strife of the late 1940's must begin with Folsom. For the story of the struggle between the conservative and liberal factions of the party in the postwar years is in no small measure the story of the sudden emergence of Folsom as the dominant political figure in the state and of the undermining of his political power by his conservative foes.

Folsom's undoing was not the work of his conservative opponents alone, however. They were aided in their task by the flawed nature of Folsom's own personality. Ironically, the very traits of character and personality that attracted the loyalty of the people he championed contributed to his political difficulties. By 1948, Folsom's political clout had severely diminished, and leadership of the Loyalists, as the progressive faction was now called, had passed to other hands. In that year of the Dixiecrat revolt, the conservative faction, the States' Righters, routed the Loyalists. The long-awaited conservative challenge had finally succeeded. The impact of these clashes between rival factions was lasting. The political cleavages forged in these years of party strife dominated Alabama politics throughout the 1950's. Their effect is still felt today.

This, then, is the story of Alabama politics in the late 1940's. It is the story of a challenge to liberal domination of the state's political life by conservatives who had been in eclipse since the advent of the New Deal. It is the story of a struggle for party control between factions whose origins are tangled in the political history of the state since its founding. It is a struggle revolving around the abiding issues of race and economics and involving the very fundamentals of democracy. It is a story, too, of a kind of persistent Populism, or perhaps more accurately, a persistent Jacksonianism in the politics of Alabama that was embodied in the personality and program of "Big Jim" Folsom.

Like most such stories, it is a tale in which symbol and myth, as well as political advantage, loom large. Race, economics, history, folklore, geography—all are bound up in the web of human experience, of which this is but an episode. It is a tale in which the echoes of past failures haunt a people's hopes for the future. The burden of its telling compels recounting the ancient and unsolved puzzles of democracy and of race. As with all such stories, so too with this one: it is less than a success story and it is not ended. Indeed, it bears within it the seeds of a larger failure which we are only now experiencing. But tragedy has pleasures of its own. And nobility and edification are not found alone in stories with happy endings. May the people of Alabama, for whom it is written, receive something of both from its telling.

1

POPULISM REVISITED:

The Emergence of Folsom

In the spring of 1946, Dr. H. Clarence Nixon sought to explain the supposedly "reactionary South." Nixon was a professor of political science at Vanderbilt University in Nashville and a sensitive chronicler of the mores and folklore of his native Piedmont, that triangle of mountainous land bounded by Birmingham, Atlanta, and Chattanooga.

Nixon wanted "to show why it is that the South seems so reactionary when actually its people are not that way." [1] His was a task repeatedly returned to by hopeful Southern liberals. In part it represented the human bent toward self-delusion, in part a realization that the region was in truth misunderstood. In great part, however, it represented a persistent desire to discover the "true" liberal past of the South in order to foster a genuine Southern liberalism in the present. Many may argue that this was an exercise in futility. But it was not without a certain nobility, and it was eloquent testimony to the truth of the adage that hope doth spring eternal in the breasts of sanguine Southern liberals. Nowhere else does it flourish so handsomely.

i   "The Southern states are honey-combed with political imbalances," Nixon argued, "with a consequent wide inequality between sections, between races and between economic groups." The effect of these inequalities, he wrote, was "to distort the picture of the real south and support the impression, as recently stated by a writer in *The New Yorker,* that this region is 'almost solidly right wing.' "

Yet only a cursory look at the "politics of the hills," Nixon contended, would show "that the South inherently is neither solid nor completely right wing. . . . I will show that conservative or reactionary elements exercise an undue and unfair share of power through inflexible patterns made long ago."

6

Thus, the triangle formed by Birmingham, Atlanta, and Chattanooga —America's Ruhr, Nixon called it—was subject to a "tenacious dominance from the lowlands, where river bottom agrarians arrived early and established priority in the exercise of power." This political inequality between regions within the states appeared most often in legislative apportionment and in the impact of a restrictive suffrage. Its effects were also apparent in party management, in the gerrymandering of Congressional districts, in tax policy and in almost every other sphere of legislation.

Nixon was chiefly concerned with his native Alabama. In Alabama, there existed "a rotten borough" system and a multitude of restrictions upon the suffrage—"an accumulative poll tax . . . , permanent registration, and educational or property tests" as well as stringent residence requirements. He sought to trace the history of this "constitutional-political arrangement," a history more familiar today through the works of V. O. Key and C. Vann Woodward.[2]

The political arrangement by which conservative interests controlled the state was made effective, Nixon maintained, "on the heels of the Populist threat to the 'Solid South.' In that threat there were gestures toward getting together by Black Belt Negroes, up-country whites and Republican politicians." But by raising the specter of Negro rule and by the judicious use of ballot fraud and intimidation, the conservative leaders turned back this challenge from agrarian insurgents. The upshot was that "white supremacy became Black Belt supremacy," and "the checks on black Republicans became checks on the republican form of government."

The state legislature had not been reapportioned since the adoption of the 1901 Constitution, despite the clear constitutional mandate that this be accomplished after each federal census. Inequities in apportionment were glaring. Jefferson County, the state's largest, had a population of 460,000 in 1940, and was afforded but one of the thirty-five state senators. By contrast, Lowndes County, in the heart of the Black Belt, had a population of 23,000—over 85% non-voting Negroes—and was also represented by one senator. The southern half of the state, according to Nixon, had "much less than half the state's people, wealth, or tax burden but a clear majority in both houses of the legislature." And this in clear violation of the state constitution.

The political impotency of the more progressive portion of the state was "old stuff" to informed Alabamians, Nixon contended. But what were the prospects for change? The nationalizing effect of wartime prosperity and continued industrialization could not be discounted. Moreover, Nixon thought he discerned on the near political horizon "a crop of social Democrats, with opportunities for new leaders to battle the old."

The Birmingham *News,* in commenting editorially on Nixon's argument, added simply, "Let us hope he is not seeing mirages." Over two decades later, one is tempted to concede that Nixon was seeing just that. Still, this hopeful man could have pointed to one very tangible and immediate representative of the new "crop of social Democrats" he hoped for. For even as Nixon wrote, James E. Folsom was embarked on a successful campaign for governor in Nixon's native Alabama. It was a turning point in the state's political development.

ii   Folsom's emergence as the most powerful political figure in Alabama in 1946 was a surprise even to the progressive New Deal faction of the Democratic party. But to the conservatives within the state party, it was a fundamental challenge to their hopes for a postwar and post-Roosevelt resurgence. For Folsom represented the most radical and serious threat to conservative power in state politics since the agrarian revolt of the 1890's. Progressive governors like Bibb Graves might offend proper notions of good government and economy, and New Deal senators like Lister Hill might support TVA and other New Deal reforms, but they had not seriously threatened the institutional basis of conservative strength—a limited electorate and a malapportioned legislature. Theirs was not so radical a challenge to the permanent sources of conservative power. Folsom's was.

Folsom, like his Populist predecessors, met repeated defeat in his efforts to liberalize the suffrage and reapportion the legislature. But Folsom shared more than a common fate with the Populists. For as V. O. Key recognized twenty years ago, the remarkable thing about Alabama politics in the late 1940's was how little had changed since the 1890's, how strikingly similar political arguments and alignments were.[3] The principals had changed, at least in name. Reuben Kolb, "Evangel" Manning, Thomas G. Jones, William C. Oates [4]—those names had faded from living memory. But both the roles and the character of the players seemed static creations, impervious to the passage of half a century.

In rough-hewn rhetoric as well as in program, Folsom echoed the cries of the Populists. A champion of the common man—more particularly, the small farmers, the laborers, the "real people"—he drew upon the social and political outlook, as he understood it, of his historical hero, Andrew Jackson.

His enemies, in his view, countered his faith in the people with the demands of property and of privilege. And they, like their historical forebears of the 'nineties, were driven in desperation to defeat the people's champion, to deny in fact the very democracy they gave rhetorical homage to. This time they did not have to stoop to the crude means of ballot fraud and outright intimidation to accomplish their aims. They were called Bourbons, but they were more than the name Bourbon implied.

For they had learned the lesson of the 1890's all too well and had enshrined in the 1901 constitution the means by which to perpetuate their power and privilege through restricting the size and composition of the electorate. They had done their work enduringly well.

iii   Folsom represents the persistence of Populism in the politics of the South. But he represents a political tradition older than the Populists as well, as old as the state itself.

Antagonism between small farmer and planter shaped the political history of the state from the time of its admission in 1819.[5] This conflict had its roots in divergent economic interests. But, as in other Southern states, it was heightened by differing sectional interests and attitudes.

Northern Alabama was the center of small farmer strength. In an era when the pattern of river commerce was all important, north Alabama was cut off from the remainder of the state, unconnected with the great complex of river systems that drain the central and southern portions of the state. Served by the Tennessee, north Alabama looked eastward to North Carolina and east Tennessee, westward along the Tennessee to St. Louis and down the Mississippi River to New Orleans. Central and south Alabama looked to the south, to Mobile.

This geographical influence on the pattern of state politics manifested itself in other ways as well. North Alabama was settled chiefly by migrants from the hills of Tennessee and North Carolina. In central and southern Alabama, migration from South Carolina, Georgia, and Virginia was more common. Each band of settlers brought with them the political and social attitudes prevalent in their home area. These divergent origins and attitudes tended to reinforce the natural geographic divisions in the state.[6]

Moreover, the character and quality of the land itself determined the kind of agriculture which came to predominate and, in turn, influenced the nature of social organization as well. Except for some areas in the western Tennessee Valley, the broken, rolling, sometimes mountainous land of north Alabama was ill-suited for the cultivation of cotton or other staple crops. The land was less fertile than in the Black Belt and less adaptable to the plantation system. As a consequence, north Alabama, like the Wiregrass area in the southeastern corner of the state,[7] was a region where farms were small and subsistence farming the chief occupation. Here slave holdings were small or nonexistent, and hostility to the great slave-owners of the Black Belt was endemic.

Planter strength centered in the fertile Black Belt, a swath of rich, black, alluvial soil stretching from the east and south of Montgomery westward, past Selma, thence northward, widening as it nears the Mississippi line. Here land holdings were large, cotton was the rule, and the concentration of Negroes was the greatest.[8]

Clashes between the two great sections of the state appeared repeatedly in the state's history. The location of the state capital, the basis for apportionment in the state legislature, national contests between Whigs and Democrats—all were issues on which sectional division appeared. Sentiment for Andrew Jackson in the 1830's and against secession in the 1860's was strongest in the north Alabama hill country. The Populists drew their support from north Alabama and the Wiregrass, though they also received aid from the nascent labor movement in the mineral district of north-central Alabama.[9]

After the defeat of the Populists and the consolidation of the one-party system, these sectional divisions continued to serve as a basis for a rough bi-factionalism between progressives and conservatives in the first four decades of the twentieth century.[10]

The power and influence of the pre-Civil War planters had been grossly disproportionate to their numbers. After the war, when industrialization wrought an economic transformation in and around Birmingham, the Black Belt remained politically potent. Now in league with conservative industrial interests in Birmingham and Mobile, the Bourbons of the Black Belt dominated state government in the last three decades of the nineteenth century.[11]

Having weathered the flare-up of agrarian revolt in the 1890's, conservative forces within the state consolidated their control over state government (whose taxing powers were increasingly curtailed) with the constitution of 1901. Both Negroes and many poorer whites were effectively disenfranchised. With the electorate increasingly weighted in their favor, the Black Belt leaders with their industrial allies dominated state government for much of the twentieth century.[12]

At times a candidate for governor would defy the conservative alliance. If the times were right and the candidate had the personal magnetism of a B. B. Comer or a Bibb Graves, he might win a state-wide race. Comer had ridden to power on the issue of railroad regulation in the progressive surge of 1906. Graves had first been elected in the mid-twenties by a coalition of groups which stood to benefit from an expansion of state services. He also had the support of the revived Ku Klux Klan.[13]

Though progressive candidates such as Comer and Graves succeeded in winning the governorship, conservatives forces remained entrenched in the state legislature. There they could not always prevent progressive measures from being enacted, but they were able to forestall any far-reaching changes that might threaten their power.[14]

This bifactional division between liberals and conservatives, underlain as it was by a persistent sectionalism, constituted the political milieu within which James E. Folsom operated and of which he was well aware. And it was within this political context that the intra-party struggles between the conservative and liberal factions of Alabama Democracy were fought in the 1940's.

iv   James E. Folsom was born in 1908, the fifth of seven children. His family lived in a small rural community known as Farmer's Academy in Coffee County, one of the Wiregrass counties in the southeastern corner of the state. The Folsoms were not wealthy, but they were solid rural middle class.[15]

When Folsom was a child of two, his family moved to town, to Elba, a thriving community of 1000.[16] There he spent his youth and early manhood. Within the confines of the town and county, the family was prominent socially and active politically. At one time or another, Jim's father served as tax assessor, deputy sheriff, and county commissioner.

Elba was the county seat of Coffee County, and the county seat was the economic, political, and social center of life in the rural South. Each Saturday farmers from throughout the county would flock to Elba to transact their business dealings and gather in small clumps under the shade trees surrounding the county courthouse. Here the weather, the crops, the latest murder or scandal were the staples of conversation. That and politics.

Young Jim Folsom was raised on a typical Southern diet of grits, greens, Sunday chicken, pork—and politics. From his father and his colleagues, young Folsom heard tales of storied contests between the political giants of the past, of Andrew Jackson and more recently of William Jennings Bryan. And he readily absorbed the whispered rumors of the political present.[17]

Politics was not something one talked about occasionally or complained about casually. It was something one *did*. It was something you were a part of. And there was a continuity about it all. Political contests of the past were not the stuff of textbook history: they were real and they were reenacted in the present, though with new and different actors.

It is not surprising, then, that politics became an abiding passion with that young boy who dogged his father's footsteps as he went about the county's business. Nor that he was to feel an identity with the political past by which he located himself politically, economically, socially, in the present.

Folsom was an indifferent student, though he did well in the courses that captured his interest—geography, history, and civics. After graduation from high school, he attended the University of Alabama for a year and then transferred to Howard College in Birmingham in hope of playing basketball. His ambition at the time, as befits the 1920's, was to become a corporate lawyer. That ambition and his college career ended abruptly, however, in March of 1929.

The Pea River, which flows through the heart of Coffee County and meanders through the town of Elba, overflowed its banks in a disastrous flood that spring. Water was head-high in parts of town, and economic losses were staggering.

The depression which hit the rest of the country in the winter of 1929 had blighted the economy of the rural South since the early twenties. But the flood was unlike the continuing decline of farm income which had plagued the area. However cruel, that decline extended over a period of years and, because it was gradual, could be adjusted to. The flood was quick and devastating. It wrought havoc not only to the economy of the area but to Folsom's hopes for a legal career as well.

Folsom left school to help reestablish his family. Except for a few courses in public speaking and political science at George Washington University in the late thirties, this was the end of his formal schooling. Because he never completed his formal education, Folsom's political opponents in later life often depicted him as a rather ignorant country bumpkin. Shrewd, yes, but without sophistication, the inner self-control and self-assuredness that come from the disciplined application of a receptive mind to formal studies.

There is some truth to the charge, and Folsom himself contributed to the creation of that image by his rustic manner and unorthodox campaign theatrics. But he grasped what his opponents sometimes did not— that politics performs functions other than the rational resolution of political questions; that it is also a means by which a people assuage their fears, articulate their aspirations, achieve rhetorical victory over their assumed enemies and triumph over all the ills that beset them.

Folsom was more than the smart fool, the shrewd manipulator of the people he purported to champion—though that is an archetype not unknown to Southern politics. Folsom's reading of history had not been deep but it had been wide and purposeful. And the history he read had a profound influence upon the nature of his political career.

The history Folsom absorbed as a youngster and as a student of A. B. Moore at the University of Alabama was an amalgam of Enlightenment attitudes, George Bancroft, the "new history" of the Progressive era, and a popular folklore that together elevated Jefferson and Jackson to the pantheon of American political heroes.

Simply told, the history of the West since the Middle Ages had been part of the ceaseless struggle between liberty and tyranny. It was the story of western man's attempt to cast off the dual tyrannies of mitre and sceptre. It was a history secular in outlook but Protestant in tone. From the vantage point of a modern and secular liberalism, it roundly condemned the cruel and repressive practices of the medieval church, the Inquisition, the persecution of dissenting sects. It was a history which chronicled the struggle of the European peoples to free themselves from the yoke of lords and nobles, dukes and kings, and which championed each milestone along the road to liberty: the Magna Carta, the Glorious Revolution, the American Revolution and the Declaration of Independence, the French Revolution and the Rights of Man.

The history of the United States held a special place of prominence in that history. The New World, like the Old, saw a renewal of the struggle between the forces of liberty and those of repression, between "the people" and the privileged, the masses and the classes. From the demise of the Dominion of the New England, through Bacon's Rebellion, the South Carolina Regulators, and the American Revolution, the story of early America had been one of struggle against the tyranny of the English monarch and the unresponsive rule of a nascent colonial aristocracy. That struggle was crowned with success—at least temporarily—by the American victory in the Revolutionary War.

In the early days of the republic, the struggle between the people and the privileged was renewed and embodied in the political struggle between Jefferson and Hamilton. Indeed, the whole of American history since the nation's birth was cast as a struggle between the historical and political heirs of these two founding fathers.

Always the cause of democracy, of an ever-widening suffrage, was opposed by the conservative followers of Hamilton, who feared the people and prized their own power and privilege. And always that cause was championed by strong men, such as Jefferson and Jackson—forceful executives who embodied the spirit of the age and who spoke the people's will.

For Folsom, this history was not something one apprehended intellectually, out of a textbook. It was something of which one was a part, to which one connected. One read such history as it was meant to be read—with a visceral identification with the cause of liberty, with "the people."

For some men the study of history is a detached delight in the discovery of a past way of life; for others it is a burdensome bore which must be endured as part of the traditional school curriculum. But for some, as for Folsom, it is an extension of the present backward, and it is alive with import for the present. One locates oneself politically, morally, in the present by reference to that past, and one recounts the epic political battles of the past with the relish and rhetoric of an actual participant. And so it is that a note of fire and of urgency still enters Folsom's voice when he recounts his version of Andy Jackson's victory over the monster bank and of how the Black Belt stole the state capital from north Alabama in the 1840's. Or that the medieval legacy of political oppression and religious persecution is recounted not in abstract terms but as something which happened to his forebears.[18] His antipathy for the British (reminiscent both of Jackson and of some Populists), his sympathy for the Irish, his disdain of monarchy, his identification with colonial peoples, his racial and religious tolerance—all stem in part from his reading of history.[19]

Within this amalgam of folklore and history, there are nuances in Folsom's rendering of it, stresses, emphases, that are important. If Jefferson and Jackson are the patron saints in the popular version of American political history, still it is revealing that some men feel more closely drawn to Jefferson than to Jackson, or the reverse. Folsom's preference is clear: Andrew Jackson.[20]

Victor over the British, champion of the common man, and scourge of "the interests," Jackson was for Folsom both hero and model. His campaign techniques, his rhetoric, his inaugural—all were reminiscent of Jackson. His eldest daughter he named Rachel, and his second son Andrew Jackson Folsom. During his lifetime he was drawn to national politicians cut from the Jacksonian mold.

The Jacksonian era was the source of much of his political and economic outlook. His disdain for civil service or for any effort to "take politics out of politics" was typically Jacksonian and alien to the high-minded reform sentiment of the "best men" in the late nineteenth and early twentieth centuries. Patronage was an integral part of the political system; it was one of the few weapons an embattled executive could use to implement the popular will and reward the politically faithful. Folsom's belief in a strong executive as guardian of the public interest, his distrust of those who would use the "false" issues of race or religion or a misplaced Southern sectionalism to stifle the "real" economic issues that transcended divisions of race and section—these all had roots in the age of Jackson.[21]

And from that era also came two secondary characters to whom Folsom was drawn: Thomas Hart Benton and Sam Houston, next to Jackson, his favorite.[22] Folsom's admiration for these men provides a key to his political orientation in his own time. They were all sons of the frontier and spokesmen for the common man. Jackson and Houston were both Southerners influential in national politics who championed the common man *and* the federal union. Jackson challenging Calhoun and the hotheads of South Carolina in the Nullification Crisis and Houston attempting to forestall the secession of Texas in 1861—the example of each molded the thought and action of the man who fought the Dixiecrats in 1948 and the Nullifiers of 1956.

v   The depression that ended Folsom's hopes for a career as a lawyer reinforced this Jacksonian amalgam of political and economic attributes. Once again the sins of speculators and of financiers were visited upon a helpless people. And once again it was to the national government that the people looked for aid and solace. The depression also affected Folsom's attitudes toward the question of race, reinforcing a native Populistic tolerance.[23]

Folsom's bountiful empathy for the little man, the downtrodden, the oppressed, the exploited, carried over to the Negro. Genuine sympathy and concern for the Negro was not absent, as it was from many hill country politicians who, like Hinton Helper before the Civil War, were disturbed more by the power of the Black Belt planters than by the plight of the Negro.

Again, Folsom's reading of history reinforced his initial inclinations. Folsom felt that race had always been used by conservative spokesmen as a smokescreen to divide black and white, to divert the attention of poor whites from their mutual economic grievances with Negroes. Race and appeals to a misplaced Southern tradition had enthralled north Alabama since secession, persuading her against her interest to continue to submit to the oligarchic rule of planters and business interests. It was an indispensable prop of the conservative oligarchy who controlled the state's affairs.

The problem facing Folsom as candidate and governor was how to enlarge the Negro electorate, so that by their suffrage they might protect their own interests and join with their natural economic allies in defeating the conservatives, without simultaneously antagonizing his own followers, among whom racial feelings could still be aroused. In the end, the task proved impossible. But he had vowed never to use the race issue and he never did, even when it might have forestalled political defeat. By so doing, the man regarded by many as a buffoon and a scoundrel retained more of his dignity than many politicians of his age. It was, however, a tragic honor.

The depression reinforced his feeling that the economic well-being of white and black were intertwined. It confirmed his view that the issue of race had been used to blind whites to their common economic interests with the Negro. And it strengthened his native resolve to forego appeals to racial or religious hatred. It also strengthened his nationalism, just as had his reading of history. When the crisis of the 1950's came, a crisis which challenged both his nationalism and his liberal outlook on race, he knew where he stood.[24]

This was a long-term influence, however. The depression had a much more immediate effect upon the young man of 20, forced to leave college and abandon hope for a career as a lawyer. By the early 1930's the Folsom family had weathered the immediate effects of the Pea River flood, and young Folsom became, like many victims of the depression, a wanderer. He joined the Merchant Marine and circled the globe twice. He lighted for a while in New York, where he worked as a tourist guide and as a theater doorman.

In 1933 Folsom returned to Alabama and went to work with the WPA in Marshall County in the northern section of the state. Two years later, when the Marshall County office of the WPA was closed and its duties shifted to the district office in Decatur, Folsom secured a position with the main offices in Washington.

Folsom's stay in Washington was short, but his interest in politics was heightened. When he returned to his native Elba in 1936, he was running for Congress. His work with the WPA in Marshall County had deepened his awareness of the plight of a people afflicted with economic catastrophe, and his work in Washington had made him aware of the advantages which accrued in the 1930's to candidates associated with programs designed to relieve economic misery.

Folsom ran for Congress against incumbent Representative Henry B. Steagall, the powerful chairman of the House Banking and Currency Committee.[25] Steagall was a patriarch of the House, a member of the official Democratic family, while Folsom embodied the strain of radical impatience apparent in the mid-thirties. Here, in the beginning of his political career, Folsom represented the challenge of the outsider, as much a challenge to the New Deal establishment as to the conservative business and industrial interests he damned.

Folsom ran as an advocate of the Townsend Plan to grant each individual over the age of sixty a pension of $200.00 per month. He also favored federal aid to education, expanded farm relief and easier rural credit, rural electrification, and pensions for the widows of deceased veterans. This brand of bread-and-butter liberalism appealed to the poor, rural constituency of Alabama's third district in 1936. But Steagall was too entrenched and too closely associated with Roosevelt and the New Deal for Folsom's appeal to make much headway. The thunder on the left in 1936 was more a warning signal to Roosevelt than a harbinger of a new radical outpouring. At least the political lightning did not strike Jim Folsom.

Steagall defeated Folsom handily, carrying every county in the district except Folsom's home county of Coffee. Nonetheless, it was a fair showing for a political novice of 27. He won over 38% of the vote against an esteemed and powerful veteran who had the backing of the immensely popular Roosevelt.[26]

Two years later, in a similar campaign, Folsom ran against Steagall again. This time, however, he had a competitor for the votes of the disaffected. In a three-man race, Folsom ran third, with only 25% of the total vote.[27]

After two political defeats, Folsom sought to make a decent living for his growing family. He had married the daughter of the probate judge in 1936 and now had two daughters of his own. He and other members of his family participated in the organization of a fire and casualty insurance company, and Folsom worked as an insurance agent, making the rounds of his rural neighbors much as he had in Marshall County when he worked for WPA.

In part because of that experience in north Alabama, Folsom was made general agent for the northern half of the state, and in 1938 he moved to Cullman, county seat of the county of Cullman, just to the east of Marshall. Cullman was the center of a fertile area of small farms. Founded late in the nineteenth century by a group of German immigrants, the area was noted for its attractive and efficient farms. Many of the German settlers had been Catholic, and Cullman remains today something of a Catholic outpost in predominantly Protestant north Alabama.[28] The German immigrants arrived in Cullman with the anti-slavery, pro-Union sentiments shared by most of their compatriots in this country. Many soon adopted the Republican politics of many of their hill-country neighbors. Here Folsom made his home. Cullman and surrounding counties became the political base from which he ran for governor in 1942.

vi   The 1942 gubernatorial primary seemed to take shape as another in a long series of contests between progressive and conservative wings of the Democratic party in Alabama. Bibb Graves, who had served two previous terms as governor, once again led the liberal wing of the party. He was conceded to be the frontrunner. Chauncey Sparks, who had run second to Frank Dixon in 1938, became the candidate of conservative interests almost by default. No one paid much attention to the late entry of Jim Folsom.

Graves first won the governorship in 1926. As with many Southern progressives in the 1920's, Graves had flirted with the revived Klan and had received its backing. But he broke with the organization when it took a violent turn in the late twenties. Graves easily made the transition to ardent New Dealer in the 1930's. Along with Hugo Black, Lister Hill, the occasionally reluctant Bankheads, and, later, John Sparkman, he had been a dominant leader in the New Deal faction of the Democratic party in Alabama.[29]

Graves' administrations had greatly expanded the role of the state government. In the effort to finance his ambitious programs, he sought to place a larger share of the tax burden upon the corporate interests of the state, particularly upon the utilities.[30] He thus bequeathed the state a kind of rough bifactionalism that cast political contests in the state largely as struggles between liberals who favored expansion of the social services of the state paid for by shifting the tax burden to the corporate interests and conservatives who promised efficiency and economy in government and an end to the political spoils system that had grown up as state programs had expanded.

Graves' administrations elicited the same conservative criticisms that were leveled at Roosevelt's New Deal. They were wasteful, extravagant, corrupt, contrary to the spirit of American self-reliance and initiative. They sapped the vitality of the American system of free enterprise and created a political machine of perpetual office-holders and hangers-on.[31]

The conservative wing of the party, led by incumbent-Governor Frank M. Dixon, long a hostile critic of the New Deal, was determined to prevent Graves' reelection. Conservatives could thus continue to lay the groundwork for a full-scale assault upon the New Deal and its adherents within the state. The problem for the conservative wing of the party was to find a candidate attractive enough to counter Graves' personal charm, his political machine, and his identification with Roosevelt and the New Deal. The logical candidate for the conservatives was Chauncey Sparks, "the Bourbon from Barbour," as the press had dubbed him. Sparks had run second in 1938, and it was an adage in Alabama politics that the runner-up in one election year won the next. Though a member of the conservative "economy bloc" in the legislature during Graves' second administration, Sparks was at base a non-ideological politician. He had ingratiated himself with the conservative faction in the state party by declining to force a run-off against Frank Dixon in 1938.[32]

Sparks believed that he was the only viable candidate for the anti-Graves faction in 1942. He thought he deserved the support of the conservative wing of the party against Graves. But Dixon and his conservative followers were dissatisfied with Sparks as their candidate. He lacked color, they said, and could not fire the popular imagination. He could not win. Some conservatives were so despondent at the poor prospects of beating Graves that they considered letting the election fall to Graves without contest. Others floated trial balloons for alternative candidates, including Chris Sherlock.[33]

Sherlock had been highway director in the Graves administration, and the announcement of his candidacy in late February, 1942, shocked the Graves forces. It was widely rumored at the time that Governor Dixon was the architect of Sherlock's announcement, presumably to see if Sherlock could elicit greater fervor from the anti-Graves faction than Sparks. Sherlock claimed he was running because Graves was near death and could not live out another term. Graves' candidacy in the face of the seriousness of his illness, Sherlock charged, cynically masked the selfish interests of his political retinue.[34]

Graves' health was of great concern to his backers. Plagued with a recurring kidney ailment, he entered Johns Hopkins in January. Despite the reassuring bulletins from Baltimore and from Florida, where Graves went to recuperate, rumors of his declining state of health were rife.[35]

Graves died in mid-March. His death caused a mad scramble in Alabama politics as politicians of all persuasions flocked to Sparks' banner.

Overnight Sparks became the odds-on favorite rather than the likely also-ran. Despite Chris Sherlock's diversionary maneuver, Sparks had consolidated his support in the conservative wing of the party, partly by taking a tough anti-labor stand. Now his campaign was bouyed by the support of a majority of the local and state officials who had earlier supported Graves. What else could the Graves men do? Sherlock was now anathema to them; Graves' death had made him appear an ingrate, an apostate. They could not support him. It was too late to enter a substitute candidate. No one took Jim Folsom's candidacy seriously. So despite the harsh words Sparks and his advocates had spoken about Graves earlier in the campaign, the majority of Graves' men among city and county politicians took the course of political realism and supported Sparks. The conservative wing of the party seemed likely to win by default.[36]

A small group of Graves' lieutenants broke ranks, however, and supported Folsom. A few weeks later the newspapers reported that "one of the mild surprises of the campaign" was the overnight strength of Folsom, "who had looked down in bucolic bewilderment when he found a group of Graves' men had decided to have a fling with him." Folsom's candidacy was being pushed, the Birmingham *News* reported, by a "comparatively small but potent group" of Graves' followers who felt they could not support Sparks or Sherlock and who hoped to force the two into a run-off to enhance their own bargaining position.[37]

vii   Folsom's campaign was unlike any other in Alabama before or since. Familiar with the techniques of other mass leaders of the South, he drew upon their innovations and adapted them to his own use. Remembering Jackson's ploy of brandishing a hickory broom and promising to sweep the rascals out, Folsom acquired a corn-shuck mop of his own. Up-country bands, the passing of the bucket, the outlandish rhetoric damning the corrupt politicians and the special interests they served —all became his stock in trade.

These have been the techniques of men both of good intention and ill. Folsom mastered them for his own purposes. But his greatest asset was himself. He was not a grand orator of the old school. He did not stir the masses with fevered phrases. He was not grandiloquent. No, it was not Folsom's oratory that captured the allegiance of the plain and simple folk who heard him. Indeed, he was the antithesis of the great orator, more akin to Will Rogers than to anyone else. He was tall—six feet eight, and when introduced he would walk to the podium with a rather ambling gait, almost a shuffle. His hulking frame encased in a dark business suit or in shirtsleeves, a dark shock of hair falling down over a broad expanse of forehead accentuating the warmth and openness of his large brown eyes and handsome features, he would speak to his listeners in long, loping sentences that resembled more the across-the-fence talk of rural neighbors than the heightened periods of a politician's speech.[38]

It was low-key, despite the inflated rhetoric and pungent phrases. Replete with anecdotes drawn from rural folklore, his performance was captivating. He was every town's overgrown boy, faintly bashful, full of mischief but easy to forgive. He exuded a sincerity of purpose and an integrity of intent that found ready adherents among those who heard him. To men he was the essence of the perfect companion—genial, a fellow to swap yarns with or to josh with with immediate ease. His appeal to women was unique. From older women he evoked maternal warmth; to younger women he was darkly handsome and surrounded by an aura of excitement.[39]

Folsom's campaign was run on a shoe-string. He lacked support from the traditional courthouse politicians who had switched to Sparks when Graves died. And he had no large financial backers. He took the only course open to him, appealing over the heads of the political establishment directly to the people, crisscrossing the state by automobile, traveling from small town to rural crossroads, back into the brush arbors and the hills.[40]

With Graves no longer living, each of the remaining candidates sought to wrap himself in the dead leader's mantle. Richard Rives, Graves' former campaign manager, spoke for much of the state's liberal faction in now supporting Sparks. Folsom and Sherlock, Rives contended, were "two self-styled liberals" and it would be "a sad day for the true liberals in Alabama if . . . either . . . should be elected." [41]

Rives' efforts to portray Chauncey Sparks as the "true liberal" in the race was unconvincing. Sherlock's campaign advertising highlighted Sparks' conservative legislative record. Sparks was "a born aginner," Sherlock said, "a reactionary bourbon from Barbour" who "fought every humanitarian program that Bibb Graves ever advanced." Sherlock pointed to himself as the genuine "New Deal" candidate. Organized labor also refused to accept Sparks' recent conversion to liberalism, particularly after his harsh criticism earlier in the campaign. The A.F.L. refused to endorse anyone, though indicating that they would have endorsed Folsom if he had a chance of winning. The C.I.O., however, switched its support from Sherlock to Folsom in mid-campaign.[42]

Folsom also sought to identify himself with Graves, to cast himself as the genuine liberal in the race. He was pleased, he said, that Alabama had turned to "a real Democrat who believes in the principles of our leadership in Washington and in the political philosophy practiced by that great humanitarian, the Hon. Bibb Graves, who has just passed on. . . . I will carry on from where he left off." [43]

Despite last-minute charges by Sherlock, a Catholic, that Sparks was guilty of religious prejudice and that he had avoided military service in World War I, Sparks won by a small majority. Predictions that he would garner sixty to seventy-five percent of the vote were wide of the mark, however. Folsom ran a surprising second, and whether or not there would be a run-off was in doubt for several days. But when the official count was released, Sparks had a margin of 6,071 votes out of the 279,000 cast. A run-off was unnecessary.[44]

With Sparks' victory, the conservative anti-New Deal wing of the Democratic party in Alabama seemingly retained control of one of the few elected posts they occupied. Sparks was to prove an independent governor, however—perhaps he remembered the reluctance of a great many conservatives to support him—and his administration disappointed some and surprised others by its progressive cast.[45]

viii   In this 1942 election, as in others in which Jim Folsom was involved, the historic sectional divisions within the state were apparent. Folsom ran strongest in a band of eleven contiguous counties stretching from the northeastern corner of the state, down the southern bank of the Tennessee, dipping into the mountainous mineral district and then on west to the Mississippi line. A second pocket of strength lay in a group of five counties in the southeastern corner of the state, the Wiregrass.[46] These were areas that historically had supported insurgent candidates. They had a tradition of dissent in state politics.

The region of Folsom's greatest weakness was the Black Belt and the Gulf Coast counties of Mobile and Baldwin. Here Folsom received less than fifteen percent of the total vote. There were a few scattered counties in which, because of local or other factors, he ran poorly. But the pattern of his weakness is clear.[47]

Folsom's rhetoric, his campaign style, his progressive program, the accident of his birth and residence had all combined to bring forth once again the historic, economic, and political divisions within the state. It was a pattern that would persist as long as Folsom was a factor in Alabama politics.

ix   Folsom campaigned in 1942, and in later years, as the champion of the little people, the outsiders, those mistrustful of all established authority but especially the authority of those in power, the "establishment," whether liberal or conservative, the wealthy, the giant corporations headquartered in the alien city. Four years later, the little people elected the "little man's big friend" governor. But for the moment, at least, 1946 could wait.

There were matters more immediate at hand—a return to Cullman, to his insurance business and to his family, a return made more mandatory by the unexpected death of his wife in 1944.

The 1942 defeat was Folsom's third in three tries. But he had made a striking showing for a candidate without a statewide reputation. As late as mid-April, the conservative magazine, *Alabama*, had reported the "virtual collapse" of his candidacy, had called it a "flash-in-the-pan," and predicted that Sparks would receive over seventy percent of the vote.[48]

Sparks, with conservative backing, had won in 1942. But it was not a clear test of the state's political sentiment. The most powerful leader of the liberal faction, Bibb Graves, had been removed from the contest by death, and factional lines had been blurred when most of Graves' supporters swung to Sparks. Folsom's candidacy and his surprising strength, nonetheless, demonstrated that, despite the lack of support from the liberal establishment or from the courthouse rings or newspapers or wealthy backers, a candidate with a good deal of personal charm and a New Dealish appeal could attract a sizable following.

Conditions had been propitious, of course, and that had aided Folsom's campaign. Despite his more immediate concerns, Folsom could look forward with some confidence to 1946. It had become customary for the runner-up in a gubernatorial primary to be elected four years later. A man ran once, it was said, to make himself known. If he did well, particularly if he ran second, he ran the next time to win. Certainly that was in Jim Folsom's mind when he conceded defeat in 1942. And certainly neither the conservative nor liberal wing of the party foresaw the impact his candidacy in 1946 would have.

2

FOLSOM TRIUMPHANT:

The Gubernatorial Election of 1946

In 1946, conservative hopes of capturing the gubernatorial chair seemed bright. For the first time in decades, the liberal-progressive wing of the party was badly fractured. The death of Bibb Graves in 1942 had left a vacuum among liberal ranks, one that his chief lieutenant and apparent heir, Lt. Governor Handy Ellis, seemed unlikely to fill.

The close race of James A. Simpson against Lister Hill in 1944 had buoyed conservative hopes for 1946. With the war over, with Roosevelt and the New Deal increasingly a memory rather than a political rallying cry, the time to reassert conservative control of the state's life, to regain the advantage that had lain with men like Graves and Hill since the early 1930's, seemed at hand.

The hopes of conservatives must have soared when they viewed the disarray that prevailed in liberal ranks. Though Handy Ellis had inherited most of Bibb Graves' organized support, the progressive wing of the party was divided and badly enfeebled. Ellis, like Graves, had been identified with the Klan in the 1920's, but he had repudiated it and labored long and hard in the liberal vineyards of the 1930's. Ellis tried to hold together Graves' coalition of oldsters, educators, organized labor, and local officials. Even outgoing-Governor Sparks lent his support to Ellis' candidacy, but Ellis was hampered by his age and by a lack of the personal magnetism that Graves had possessed.[1] His efforts to hold together the Graves coalition were also undermined by vigorous challenges to his leadership of the liberal forces. Two young and attractive men of the liberal persuasion, Gordon Persons and James E. Folsom, vied with Ellis for liberal support.

Persons was a consumer-oriented member of the state Public Service Commission, which regulates utility rates. Earlier in his career, he had been associated with the Rural Electrification Agency, and he hoped to join support from rural voters with that of urban labor.[2] He was young, attractive, with an appearance that was the epitome of rectitude—a clean-cut profile capped by a shock of prematurely-gray hair.

Persons attracted suppport from the younger and better-educated liberals in the state—men such as Neil Davis, the editor of the Lee County *Bulletin*—urbane progressives who were perhaps repelled by the shop-worn image of an Ellis or by the undisciplined rustic radicalism of a Folsom. Persons was hampered, however, by a heart condition, and mid-way through the campaign he was forced to curtail his activity.[3]

Because of his failing health, Persons was no threat to Ellis' hopes of preserving intact the old Graves coalition. Rather that threat came from Jim Folsom.

By historical precedent, Folsom should have been considered the frontrunner. The last four men to serve as governor had first been elected after running second four years earlier.[4] But Folsom's showing in 1942 was dismissed by many commentators as a one-time fluke, a sport.[5] Many still did not take seriously the ballyhoo artist from Cullman, with his rube band and unorthodox campaign theatrics.

There were those, however, who were worried about Folsom's candidacy. For the professional politician, Folsom was an unknown quantity. As one perceptive newsman put it, "the new thing in the gubernatorial race is that Folsom . . . makes all the candidates nervous." He had surprised both the commentators and the politicians in 1942, and the infectious appeal of his personality and the importance of his labor support were difficult to guage. His opponents were worried. They only hoped that Folsom would "light long enough . . . for people to look past the razzle-dazzle and see what all isn't there." [6]

They hoped, too, that he might run for Congress rather than enter the gubernatorial race, for there had been speculation that Folsom intended to run against incumbent Representative Carter Manasco, who had opposed the Truman administration's full-employment bill. Again it was said he might run for the Public Service Commission or that he was delaying his announcement for governor, perhaps permanently, because he had not received the financial support he had expected as the 1942 runner-up.[7]

Folsom ended all such speculation on January 19 when he filed for the governor's race. Two months later, the C.I.O. declared for Folsom, thus ending Gordon Persons' hope of uniting the farm and labor vote under his personal banner. Folsoms' entry brought only joy, however, to the political camp of Joe Poole, Black Belt plantation owner and candidate of the conservative business interests in the state. Another liberal candidate in the race to further split the progressive wing of the party—it was already split between Ellis and Persons—could only redound, Poole must have thought, to his advantage.[8]

i   Joe Poole had been state Commissioner of Agriculture and a conservative member of the state legislature. As in 1942 with Chauncey Sparks, the industrial interests were not wholly satisfied with Poole as their candidate. In the absence of a plausible alternative, however, they joined their traditional ally, the Farm Bureau, in support of Poole's candidacy.[9]

Poole was a colorless politician, and his conservative backers feared he could not attract popular support. Conservative discomfort with Poole mounted when he handled the issue of prohibition ineptly. Prohibition is so indelibly associated with the 1920's that it is somewhat jarring to encounter it as a political issue in 1946. It seems rather anachronistic. Most Alabama politicians knew that prohibition was no longer a live public issue—but not Poole. The failure of prohibition's last hurrah in 1946 marked with finality the passing of an era in Alabama politics.

Prohibition is not presently regarded as a "progressive" measure. But the historic reality of Progressivism is sometimes at odds with the value-laden adjective "progressive." Prohibition sentiment had been strong among the Progressive forces in the South. Prohibition was just one among the many economic, political, and social reforms that constituted that curiously polyglot movement, Progressivism. The strength of its appeal in the South may represent, as Dewey Grantham suggests, an enduring conservatism in matters moral and social, an essentially romantic willingness to be distracted from the hard, real problems of economics and class interest by quixotic crusades for some mystical goal of publicly enforced moral purity.[10]

Precisely because of the appeal of prohibition to those who supported economic reform, the cause of prohibition and other "spurious issues" had at times been championed by economic conservatives who hoped to divert reform sentiment and to smooth "over the more natural patterns of conflict . . . [by shifting public] attention from more pressing economic and social problems." The conservatism of the Southern masses on social issues could thus be used to gain support conservatives would not have garnered on economic isues.[11]

Poole and his supporters attempted such a diversionary effort in 1946. In March, a Committee for Better Government, Temperance, and Public Morals in Alabama was formed and announced its support for Poole. The committee was headed by Herbert Stockham, a leading Birmingham industrialist. Throughout the campaign, Poole charged that Ellis was supported by the liquor interests, that he was a traitor to the drys, the "pride and joy of the honky-tonk and gambling fraternity." [12]

It was soon clear, however, that Poole's strategy was not working. Poole was himself a personal dry and had promised the leaders of the prohibition forces that he would push for a statewide prohibition referendum. But he had seriously misjudged the strength of the dry forces and the relevance of the referendum issue in 1946. The capital reporter for the Birmingham *News*, Hugh Sparrow, whose career represented one continuous crusade against governmental waste and increased taxes, quickly pointed out that the state liquor monopoly was the major source of revenue for the state's general fund. With most taxes specifically earmarked for schools or roads, the general functions of state government rested primarily upon tax revenue and profits generated by the network of state-owned liquor stores. Destruction of the system would force the state to impose additional taxes to replace lost revenue. This was not a prospect that Poole's conservative supporters relished.[13]

The prohibition issue posed few problems for the other candidates. After 1933, most progressive Southern politicians, who had earlier supported the great crusade, were forced to choose between moral reform and economic liberalism. For the New Deal, which brought much that many Progressives had been striving for in the way of economic reform, also brought near-beer and eventual repeal of the eighteenth amendment.

For many dry leaders, particularly those active in politics, the choice was rather painless. Their general liberalism, combined with their desire for political success, overrode their committment to the dry cause. This had been the case with Handy Ellis and with many of his supporters. Certainly by 1946, Ellis sensed, as Poole did not, that the issue was no longer a viable one. Though Poole may have hoped for significant support among the general populace on the isue, most of the old-line progressive leaders supported Ellis.[14]

The prohibition issue, as most candidates realized, no longer occupied the public mind, and they seldom felt it necesary to debate the issue. They quietly and unobtrusively let their positions be known. But Poole had made prohibition *his* issue, and it plagued him throughout the campaign. When the difficulties involved in his position became apparent, Poole tried to straddle the issue, to back away from his earlier commitment to the drys in order to propitiate his conservative backers. "I am neither extremely dry, nor am I really wet," he remarked in an attempt to dispel the confusion. On this issue, as on others, he was increasingly vague, noncommittal. His candidacy lost momentum. Some of the rank-and-file prohibitionists became so irritated at his equivocation that they looked elsewhere for another and drier candidate. By the end of the campaign, Poole had dropped all reference to a referendum on the liquor issue, and his initially strong support from the prohibitionists began to seep away to Persons and to Elbert Boozer, a successful business executive from Anniston. Both Persons and Boozer had perfunctorily promised the drys a referendum.[15]

ii   As the campaign rhetoric heated up, the race seemed to boil down to a contest between Ellis and Poole, with Ellis comfortably in the lead. Each campaigned chiefly against the other, ignoring Folsom and the other candidates. Ellis was depicted as a traitor to the drys, among whose ranks he had once been counted. Poole cast himself as the farmers' candidate, the only true man of the soil in the race. But the wealthy plantation owner, backed by large industrial interests, was unconvincing in the role of an honest dirt farmer.[16] Those among the agricultural aristocracy, who identified with the Farm Bureau, may have been amused or flattered by Poole's efforts. But the far more numerous small farmers and tenants were drawn to the warm and folksy manner of Folsom. For him it was an advantageous contrast.

Ellis attacked Poole's tax program, charging that it was written by, or at least tailored to, the large industrial interests. He saw the invisible hand of former-Governor Frank Dixon behind these reactionary policies. In his baiting of the interests and in his attacks upon the "big mules" among Poole's backers, Ellis displayed his old progressive bent.[17]

Ellis was endorsed by most of the state's dailies and weeklies, including the Birmingham *News*. In its editorial endorsement, the *News* cited Ellis' experience in government, his "balanced progressivism," his "know-how." Ellis is "a sort of conservative liberal," the *News* argued, ". . . basically liberal in his concern for the welfare of all the people and his realization that life is change and that the good life demands growth, as well as fidelity to the unchanging truths and values." In short, Ellis was "a careful progressive." [18]

While Ellis was receiving considerable backing from the state's press, Poole continued to consolidate support from the business community. Herbert Stockham's Committee for Better Government, Temperance, and Public Morals continued its support of Poole as "the only candidate who can win against the whiskey candidate," Ellis. And in early April the former president of Associated Industries of Alabama, a conservative lobbying group supported by the larger industries of the state, announced his support for Poole. Paul Redmond, then president of one of the state's foremost textile mills, argued that "what Alabama needs is not more tax revenue and more laws, but honest handling of the state money and practical common-sense administration of existing laws." A majority of the textile operators in the state, Redmond said, supported Poole.[19]

And so it went—Ellis and Poole attacking each other and capturing the headlines. Still there were three other serious candidates in the race. Folsom went about the state chiding his opponents and lumping them all together as "the Montgomery clique," "the Sparks-Ellis Goat Hill Protective Association," "the SPARKS-ELLIS-POLITICAL MACHINE." He was generally conceded third place.[20]

In any other year both Elbert Boozer and Gordon Persons might have made a better showing than they did. Joe Poole had pre-empted Boozer's natural constituency among the business community, and Boozer's campaign was overshadowed by Poole's well-financed efforts. Nonetheless, Boozer had pockets of support in his native northeast Alabama and among many of the small businessmen of the state. As the drys became disenchanted with Poole, he also gained support from their ranks. In another election year, Boozer's reputation and ability might have made him a leading candidate. But not in 1946.[21]

Gordon Persons, the attractive young progressive from Montgomery, was hampered by his uncertain health. An untimely attack upon the mayor of Montgomery, who supported Ellis, also hindered his efforts.[22] Though in the end he ran last among the five leading candidates, he had laid the ground for a successful race for governor in 1950.

iii   It was Ellis and Poole. The pundits were certain. Folsom was running a close third, they said. Grover Hall, Jr., the editor of the Montgomery *Advertiser* and an astute observer of Alabama politics, had predicted as early as March that "Ellis and Poole will lead, and in that order. Probably they will run it off and certainly Ellis, in the absence of the unforeseen, will win it handily." Why, then, go to all the bother of having a run-off? "Why not get it over with" by giving Ellis a majority in the first primary? [23]

Ellis had succeeded, it seemed, in holding together Graves' progressive coalition. Most of the adherents of Roosevelt's New Deal supported him, including the self-confessed "ardent, unflinching and unapologetic Rooseveltian," Grover Hall, Jr.[24] Hall was amused that the *Advertiser*, which had opposed Ellis in the 1920's—the paper had dubbed him the "bellhop of the Klan"—now threw verbal nosegays to him in its columns.[25] But he, like many other young liberals in the state, including Dorothy Vredenburgh, secretary of the Democratic National Committee, now supported Ellis.[26] Who else was there? Certainly not Poole or Boozer. It was not yet time for Persons. Folsom? They did not take him or his liberalism seriously.

The race seemed to take shape as another in a long history of struggles between conservatives and progressives. Ellis had called for a "liberal and progressive" state government and charged that former-Governor Dixon was "the mastermind of the Poole reactionary forces." According to Ellis, Dixon and the leaders of the Associated Industries of Alabama acted as a "board of strategy" for Poole's campaign, operating out of the Comer building in Birmingham. The tax program they had concocted would benefit a number of large corporations, he charged, but it offered nothing for the small taxpayer, the schools, the small farmer or homeowner.[27] Poole responded with charges of extravagance that had been levied against Graves and against the New Deal. To Poole, this governor's race was once again a contest between "a businessman who will give you a sound functioning government [and] a group of politicians eager to get their snouts in the public trough." [28]

Had 1946 been a normal political year, the factional lines might have fitted the historic pattern. Poole and Ellis—just two new names in the continuing struggle between the conservative and progressive wings of the Democratic party, each vying for the gubernatorial prize. But 1946 was not a normal political year.

iv   There were several factors new to Alabama politics in 1946. Perhaps the most important were the thousands of returned G.I.'s. Exempt from the poll tax, these men had registered in large numbers and their impact was great.[29]

The soldiers who returned to their homes at the end of World War II had grown to manhood in the depression years. They had seen both the hunger of the depression and the horror of war. That was behind them now, but it had left its mark. Their political outlook had been formed in the 1930's, when Franklin Roosevelt's New Deal had reenforced the South's traditional loyalty to the Democratic party. That loyalty was traditional, but for most Alabamians Roosevelt gave it a decidedly liberal tone.

These veterans had known little of the good life in the past. They were, however, above all else, hopeful for the future. The great war had been won. They were not content to return to the dismal days of the thirties. Perhaps because their past had been so bleak and their hopes for the future were so bright, they were more tolerant of change than their elders. Indeed, they demanded it.

They were a new breed, and they found little to attract them in the tired faces and hollow promises of politicians already grown old and familiar in the distant years before the war. Handy Ellis, despite his generous program for returned veterans, had little appeal. The essence of the professional politician, he had been active in state politics since the 1920's, and both his name and his program were somewhat shopworn. Poole had been around almost as long. He offered little that was new and much that was old and discredited. He repeated the old shibboleths they had heard uttered against F.D.R. in the 1930's. They had disparaged them then and there was little reason not to do so now.

These men seldom returned to the rural areas from which they had sprung. More likely they settled in the cities, there to join their cousins who had preceded them. They rapidly melted into the urban work force, but the attitudes and values forged in their rural past did not dissipate quickly. Both their accents and their attitudes bore continuing testimony to the legacy of their rural past.

These men looked forward to a future for their children brighter than
the past they themselves had known. They demanded new faces, new
names, new approaches. The demand for change was pervasive. Veterans
spearheaded drives to alter the form and personnel of governments in
half a dozen communities in Alabama. They were in the forefront of
moves to liberalize local liquor restrictions. And it was not uncommon
for American Legion posts to be the first to condemn blatant acts of
racial intolerance.[30] Their impact on state politics was incalculable.

There was another new factor in state politics, one which was equally
difficult to guage. And that was the power of organized labor, particularly
the C.I.O. Union labor had been more important in Alabama politics
than in many Southern states. Concentrated in the industrial district
surrounding Birmingham, unions had been both an issue and a minor
power in state politics since the late 1800's. The 1930's had brought new
prestige and power. It had also brought a new aggressiveness, particularly to the strapping young giant of the labor movement, the C.I.O.

The number of votes and the number of dollars involved in a union
endorsement was unknown. Its significance was exaggerated or under-
played according to the interests of those relating the report.[31] Grover
Hall, Jr., assumed that Folsom would get the bulk of the labor vote, but
frankly admitted that no one he had "ever talked to could tell just what
Alabama's labor vote consists of . . . ." After the C.I.O. endorsed Folsom,
Hall viewed it as a "mixed blessing. In fact, you might say that the
recipients find comfort in [the endorsement] and that their opponents
likewise find comfort." The strength of the C.I.O. was particularly puz-
zling. Hall had "yet to find a politician who could speak with assurance
or detailed knowledge of C.I.O. activity." [32]

In its endorsement of Folsom, the C.I.O.-P.A.C. lauded him as "the
one candidate in the race for governor who . . . is in step with the times.
His program and convictions . . . have convinced the farmer, the small
business man and the working man that the state of Alabama needs a man
of Folsom's caliber . . . ." Jim Folsom is young, "aggressive, a man of
vision awake to the needs of the state and its citizens, knowing that the
problems of reconversion must be solved through the industrial and
agricultural development" of the state.[33] It was high praise, but not all
labor agreed. The A.F.L. endorsed no one, though a few leaders over the
state personally supported Boozer. The railway brotherhoods supported
Ellis.[34]

v   The returned veteran with his hopes and aspirations, his
desire for change, for a better life for his children, and the assertive
labor unions with their untried political muscle—these were new elements
in Alabama politics. Ellis, Poole, and others of the older generation of
Alabama politicians had been the experts, the professionals, in the old

pre-war politics. Like all experts, they were jealous of their expertise, so much so that they were blind to the changes that had occurred around them. They performed as they had always performed. It was the only role they knew. As a result, Poole seriously misjudged the wet-dry issue, and Ellis was satisfied when he won support from the leaders of the old progressive faction. These leaders were of Ellis' own generation. They understood one another. They knew how things were done. But they did not know, and Ellis did not realize, that they had lost their followers.

The old men of Alabama politics, even those of the progressive wing of the party, had failed to capture the vague and inchoate desire for change that stirred among the young men home from war. Where they failed, Jim Folsom succeeded. Campaigning against the "Montgomery clique," the "Sparks-Ellis-Poole political machine," [35] Folsom capitalized on the multiple resentments harbored by the plain folk of the state. He articulated what many felt—a vague but general hostility towards wealth and power and towards those who possessed either. His was a campaign of the amateur against the political pros, the outsider against the ins. It mattered little that Joe Poole and Handy Ellis held widely disparate political philosophies. They were both part of the same system that had failed Alabama and her people.

Folsom reminded his audience at his opening speech in Oneonta that in natural resources Alabama was one of the nation's richest states. Yet she ranked third from the bottom in per capita income. And why was this so? "Somebody has been getting our biggest ears of corn out of our crib," Folsom cried. "It means that somebody has done been in our smoke-house and gotten our biggest hams." And in true populist fashion, the villain was the East, the wealthy, the giant corporations. "It's Chicago and New York," Folsom charged.[36]

The South's economy was a colonial one, exploited by absentee owners, discriminated against in freight rates and in tariffs. But New York and Chicago were not alone in their guilt. Alabama's politicians had connived in the exploitation of their state and people. Ellis, Poole, Boozer—it made no difference to Folsom. All were part of the system that had refused to reapportion when the state constitution required it, that kept north Alabama in a form of political bondage, that kept the poor, whether white or black, locked out of the political system through restrictive registration procedures and a cumulative poll tax.

vi   Folsom's campaign was more the expression of an attitude than a program. But he had both a program and a cluster of beliefs that together constituted a rough but working political philosophy. His platform, in 1946 and in later campaigns, was always based on a set of fundamental assumptions about the nature of democratic government. Better highways, improved schools, higher teachers' pay, increased pensions for the aged—these were always integral parts of his platform. But his was a deeper commitment, one that went beyond the specifics of any particular program. It was this dimension of Folsom as a politician that was so little understood by both his friends and opponents. It is still unknown, and unappreciated, by most Alabamians today.

Folsom is first a radical democrat with a strong sense of polity. His is the simple but powerful faith that the cure for the ills of democracy is more democracy. Basically, it is a procedural faith rather than a substantive one, one that holds that if the mechanics of political democracy function correctly the result will be the best and wisest policy. It requires a kind of absolute Jacksonian faith in the efficacy, if not the infallible wisdom, of majority rule. This accounts for Folsom's insistence upon reapportionment and his call for repeal of the poll tax and for the broadening of suffrage. The procedural nature of his liberal creed is revealed in a statement he made to a *Life* reporter in 1947. "Some folks are always tryin' to label my politics," Folsom confided. "Well, I say, if you believe in democracy you just can't be typed. You can have any kind of idea—free enterprise, regulated monopoly, like the railroads, even socialism. . . . If the instruments of democracy function right you can have any kind of set up." [37]

Folsom's faith in "the people," in untrammeled democracy, was great. It was accompanied by belief in a strong executive as tribune of the people and guardian of the public interest. The mid-twentieth-century scholar is likely to distrust public figures who prate of "the people" and whose faith in extended democracy is so simple. The whole thrust of modern scholarship, and of events in the twentieth century, has made us suspicious of such claims and acutely aware that democratic procedures do not necessarily guarantee a sane, healthy, and free society. The simple assumption, so congenial to the optimistic temperament that has lain at the roots of liberalism in the western world, that democracy was a necessary and sufficient guarantor of the open society, has been sharply challenged in recent decades. This modern skepticism is perhaps well justified, but a certain sophistication about the ills of democracy is understandably more apparent in a society in which the struggle against political inequality has largely been won. That was not the case in Folsom's Alabama, and given the state of political development, his political primitivism—for such it would appear to many—is understandable.

Folsom's faith in the people, in majority rule, was not entirely unqualified, however. For it was countered by a kind of absolute commitment to the human liberties guaranteed by the Bill of Rights. There were restrictions on what the majority, through the state, could do. A man had the right to believe what he wished, and to be "a good American" did not require one to swear allegiance to any particular

economic system. But it did require fidelity to the procedural guarantees
of a free society, the Bill of Rights.[38]

vii   Folsom's campaign was more than the articulation of the
pent-up resentments of the plain folk, the outsiders, the little people. His
platform was more than a reiteration of the fundamentals of the democratic faith. A vicious man may win election by preying upon the fears
and hostilities of the masses. A simple man may win by repeating the
popular homilies and shibboleths. Folsom was neither vicious nor simple.
He offered his people a program of expanded governmental services designed to improve the quality of life in Alabama.

In advertisements that cited Folsom as the only veteran in the race,
the general planks of his program were fleshed out with specific detail.
His was "the People's Program," and he advocated free textbooks, increased salaries for teachers, and an accelerated school building program.
To the aged, he promised a $50 minimum monthly pension. To the vet-
eran he pledged every effort by the state to insure each man "a good
job at good wages" and a $5000 homestead tax exemption. For labor, he
advocated repeal of the state's right-to-work law, a department of labor
headed by a labor man, and increased workman's compensation. To the
farmer, he pledged expanded state efforts to improve farmers' markets
in the cities, to make both electricity and a telephone available to every
farm home, and to pave a vast network of farm-to-market roads. For the
small merchant, he offered to abolish the nuisance of sales tax tokens
and to lower the state privilege tax. And, under the heading "General
Welfare," he promised honest and efficient government, an effort to repeal the poll tax, construction by the state of its own roads, and state efforts to insure "full medical attention for every man, woman, and child
in Alabama." [39]

It was in many ways an outlandish program, as several commentators
were quick to point out.[40] It was, however, a program that captured
something of the hope for a better future that suffused the Alabama
electorate. It was a program that the needs of a poor state made impera-
tive but that its poverty made impossible. Logic was indeed on the side
of the opponents of this program of vastly expanded social services. But
logic does not always win elections or gratify a people's hopes. Many
who voted for Folsom undoubtedly did not expect his proposals to be
enacted. They took those promises more as an indication of what he
would like to do. And to many voters, purity of motive and honesty of
intent is more important than a realistic appraisal of limitations imposed
by political and economic reality.[41]

viii   Folsom's strong support for reapportionment won him
some adherents, particularly in north Alabama. The specific benefits

promised in his program attracted others. But his appeal was based on something more intangible than either the specific or the general planks in his platform. Other candidates in other times and in 1946 had promised much the same without evoking the loyalty and enthusiasm Folsom elicited.

He had that indefinable ability to captivate those who heard him. His rustic humor was entertaining, his personality was engaging, his hill-billy band, the "Strawberry Pickers," was lively, his antics were colorful. But his appeal transcended all of these. Somehow he managed to convey a genuine and sincere interest in the welfare of the men and women who flocked to the little towns and villages to hear him. They took pleasure in his inflated rhetoric, in his curiously jovial baiting of the interests. He embodied both their hopes and their private fears. And he evoked a devotion almost religious in character.

Folsom "excited a religious contagion," wrote Grover Hall, Jr. The voters came to the polls with "a hallelujah look and a hosanna feeling," and nothing the newspapers, the probate judge, or anyone else said or did could deter them. John Temple Graves saw Folsom's hypnotic effect upon the voters as a hex. And Irving Beiman of the Birmingham *News* observed an old man put a fifty-cent piece in Folsom's suds bucket in Fort Payne. "There was a hopeful gleam in his eye and he looked up at Folsom as though the man were preaching a gospel he could believe in." [42]

These humble people did believe in Jim Folsom, as they believed in other mass leaders before and since. Theirs was a region in which political rallies and camp meetings had traditionally been difficult to differentiate, and they were a people, white and black, drawn to the charismatic leader.

ix   Folsom campaigned as no candidate before him had. Alabama politics had been something of a closed corporation since the adoption of the 1901 constitution. Complicated registration procedures and a cumulative poll tax to be paid far in advance of election day had produced a small and restricted electorate. This bolstered the power of the conservative oligarchy and the influence of the courthouse rings. Local officials had been an integral part of Bibb Graves' coalition, and each candidate sought the support of the probate judges, county commissioners, and city officials.[43]

As in 1942, Folsom had little support from the courthouse politicians. Most supported Ellis as Graves' successor and as the candidate most likely to win. Most of the big money, on the other hand, was behind Poole, as the candidate most conservative and most likely to defeat Ellis. Folsom was forced by circumstance to circumvent the usual political channels. It was a task for which he was suited by both temperament and attitude.

Folsom went to the people. He appealed over the heads of the politicians and the leaders of established pressure groups, even the liberal ones. He, and the other candidates, attended the annual convention of the Alabama Education Association in Birmingham, despite the fact that, as Grover Hall, Jr., put it, "Handy Ellis, once a school teacher himself and a money-raising champion of education, long ago received the nod from school forces." Folsom "bluntly told the school principals that they represented a heirarchy and that he wanted to talk to the teachers," to the rank and file.[44]

Folsom did not make the customary rounds of the county courthouses. Rather, he went from town to town, from village to village, to the "brush arbors" and to "the forks of the creeks." Without benefit of an organization in the usual sense and without elaborate advance billing, he would simply turn up in town. His opponents were dumbfounded at the crowds he could draw in these little crossroad towns with such little organization and publicity.[45]

On the appointed day, a short while before Folsom was to arrive, his advance man, John Stiefelmeyer of Cullman, would show up in town and "ballyhoo." He would spread the word that Folsom was coming. Soon the cars and trucks and wagons would pour into town from the surrounding countryside, alerted by R.F.D. that Folsom was to appear. A sense of excitement and anticipation mounted as the crowd milled around the mainstreet square. Soon Folsom and the band would arrive. The band would play, Folsom would speak a few words, and the band would play again while the "sudsbucket" was passed. "You furnish the suds and I'll do the scrubbing," Folsom would shout, waving his corn-shuck mop and promising to sweep the rascals out.

Folsom was unlike most of the mass leaders common to Southern politics. His speeches did not raise his listeners to a fever pitch of emotion. Rather, he entertained, he cajoled. He was more "an accomplished clown" [46] than a vicious demagogue. Grover Hall, Jr., covered his opening speech in Oneonta in March of 1946 and found that "it was not the show we expected. It was, in fact, flat, nasal, and devoid of pageantry." Folsom reiterated the points of his program. He favored a pension for all over sixty-five, especially for rural people who were not covered by social security. He pledged retention of the merit system for technical or clerical employees but felt that the governor should have the power to fill all policy-making positions. He would abolish the sales tax tokens, and he favored a more liberal workmen's compensation law. Hall thought the crowd of farmers and small-town folk "unresponsive." "The Folsom show had no pace and the lines were neither bright nor sharp. I was unable to see," he wrote "that Folsom awakened much enthusiasm, save when he talked about the demonstrable wonders of a corn shuck scouring broom or spoke bitterly of John Barleycorn." [47]

Hall was unimpressed. He was unaccustomed to judging the reactions of an undemonstrative rural folk, however, and admitted that "the keenest politician" in the county thought he was mistaken in judging the crowd unresponsive. "It was just not in the nature of Blount citizens to show enthusiasm." That politician was the editor of the local paper. He favored Boozer but flatly predicted that Folsom would carry the county.[48] And Folsom did, with almost 50% of the vote in the first primary and over 75% in the run-off.

Hall continued to cover Folsom's campaign, following him into south Alabama in late March to see if he had changed the style or substance of his remarks, "to see if his act had improved and [to] learn what he was hammering on in his speeches." And what did he find? "That it's hard to judge [Folsom's] progress because he does not bother with organization, that his act is much the same as it was in his opening a month ago and that his speech is preçisely the same." Even in south Alabama Folsom repeated his charge that "for two generations your political and economic life has been dominated by a small clique in Montgomery." There was one difference in his remarks, however. He took time to explain that he called his scrub tool a mop in south Alabama " 'cause that's what they call it here, rather than a broom, as it's called in north Alabama." [49]

Near the end of April, Folsom invaded the capital city itself, and Hall was there once again to judge Folsom's progress. "The Big Boy . . . ," he reported, "was in good form. The timing on his gag lines was good. His gestures and inflections have married and live in happy harmony. He was booming, good-natured and apparently confident." Folsom "delighted the crowd. They laughed and clapped, and sometimes it seemed that he would next have them gurgling." Even members of the opposition, who had come out of curiosity, were beguiled. "One Ellis manager was seen to bang his knee and punch the lady next. In the loge two Persons workers . . . roared and [then] grimaced in this direction." [50]

The chief issue of the moment, Folsom told the crowd in the Montgomery auditorium, was which of his opponents had "done the most robbing of the state treasury." He criticized foreign aid and resurrected the old Populist suspicion of the English: "England is trying to borrow four billion dollars that she won't pay back, that she'll squander." And he criticized the current merit system as inadequate. He proclaimed that he was "publicly against that [Boswell] amendment," designed to prevent registration of large numbers of voting-aged Negroes. And he discoursed on the poor quality of goods available through the state liquor stores.

There was applause. A man in the balcony made weak attempts to heckle, but Folsom ignored the content of the remarks and simply nodded, "That's right, that's right." The heckler subsided, and "two of Big Jim's factotums began passing the suds bucket down the aisles just as a church platter is passed. And as in church, there was a shifting and an apprehensive wave of sidelong glances to note the intentions of the person next. It was something new for Montgomery to pay candidates to ask them to vote for them."

"Play it boys!" the candidate shouted. " 'Up Yonder in the Governor's Chair'! Just listen at 'em go!" Hall's discomfort mounted. "The great minstrel's bucket got to my row. It was half full of lettuce and I was sitting in the middle. I felt people looking at the back of my neck." He fumbled through his pockets and fished out a fifty-cent piece. As he dropped the coin into the bucket, he wondered what the office was going to say when he entered this item on his expense account. And he knew he was going to hate himself when morning came.

x   As the first primary drew nearer, the major papers in the state began to devote more space to the Folsom campaign. He was gaining ground, though most commentators felt he was still running third behind Ellis and Poole. Few yet believed that the candidates of the two historic factions within the Democratic party would not run first and second.

But Folsom's appeal spilled out of the traditionally divided mold that was the Democratic party in Alabama. His was a campaign difficult to counter, for Folsom embodied more an attitude than a reasoned program of specific measures. Editorially, the Birmingham *News* might remind its readers, with veiled reference to Folsom, that good intentions often lead only to tragic failure when unaccompanied by experience and expertise.[51] But such obscure references were not enough to undercut Folsom's magnetic appeal. Neither Handy Ellis and the leaders of the old progressive coalition nor Joe Poole and his conservative backers had found a way to break Folsom's growing hold on the public imagination.

The voters went to the polls on May 7. What they wrought stunned Alabama's politicians and political pundits. Just as in 1942 when on the eve of the election Chauncey Sparks privately told his closest advisers that Folsom would take only 20,000 votes[52]—he drew 75,000 and second place—Folsom once again surprised his opponents. Despite Folsom's growing strength, Ellis' closest lieutenants thought Ellis would lead but be forced into a run-off with Poole. On election eve Ellis himself had confidently remarked to friends that the run-off would be between himself and Poole.[53]

Folsom not only made the run-off, he ran first. With 104,000 votes of

366,000 cast, he ran over 15,000 votes ahead of Ellis. Poole was third with 70,000 and Boozer and Persons trailed fourth and fifth respectively.[54]

The prospects of a run-off against Folsom must have bewildered the Ellis camp. Poole had been the expected opponent, and had he made the run-off there would have ensued the typical progressive-conservative battle that had characterized Alabama politics for decades. Ellis knew how to deal with that, but now he had unexpectedly run second. And he had a new and unmanageable foe.

xi   Folsom's unexpected showing turned Alabama politics topsy-turvy. Folsom had not only stymied the long-expected conservative resurgence, he had run ahead of the leader of the old New Deal coalition as well. Former-Governor Dixon, the leader of the conservative forces in the state, recognized the threat that Folsom represented. Ellis could be expected to operate in the old progressive tradition of expanded state services and increased expenditures. But he would have to make his compromises with the conservative forces that controlled the legislature. Ellis was a known quantity. Folsom was not—and that is what frightened conservatives like Dixon. What if Folsom overwhelmed the legislature? What if he were successful in having the state constitution revised? The constitutional restrictions on the taxing powers of local and state governments might be rescinded, reapportionment might be accomplished, and the restrictions on the suffrage loosened.[55]

Dixon was dejected. He had supported Poole, and Poole had run third. To a friend and fellow conservative, Horace Hall, editor of the Dothan *Eagle*, Dixon wrote bitterly, "If the people of Alabama want that kind of government, they are of course entitled to it." And to a Black Belt lawyer, he confided that "under the circumstances there isn't anything anyone who loves his state as I do can do except to support Ellis." [56]

It was an uneasy alliance, this movement of Poole's conservative industrial backers to Ellis' standard. Ellis himself was uncomfortable at the unaccustomed closeness to his traditional foes.[57] Still, Ellis must have derived a saccharine satisfaction from the support of men who had opposed him throughout his political career.

There was little else to comfort Ellis. Folsom had the momentum now. Not since 1914 had a candidate who led in the first primary failed to win in the run-off. Nonetheless, there were those who thought victory was salvageable for Ellis. John Temple Graves thought Ellis would be the natural beneficiary of votes that had gone to other candidates, that he was "heir apparent to most of the votes cast for Poole, Persons, and Boozer . . . ." And, Graves added, "Alabama is fortunate that it is so." [58]

Not all the movement was to Ellis, however. Graves' analysis of Ellis' prospects did appear logical, but it overlooked the great psychological advantage that now lay with Folsom. He had run first. Overnight he had been transformed by a kind of electoral magic from a colorful, humorous, and harmless also-ran into the likely victor. Perhaps the clearest indication that Graves' argument was as much wistful thinking as hard analysis was the announcement of support for Folsom by Richard Rives of Montgomery. Rives, who had supported Gordon Persons in the first primary, had been a long-time supporter of the late Bibb Graves and was a close political associate of Senator Lister Hill. Rives' business was politics, and he had a sharper perception of the shifting political winds than did John Temple Graves.[59]

Folsom surprised many when he received the support of two of his opponents. Both Joe Poole and Elbert Boozer endorsed him. Poole's conservative backers, like Frank Dixon, generally lent their support to Ellis. But Poole, like Boozer and Rives, had a more accurate reading of public sentiment and as a practical politician sought to place himself on the winning side while extracting as many concessions as possible for his support. Folsom agreed to sanction the election of Poole's campaign manager, the conservative and able Bruce Henderson of Wilcox County in the Black Belt, as president pro tem of the Senate. Folsom also agreed to appoint both Boozer and Poole to a five-man unofficial committee to advise him on policy and patronage.[60]

That Boozer and Poole came to Folsom was an indication of the desperate straits Handy Ellis' campaign was in. On the face of it, it seemed logical, as John Temple Graves argued, that Ellis would inherit all of Poole's support, much of Boozer's, and much of Persons'. But it was Folsom who had the momentum, the color, the dash. And Handy Ellis knew it.

The old progressive found himself in an unaccustomed position. His traditional role was reversed, for now *he* appeared the more conservative of the two candidates. He was desperate for an issue to counter Folsom's personal appeal. The editorial writers of the state might coolly analyze Folsom's showing and reiterate their support for Ellis' "balanced progressivism"; they might retain a measure of objectivity and calm, but Handy Ellis' political career was at stake.

Ellis felt, and with some justification, that the governorship was by right his. To have it snatched from him when he was so close to the culmination of a long career was intolerable. And to be felled by a political upstart of outlandish proportions and program added naught but cruelty to the farce. It was enough to goad almost any man, especially any political being, to extreme measures. Handy Ellis needed an issue. He found one and he proceeded to wage a campaign that bordered on the irresponsible. He called upon the darker passions in the body politic, foreshadowing the political hysteria of the late 1940's and early 1950's.

To the dismay of some of his backers, Ellis seized upon the C.I.O.'s endorsement of Folsom as his bugbear. And he preyed upon provincial distrust of the alien, the outsider. Increasingly, too, he made explicit reference to the race issue, stooping to use the one issue that had been used so often and so recently against his fellow candidates of progressive bent.[61]

Within a week of the first primary, Ellis was proclaiming throughout the state that the foremost issue in the campaign was "the people of Alabama versus the C.I.O." The C.I.O.–P.A.C. program was a threat to the well-being of labor, agriculture, and the general public, he charged. And it would "disrupt our fine and wholesome race relations by breaking down our segregation laws." [62] To his credit, Ellis did not wage the gallus-strapping "nigger-hating" campaign still prevalent in Mississippi and Georgia. But as he grew more desperate, his remarks moved increasingly in that direction.

The people had had their "small fun" in the first primary, Ellis said, and now was the time to face their duty seriously. "The time has passed for clowning and hippodroming and putting on a medicine show," he said.[63] He tried to talk about the issues, about his qualifications, but the direction of his campaign was set. His ire was up, his political career was in the balance, and he was scared. He took the road of a man frightened and attacked without quarter and without reason.

Ellis pledged to protect Alabama's institutions and traditions from being victimized by "a ruthless, radical outside political machine bent on exploitation and domination of our state government." To "Keep Alabama for Alabamians" became his keynote. He did not mean to impugn all of labor, he assured his audience, just the C.I.O., and he quoted the president of the A.F.L. as authority for the C.I.O.'s being "saturated with communism." No, his was no anti-labor fight, Ellis contended. Rather, "this is a fight against a group from outside our state who seeks to dominate our social and economic affairs in the exclusive interest of its own selfish aims." [64]

Ellis sought to heighten the normal human fear of the outsider that sometimes seems so exaggerated among Southern and rural folk. And he sent forth a call for unity in the face of the alien foe.[65] To "all citizens of Alabama who cherish the traditions of our state and the heritage of our fathers," he issued a challenge "to stand together in this battle to preserve those things we hold dear." [68]

Ellis called upon the voters to "turn back the most serious threat that has faced us since reconstruction." If the danger of domination by the C.I.O. seemed remote and unreal, he sought to personify the evil, to name for the people's enlightenment the particular man who was masterminding this diabolical plot. "The principle involved in this campaign," he asserted, "is whether a political agitator and rabble rouser, a man who was born and reared in Russia, can fasten his greedy clutches on the free Americans in the State of Alabama, slap a ring in their noses and tell them what they must do in a local Democratic primary." Sidney Hillman of the C.I.O. made a convenient target as the alien, the unknown, the feared. In references to this "alien doctrine," to "the radical hotbed in New York, where Hillman maintains his headquarters," and to Hillman as "head of the Communist leftwing C.I.O.," Ellis decried the threat from the "outside." [67]

And what was the specific nature of the threat from the C.I.O.? At first it was simply a vague and generalized fear of the foreign, the unknown. Increasingly, however, it took specific form as a threat to white supremacy. Ellis was forced to resort to the old stand-by for Southern politicians who think they cannot win on other issues, the inflammatory issue of race.

The C.I.O. program posed a threat to "our segregation laws," he said. What if Sidney Hillman should influence the appointment of voting registrars? "What then," Ellis asked rhetorically, "what then would become of our Alabama voting laws and regulations? I'll tell you. They would vanish like tissue paper in a bonfire." This was "a new group of modern carpetbaggers" descending upon a helpless state, and Ellis warned his audience to be wary of the man with the scouring mop and promises to sweep the capitol clean. "Our capitol has been swept out once before," he said, "by the carpetbaggers, and we are still feeling the effect of that mop-up." [68]

As election day neared, the charges became more graphic. The C.I.O.–P.A.C. was "hatching a dark and ugly plot against our institutions, our cherished traditions, our free Democratic institutions. . . ." The C.I.O. program, and by implication the election of Jim Folsom, would mean "the complete destruction of our segregation laws—laws which are best for the white man and the colored man—laws under which our white folks and colored folks here in Alabama and the South have lived in peace and harmony and friendly understanding." It would mean repeal of the poll tax and the weakening of voter qualifications. It meant the end of "the Southern way of life." [69]

xii   Ellis' tactics upset some of his followers. Grover Hall, Jr., wrote that he "never did like the C.I.O. issue . . . ." Hall could not understand "how anybody who had been a Roosevelt-lover and a Hill supporter [as Ellis had] could very well rebel at Folsom's candidacy on the grounds of C.I.O. support." He could not see "that there is a difference between the C.I.O. entering Alabama politics and the Big Mule corporations . . . [who] advised Ellis that they had spent so much money on Poole in the primary that they would be 18 months writing the expenditures off on their books. Both groups spent their money to further their own causes." That was "either fish and fish or fowl and fowl," as Hall saw it. Hall also objected to "Ellis' partisans' harping on the fact that Sidney Hillman was 'foreign born.' So what?" he asked. "Of what do they think this country is composed? Do they think America's population is largely . . . descended from the English?" [70]

There were others among Ellis' supporters who were equally dismayed at his emotion-laden attacks upon the C.I.O. The Birmingham *News* looked forward to a Folsom administration with "deep trepidation" but it did not approve of Ellis' emphasis upon Folsom's C.I.O. backing. Ellis, who had earlier sought labor's support, could have accepted that support, the *News* maintained, without fear of domination by the C.I.O. So could Folsom. Neil Davis, editor of the Lee County *Bulletin,* "a thorough progressive . . . [and] discerning liberal," had first supported Persons and now supported Ellis. But he, too, was disappointed in Ellis' attacks upon the C.I.O.[71]

Ellis was not the only one whose emotions got the better of him, however. John Temple Graves, the usually urbane and sensitive syndicated columnist from Birmingham, became increasingly shrill as election day approached.

Graves had been, like Hall, an ardent Rooseveltian. He was a man of progressive and enlightened views. But by 1946 he had already begun the rightward movement that was to end in sullen resentment before his death in 1961. Still, unlike many of similar bent, he was unwilling to repudiate his past loyalties. "Bitter *ab initio* enemies of the New Deal" were not acceptable to him as the South's leaders in the postwar era, "because a majority of us have been New Dealers . . . and will not damn it now even though we have had enough." He still favored repeal of the poll tax—it was "an abomination" to him—but by state, not federal action. Vehemently opposed to a federal fair employment practices commission, he favored "in each Southern state a commission devoted officially to the exercise of influence, watchmanship and adjustment in behalf of truly fair employment practices for the Negro." Adamant that there be no breakdown in existing segregations laws and no further federal invasion of states' rights, he nonetheless was acutely aware that the defensible position of states' rights had been abused and sullied by its connection with indefensible causes. Still, he felt that "the states' rights cry is a healthy one, no matter how many selfish and unsocial ones come fellow-traveling . . . . no matter how many . . . [reactionary] lost souls string along." [72]

Graves was consistent in his conservative view of the franchise. Whatever qualifications were required by law had to be applied without discrimination. "Don't think I believe 'qualifying' is something for colored people only," he warned those perhaps a bit too eager to seize upon his defense of voter qualifications. "There is no Jim Crow line for that." Still he argued that as a whole the Southern Negro was not ready for the suffrage, "no matter whose the fault," and "we'd do well to have a gradual increase in Negro voting based upon qualifications." [73]

Graves had been surprised at Folsom's showing in the first primary, but he was not worried. Ellis seemed likely to draw the votes of the other candidates, and Folsom had probably drawn his peak support in the first primary. It was good that this was so, "for with all of Big Jim's charm and good temper, his election would be a victory for forces [of reform] which needed expression here in the 1930's but [which] have dangerously overreached themselves in the 1940's and must be stopped." Still, "Big Jim's showing wasn't just [the result of a] hillbilly band and showmanship, any more than it was to be attributed solely to a failure of the farmers throughout the state to understand that he was the C.I.O. choice. It was charm," Graves thought. "Even without his band and theatricals he is a winsome fellow, full of personality, with a fine voice and presence and a happy-go-lucky amiability that is as appealing in this world of trouble and problem as going fishing when you should be mining coal (and as wrong). No one else in the race compared with him in political 'it.' That's why the P.A.C.–C.I.O. selected him. They have political sense . . . ." [74]

Such cool, reasoned, and well-phrased appraisals represented Graves at his best. As May gave way to June and run-off day neared, however, his pen grew shriller, his sentences shorter, more pointed. His cool analysis became impassioned polemic. Still, there was an underlying element of truth in his devastating parodies of Folsom's manner.

"The farmers gave and the farmers will take away," Graves wrote. The rural folk had been captivated by Folsom's clowning, but in the run-off when they discovered the true nature of "the elements behind amiable Jim which have come from afar to threaten disunion and collectivism," they will desert Big Jim. "Our farmers don't care for Sidney Hillman, Walter Reuther, and company." [75]

In following Folsom, Graves maintained, "the people of Alabama don't know in the least where they are going, are glad only to seem to be on their way . . . ." Never before, he wrote, "have Alabamians followed as little qualified a man . . . . Never have they let themselves be won so by mere entertainment and careless promises." The tone of his comments belied the confidence he expressed in Ellis' chances. "When and if the victory is won [by Folsom], Sidney Hillman in New York will issue a jubilant statement that his P.A.C. has won a great battle in the South. The reformers up there will issue statements, too, about a break in the South's ranks against the F.E.P.C., and on the race question generally." Nobody knows, really, what a Folsom victory would bring. "Given so little qualified a man, so carelessly willing to promise and accept and move one way and another, the result of his election would be a scramble for power on the part of all sorts of people, with the worst ones sure to come out on top." [76]

"This just isn't the time," Graves argued, "for Alabama to indulge it-self in another of the entertaining fellows. As the present national crisis tells us, we've got to know on which side our governor stands in the next four years. And we've got to have a governor who knows a lot more than fiddling and passing suds buckets and doing all the old professional tricks of other political showmen before him." Yet Graves recognized Folsom's appeal. Folsom had "put a hex on some Alabamians and it's bad." He would be no threat if the only votes he received had been those cast by voters who stand with Sidney Hillman and the C.I.O. and who welcome the invasion of these states by "communistic innovations and uncomprehending interference with our race relations." No, they and their ilk did not put Folsom in the lead. It was the farmers and they alone. And why did they vote for a man backed by such insideous forces? Why, Folsom "hypnotized" them.[77]

Yes, the farmers had been hypnotized. The hypnotic word was simple and easy to say. "It is 'fokes.' Folsom just stands up before our fine farm people and says 'fokes.' Then he says it again—'fokes.' And then he says it a few more times—'fokes'—and you begin to feel all warm and happy and careless." The effect of this hypnotic trance was stunning. "You stop noticing what he is saying, you overlook the promises that can't be kept . . . , the political tricks like the suds bucket and string band . . . , the record of the man as a light-footed wanderer utterly unfit for the job he wants, the fact that though he may be Big Jim in stature, he is very little Jim in ability and experience. You just go to sleep and sign up in a happy-go-lucky dream, dear fokes and fellow Alabamians." [78]

Folsom cried "Fokes—fokes—fokes! But it isn't our fokes," Graves charged. "He deserted his fellow Alabamians and our great farm states-man, John Bankhead, at the Democratic National Convention, in favor of Sidney Hillman's man Wallace. . . . He deserted John Bankhead for the crowd that proposes to take over the South from outside and handle all our problems for us, especially the race problem, without regard to how we feel about them or what we know is right." [79]

Four days before the election Graves' column grew even more harsh and devastating. Folsom was to speak in Birmingham the evening of May 31, and Graves announced that "Jim Folsom's in town today, fokes, so go telephone your friends. He's the biggest show on earth, fokes, an amazing amassment of amalgamated attraction, fokes, and there'll be standing room only at the Temple, fokes, because who wants to miss a show like this, fokes." [80] The usually urbane, faintly remote quality of Graves' prose had evaporated. The connoisseur of the classics, the dis-criminating poetaster, had been reduced to cheap, but effective, parody.

Graves' hold on perspective was tenuous in the closing days of the campaign, but in the waning hours before election day he realized that his recent columns had lacked their usual reasoned tone. In a column written the day before the run-off, he lamented that the emotionalism of the campaign had led him to portray Folsom and the C.I.O.-backed Congressman from Birmingham, Luther Patrick, as behorned devils. "It will be a good thing to have Wednesday come and give us back our balance," he confided. "There really aren't any devils around, least of all should the pitter-pattering Mr. Patrick or the fulsome Mr. Folsom be suspected. They are just two very pleasant and rather weak gentlemen who want awfully to be elected and who have persuaded themselves the wave of the future is what the C.I.O.-P.A.C. is riding." Folsom and Patrick, after all, "are good fellows, they have no horns at all, and when they have been beaten tomorrow"—as Graves expected them to be—"all of us will remember how we like them." But, he added, "something to remember right now, dear friends and fellow Alabamians, is that just because Luther and Jim haven't any horns, that doesn't mean there are no horns involved in this election. The horns are up in New York," he charged, "and back of them are horns from the sick lands of Europe, and Russian horns." [81]

xiii   Wednesday came and John Temple Graves may have regained his longed-for balance, but Jim Folsom had won the election. As in the first primary and as in 1942, Folsom ran well in north Alabama and in the Wiregrass. His strongest support centered in his home county of Cullman and the county of his birth, Coffee.[82]

Folsom had won. He had triumphed over the opposition of the state's business community and press. He had put to rout both the conservative candidate of the anti-New Deal faction as well as the candidate of the old progressive coalition. His victory had forestalled the postwar resurgence conservatives had hoped for, but it had also shattered or at least restructured the old liberal coalition.

3

THE DEMOCRATIC ASCENDENCY:
Sparkman, Folsom, and Hill

The dominant motif in all the explanations of Folsom's victory was the desire of the electorate for change, a desire met by neither the conservative Poole nor the old progressive Ellis. Folsom's youth, the hope he engendered among the masses, the faith in a brighter future he kindled led to his triumph, not his liberal ideology, the Birmingham *News* believed. Folsom had won while Luther Patrick, the C.I.O.-endorsed incumbent Congressman from Birmingham, had lost to a youthful, inexperienced G.I. The *News* saw nothing enigmatic about Folsom's victory and Patrick's defeat. Both were evidence of "a tremendous desire for simple political solutions in a time of great complexities." Neither Folsom, nor Patrick's successful foe, relied on "specific ideas as to how to attain the objectives they urged. They promised to do better jobs than had been done. They implied that what mattered most were the fundamentals of intention, the honest purpose, the right hope." Charles Feidelson, the perceptive editorial columnist for the *News*, agreed that ideology had played no significant part in Folsom's victory. "There is a political cycle just as there is an economic cycle," he wrote. "A time comes when the groundswell seems to have set in so that the mood of the people is turned against the 'ins,' without reference to the quality of the 'outs.' " [1]

Other analyses of the election ran in a similar vein. Neil O. Davis, the liberal editor of the Lee County *Bulletin*, who had supported Handy Ellis in the run-off, felt that Folsom was "a genius at knowing the people's mind and [had] diagnosed, as none of the other candidates could, the hopes and aspirations of the small farmers, the country storekeepers, the rural school teachers, the thousands of workers who labor in overalls and white collars." Folsom knew that "the people are restive and want a change. He knows enough history to understand that such a restless frame of mind comes always with the dislocations of war." He knows, too, "that homey, plain talk about government rule by all the people instead of by a few old-line politicians rings the bell." [2]

Grover Hall, Jr., felt that the election simply showed that "Folsom had personality, that he was a fresh breath." Hall did not doubt that the C.I.O. contributed to Folsom's victory, "but it was, above that, a matter of a colorful figure against a field of candidates whose outstanding characteristics were not personal magnetism." [3]

The role of the C.I.O. in Folsom's victory was dismissed by most observers. John Temple Graves warned that a misinterpretation of the returns was beginning to appear. "You gather that what won for Jim was his C.I.O.–P.A.C. support. . . . You gather that Perpetual New Dealism, fading everywhere else, is marching on in Alabama. You gather, even, that our farmers have gone Aubrey Williams." But, he continued, "nothing could be further from the truth. It was the farm vote . . . which elected Jim Folsom," he explained. "Does anybody believe the farmers of Alabama . . . have turned to Henry Wallace again, or are pro-C.I.O.–P.A.C., or are for more federal controls and a Perpetual New Deal?" he asked. "Of course not. They are not even for repeal of the poll tax, I regret to say." The real explanation is simple. The farmers "are for bread and circuses." Grover Hall, Jr., also felt the C.I.O. was "a minor factor" in Folsom's triumph—and pointed to the defeat of most C.I.O.-endorsed candidates and to the fact that Folsom's greatest strength lay in rural areas. No, we must "give the devil his due," Hall concluded. "He ran a truly remarkable race. He did it all by himself, with his bare hands." [4]

Hall had opposed Folsom, but he felt that some good might come of his election. "For at least one political generation," he wrote, "it will be remembered that solitary independence and defiance can win handsome rewards. That will be remembered in the same way that Andrew Jackson's fierce solicitude for the rag-tags is now part of every politician's reflex reasoning." For the moment, "the Outcasts of Poker Flats in Alabama" are the politicians. " 'Politicians,' according to the Saint James E. Version of politics are [for the most part] clanning ogres hiding under the bed and waiting for the moon to go behind a cloud before jumping out to wreck some mischief." [5] This distrust of men of power was beneficial, Hall argued. It would instill humility in the people's servants and remind "politicians that they serve and power strictly on a 'lend-lease basis.' " The professional politician, so long an object of derision, would not go away. But he might be more circumspect, more aware that he is but the people's emissary. "They'll be a much smarter bunch" next time, Hall predicted. "They all hold diplomas now from Folsom University." [6]

i   A vague, incoherent but widely-felt impulse for change had produced Folsom's "surprising and upsetting" [7] victory. And it was precisely a fear of change that had motivated much of the articulate opposition to his candidacy. For Folsom represented a far more serious challenge to conservative interests than Handy Ellis.

During the campaign, Folsom had proposed a constitutional convention to achieve reapportionment. The 1901 constitution, he charged, "was written by reactionaries in behalf of corporations" and was a barrier to Alabama's progress.[8] It had restricted the state's taxing power and had also provided checks on the fiscal policies of local governments. Conservative economic interests, whose purposes had been well served by a mal-apportioned legislature, feared a constitutional convention not only because it might end Black Belt-conservative dominance of the state legislature but also because it might remove existing restrictions on the state's taxing powers. Frank Dixon's fears were evident in a legal memorandum he prepared on the possible consequences of a constitutional convention. Existing limitations on all forms of taxation except the sales tax could be destroyed, Dixon warned. Limitations on city, county, and state indebtedness might be weakened or removed. The requirement that individuals and corporations be taxed at the same rate might be repealed. Dixon was worried. Pressure for extending governmental services is great, he cautioned, and this "would make the holding of a Constitutional Convention dangerous at this time, particularly in view of the temper of the people." [9]

Conservatives feared the possible economic consequences of Folsom's constitutional convention, but they harbored an equal and related fear of an expanded electorate. "We face difficult times . . . ," wrote former-Governor Dixon a few days after Folsom's victory, "primarily on account of the ability, under the law, of any governor to appoint registrars who will complete the registration of negro voters." It was not only the prospect of numbers of Negro voters that frightened the conservatives of the state. They also viewed with alarm the prospect of additional whites, particularly the "wrong sort" of whites, lengthening the list of eligible voters. Dixon evidently expressed to the Chairman of the State Democratic Executive Committee, Gessner McCorvey of Mobile, his fear of additional unqualified white voters in north Alabama. "I realize," McCorvey answered, "that up in North Alabama the wrong sort of Board of Registrars will register a lot of white people who have no business" voting. McCorvey, unlike Dixon, was primarily interested in the Black Belt and in the urban counties of Jefferson (Birmingham), Mobile, and Montgomery, where blacks were numerous and more likely to meet existing requirements. "We are not going to be able to do much in the way of preventing the registration of white citizens," he replied to Dixon, "even though they are of a type which has no business voting." [10]

Folsom's commitment to reapportionment did little to still conservative disquiet. Other candidates in the past had campaigned for reapportionment but once they were in office, bond issues for highways or for schools always seemed to take precedence over the long-range reform of reapportionment. Progressive governors, like Graves, had used reapportionment as a bargaining device to extract concessions from conservative legislators on other, more immediate programs.[11]

The prospects for reapportionment were not particularly bright in 1946. There was little pressure for reapportionment even from some of the areas of the state that would benefit most. The powers-that-be in Birmingham, the executives of the state's major industries, insurance companies, and banks, were not wholly dissatisfied with the grossly disproportionate power enjoyed by the Black Belt. After all, as the political columnist for the Birmingham *News* pointed out, the Black Belt might be "the tail which wags the dogs," but it is "the big mules [the large industrial interests] who are the masters of that highly versatile tail."[12]

Few had given much heed to Folsom's campaign commitment to reapportionment. But a disturbing suspicion that Folsom was intent upon basic reform began to filter through state political circles by late summer. Grover Hall, Jr., had not initially taken seriously Folsom's campaign stand on reapportionment or the poll tax. In the first weeks following Folsom's victory, Hall had believed that it was "a mistake to draw conclusions" from Folsom's platform statements. Folsom's "victory was not in the name of his poll tax and reapportionment plans. . . . Those two planks just happened to have been printed on some of his literature. . . . Folsom never bore down on these planks; he hit them glancing blows or none at all. They were chiefly things written in agate type on his campaign leaflets."[13]

Hall was always the thorough skeptic, and his commentary often bordered upon the cynical. He cast the journalist's jaundiced eye upon any politician's pronouncements, and his long acquaintance with state political figures in Montgomery had only deepened his skepticism. He too had heard it all before and could not believe it was genuinely meant this time any more than last.

By late summer, however, Hall's assessment of Folsom's intentions had changed in tone. In an August interview, Hall found Folsom "as determined as ever to have a constitutional convention, eradicate the poll tax and reapportion the legislature." This time, Hall felt, Folsom "evidently means business on these perennials as perhaps no other modern governor before him." Little more than a week later, Hall wrote that other governors had promised reapportionment but that no governor had ever really tested the opposition's strength. Folsom was different, Hall concluded. "He may be one of those amateurs who lacks the knowledge to see the difficulties and smashes ahead to victory."[14] That must have been a disturbing thought to the conservative wing of Alabama Democracy.

Conservative leaders were also concerned over the social and political views of Folsom's advisers. Gessner McCorvey was disturbed that Folsom seemed willing to rely upon the advice of Mobile's able state senator, Joe Langan, particularly in the appointment of registrars. "Joe is a pretty good sort of boy," McCorvey wrote Dixon, "but he is just as radical as the mischief . . . ." [15]

Former-Governor Dixon was primarily concerned with Folsom's economic views and sought personal information on Philip Hamm, Folsom's Commissioner of Revenue. He was told that Hamm had been born and reared in Elba and had grown up with Folsom. He and Folsom had roomed together for a while at the University. "Those who were at the University with him say he was fairly smart but extremely radical even then. He was suspicious of the fraternities and all who belonged to them, cussed them freely, was against anybody that seemingly had anything." After graduation, Hamm had taught school and "was rather outspoken in his left-wing philosophy during those years." Hamm, Dixon was told, "is a small bore school-teacher politician with an innate suspicion and hatred of those who have acquired success." As Commissioner of Revenue it was expected that Hamm would try "to secure additional revenues, to penalize and soak industry and business and not be concerned about the consequences." [16]

ii   Frank Dixon and Gessner McCorvey were not the only ones concerned about the character of those surrounding Folsom. Men of a more liberal persuasion were also perturbed. The Birmingham *News,* whose gentle and rational progressivism had led it to support Handy Ellis, had warned that there were groups and individuals who hoped to control the governor's power through Folsom. The election of Folsom would mean, the *News* had earlier stated, "a scramble for power, a confusion of purposes, a conflict of efforts that would be disastrous." Handy Ellis would have been subject to pressures, but at least he would have been head man. Folsom was so vague; no one knew what his real purposes were. This was why so many diverse and antagonistic groups and individuals supported him, the *News* asserted. "Some interests with very definite ideas and purposes see an unusual chance to advance their own causes . . . ." through him. Moreover, Folsom was "so eager to be governor, so generous in his impulse to please . . . , that he invites the special efforts of various self-seeking factions and ambitious individuals to gain places of favor with him." [17]

It must be said that Folsom had attracted an incongruous lot to his caravan. If it was not quite true, as Birmingham's staid reactionary, Hugh Locke, a progressive gone rancid, charged, that "all the gluttonous grafters" had hopped on Folsom's bandwagon, he had certainly attracted his share of political leeches. Folsom's following was as strange and variegated a menagerie as is found around any politician bound for victory. Horace Wilkinson was there, perhaps the state's most virulent segregationist and politician extraordinaire. Joe Poole and Elbert Boozer were there, too. They shared their places, in unaccustomed proximity, with liberal idealists, men such as Gould Beech, the fiery young editor of the *Southern Farmer*. Older liberals, such as Aubrey Williams, formerly of the New Deal's National Youth Administration and now publisher of the *Southern Farmer*, was there, too. Men close to Senator Hill, including Richard Rives of Montgomery, were there. And there were young men, like Philip Hamm, who had known Folsom since childhood and who shared much of his outlook. There were other young men, chiefly from north Alabama, who were attracted to Folsom. Some, like O. H. Finney of Albertville, had worked with Folsom in the days of W.P.A. Others, like the talented and sensitive Ralph Hammond, had met Folsom during the campaign and were attracted by his progressive views. Many, like Myra Leak of Arab and Bill Lyerly, a returned G.I., shared Folsom's political outlook but were drawn to him less by liberal theology than by personal faith in Jim Folsom.[18]

It was indeed a strange bag and many feared the worst. Grover Hall, Jr., agreed that "there is not one single person in Alabama who can tell you what Folsom is going to be." But he did not agree with the *News* or with John Temple Graves that Folsom would become the willing tool of some of the evil men who aided his campaign. Folsom "is not simply what you have seen on the stump." Hall argued. "He is not an easy man to understand; he is complex and sometimes inscrutable." And it was Hall's opinion that "nobody owns him. I think he is by nature independent." The story, Hall decided, "lies in this. Folsom is not lacking a brain. His trouble is, he knows nothing." Thus he will have to proceed "intuitively, by ear. And that means [he] must have a man or men around him who can tell him what seems the best thing to do." Such advisors may change "a dozen times in four years," Hall predicted. "The palace guard and throne room boys ordinarily do not enjoy long life." In the meantime, "none of us knows who these men will be. So it is idle now to speculate." [19]

Hall understood Folsom as well as anyone who commented on his political career. Folsom was indeed "by nature independent." At times he was simply mule-headed. If he felt pressured to act in a certain manner, he would often, out of sheer stubbornness, react in opposite fashion. He was first and last his own man. But the very fact that he felt compelled to prove it perhaps reveals an inner insecurity, an inner doubt. As Hall understood, Folsom was the perennial outsider. In mid-June, when Folsom had retreated from public view after his triumph, Hall noted that "Folsom apparently feels that he is not only the declared enemy of everyone holding State office, but also that he is a stranger and a kind of strange stranger to them." In July, Hall wrote that Folsom "retains the psychology of an outlander." [20] He was the little man suddenly catapulted to place and power. But he still harbored those multiple resentments of the plain folk everywhere.

Hall understood Folsom as few men did. But he was a cynical observer and often failed to appreciate one aspect of Folsom's character. And that was his sincere commitment to his basic political premises. The ballyhoo, the clowning, the rhetoric—Folsom enjoyed it all and was not unaware of the role he fulfilled to perfection. Hall knew that and relished this colorful, showy side of Folsom's character. He little knew and perhaps would not have appreciated the other. It was not the Horace Wilkinsons who became "the palace guard and throne room boys." Rather it was the young idealists, the little-known veterans who shared Folsom's hopes for the future and his disdain of the established order—men like Finney, Hamm, Hammond, and, in the early days, Beech. As Hall had predicted, the cast changed over time, roles were upgraded or diminished as some rose and others declined in influence. Over time, they themselves were hardened by their encounter with the rough-and-tumble world of practical politics and public administration. They lost much of their initial naïvete and first-blush idealism. Some became cynical and suspicious. But as with Folsom, that inner core of commitment remained.

iii   While conservatives fretted and editors mulled over the results, one reporter for a metropolitan daily interviewed individuals at random on the streets of Birmingham. The reactions were varied. Few were despondent, most were hopeful, though one dejected businessman predicted a "general raising of taxes." A former state legislator, who had opposed Folsom, was optimistic. "He's not dumb," he said, "and although he may now be ignorant of the way to run a state government, he'll learn quickly, and I look forward to a progressive administration." That very prospect was what worried one Birmingham industrialist. Folsom's policies and appointees would be pro-labor, he feared, and Folsom would be unlikely to side with management in any labor strife that should erupt.[21]

A south Alabama farmer thought the "state has a bear by the tail. . . . We can't let go now." He expected "something of a revolution in state government." Less interested in paving farm-to-market roads than in raising teachers' salaries, he maintained that "as long as we have ignorance in the state we'll have poverty and bad health, and those two things always bring bad government in their train." He looked to Folsom "to do much to raise our standards of education and health."

A Negro leader from Birmingham was also encouraged by Folsom's victory. Folsom was a man of courage and a ray of hope for the Negro people, he said. "It took nerve to oppose openly the keeping of the poll tax," he commented. "I think he made no promises to my people that he will not try to keep."

Many, even those among his supporters, felt that Folsom's campaign had "lacked dignity." But, they added, he used "his methods to get elected so that he could honestly try to improve the status of just those folks to whom the hill-billy tactics appealed the most." There was general regret that Folsom's "unconventional antics" had given the state an unfavorable image in the national press, but no one accused him of being a demagogue like Bilbo or Talmadge. In short, the *News* reporter concluded, "the shouting is over and everyone hopes for the best," though many who opposed him thought he was in for a rough time with his legislature.

The shouting was not over, however. It had only begun. It would last through a special election to fill the Senate seat left vacant by the death of John Bankhead in late May. It lingered through fall in a heated referendum that divided the state party along traditional progressive-conservative lines over a measure designed to restrict Negro suffrage. And it was revived late in the year when Folsom and conservative forces in the legislature clashed in an important symbolic test of strength. With a few additional skirmishes between Folsom and his opponents for good measure, the state was to have no respite from "politics." And when the good people of the state became increasingly weary of protracted struggles in Montgomery, they began to turn on their youthful hero. Before the first year and a half of his term was out Folsom's troubles were compounded by a scandal that cast dishonor upon his character. Folsom's opponents clearly planned the former and welcomed the latter. They profited by both.

iv   All that lay in the future, however. For the moment, Folsom could savor the sweet taste of victory. It was enough to make heady even so ambitious a man as Folsom.

The liberal faction of the party quickly sought to claim Folsom as one of its own. In August he traveled to Washington for a dinner in his honor with President Truman, Secretary of Commerce Henry Wallace, and Paul Hannegan, the Chairman of the Democratic National Committee. From Washington he continued on to New York, accompanied by Senator Lister Hill and Justice Hugo Black. Grover Hall, Jr., was bemused by Folsom's adventures among the mighty. "We can imagine [him] having audience with President Truman and feel assured that it was a natural and delightful meeting. But our imagination sags and groans when we . . . picture the New York holiday junket of this trinity of golden boys— Justice Hugo Black, Senator Lister Hill, and, just get the name right, boys—Big James." [22]

Hall was bewildered. "How'n hell did those three get together? Here's the erudite supreme court justice whose mind and soul burns like cordite and who reads Aristotle for pleasure." He does not drink and "is not the convivial type." Then there is "the lanky Senator Hill," who does not smoke but who "looks a cocktail in the eye unafraid." And, finally, "there is Big James and he is a combination of all the virtues Black and Hill have and have not." The incongruity of this threesome amused and puzzled Hall. "What's Black going to do with his judicial austerity when, in the dining room of the Pennsylvania Hotel, Big James busses a couple of waitresses and has the stewardess sit on his knee." Hall could envision Hill throwing "his head back in a loud laugh to cover his inward nervousness. But what is the unsmiling Justice Black going to do with himself? Look at his hands?" [23]

Still, the Washington-New York trip was not without significance. Hall felt that it was evident that Folsom might become a figure of national importance. "Consider it from the viewpoint of a political practitioner in Washington," he urged. "We in Alabama don't know precisely what Folsom's victory means. All we know is that it was some sort of vague, departing swing in our political temper. But to the high level makers of political cartels in Washington, who became aware of Folsom after his election, he is seen as a Liberal, some sort of out-of-this-world Ellis Arnall . . . a man who might well be put to national party uses." [24]

When those in Washington look South, "they see the man who will be the tallest Governor in the United States. . . . With it, the Washington politicians hear, Folsom has magnetism." Folsom is "accounted a Southern Liberal who can take Southern Bourbons by the scuff of the neck and shove them aside like spindly-legged newsboys. The Democratic Party, you can hear the big boys thinking, can use Governors like that." [25]

And so the Washington dinner party is arranged. ". . . All the mighty from the President to the party boss to the senators (who probably wouldn't have encouraged their cooks to buy an industrial insurance policy from Folsom five years ago), assembled to honor and at the same time examine what has been washed up on the beach. Or more accurately, what has come striding out of the sea onto the beach." [26]

President Truman, Party Chairman Hannegan, and Secretary Wallace, Hall surmised, "are having thoughts—inescapable thoughts—of the 1948 nominating convention, and, incidentally, of the Alabama delegation." If there is any man in Alabama who could control that delegation, it would be Folsom, this man "of extraordinary size and picturesque personality, this man who so recently had more Alabamians vote for him than any in Alabama history." Hill, Black, Truman, Wallace, Hannegan—"They are all like engineers regarding Victoria Falls, trying to devise a means of harnessing the turbulent force." But, Hall warned, "it is going to take some first-rate engineering talent. We all have a lot to learn about the falls." [27]

This was heady stuff even for a young man of grandiose dreams. Undoubtedly Folsom permitted himself, in unguarded moments, the luxury of private thoughts of a career of national import. His model and hero, Andrew Jackson, had been a liberal Southerner with a national career. There were others of similar persuasion who dreamed the same dream, Huey Long, Lyndon Johnson, John Sparkman, Estes Kefauver, Albert Gore. That Folsom should entertain such thoughts was inevitable.

There were, however, insistent voices at home who forecast trouble ahead and who warned of such illusory adventure. John Temple Graves reminded Folsom that he "wasn't elected by a lot of Perpetually New Dealing reformers but by highly entertained farmers." "The tide is running against those people now, not with them any more," Graves cautioned. Folsom should "take a good look at his situation. . . . The high place to which the Henry Wallace people have been taking him for temptation is crumbled now. It is a setup for a bad fall," he warned. If Folsom wants to succeed at home, Graves concluded, "he will have to forget about Henry and the high place." [28]

v   Graves' forecast of storm clouds at home proved accurate, but for the moment Folsom's name was political magic in Alabama. When Senator Bankhead died in late May, Folsom's endorsement of a candidate to fill the post was seen as a political touchstone. Grover Hall, Jr., could only marvel that a man who "three months before . . . [had been] accounted a failure who had been defeated in four forlorn races" was now endorsed by one candidate for Bankhead's seat, courted by another, and imitated by still a third.[29] As usual in Alabama, there was no dearth of candidates for Senator Bankhead's post. There were only three major contenders, however, Representative John Sparkman, Representative Frank Boykin, and former state senator James Simpson.

Sparkman was a competent and liberal congressman from the progressive eighth district in north Alabama. A veteran of five terms in Congress and already majority whip, Sparkman was still a relatively young 47. In many ways he was an ideal candidate for the hill-country South. An authentic son of a tenant farmer, "from whom even the cow was taken for debt," he had put himself through school by shoveling coal in the University furnaces. He had maintained an enviable academic record, graduating Phi Beta Kappa. Awarded his bachelor's degree in 1921, he continued his study of history and in 1924 received a master's degree. His thesis was a study of Reuben Kolb, the Jeffersonian-Populist leader of the 1890's. Sparkman also studied law and was awarded the Ll.B. in 1923. Elected to Congress in 1936, he early established a position of prominence and a voting record of progressive cast.[30]

From the opposite end of the state came the jovial but inconsequential Frank Boykin of Mobile. "Everything was made for love" in Boykin's world. He was a non-ideological being, though his voting record in the

House had been a conservative one. Boykin had served in the House for eleven years, but perhaps because he was more interested in his own burgeoning business empire, he had not distinguished himself as a Congressman.[31]

State Senator James Simpson was from Jefferson County. Together with Frank Dixon, he was one of the leading spokesmen for the conservative industrial and business interests centered in Birmingham. He held an uncommon place of esteem in the business heirarchy of the state and had important ties with other conservative forces in the state, including the Farm Bureau. In 1944, Simpson had run a well-financed campaign against Senator Lister Hill, but despite the use of the race issue against Hill, he had lost.[32] Simpson was an honest public official, a man of integrity. Certainly he was no mossback reactionary. But like economic conservatives elsewhere, as Otis K. Rice observed of the Byrd machine in Virginia, he and his supporters "made a fetish of financial integrity and frugality in government . . . at the expense of education, social welfare, highway construction, and other governmental services."[33]

vi   Massive disinterest on the part of the voters characterized the campaign from start to finish. Sparkman campaigned on his liberal voting record in Congress, on the benefits of programs he had favored for farmers and workers, and on Jim Folsom's coattails. Sparkman's eagerness to identify with Folsom amused Grover Hall, Jr. "Sparkman has been 10 years in Congress. He is now assistant majority leader (whip) of the Democrats. He is smart. All of which means that he is an encyclopedia of measures, issues, and platforms." Yet in the announcement of his candidacy, Sparkman "saw fit to mention the homespun platform devised by Folsom as a sort of second home in his own campaign." The professors, Hall concluded, "are taking lessons from the first form scholars."[34] Sparkman's efforts were testimony to the magic that Folsom's name held for the Alabama electorate in the summer of 1946 and another example of the adoption of Folsom as one of their own by the liberal faction of the state party.

Sparkman's campaign was not simply an imitation of Folsom's, however. He had already carved out a neo-Populist style of his own. He attacked Simpson as a man "who is supported by and preaches the same doctrine as . . . large corporations, Republicans, and other selfish groups," a man who has been "a life-long corporation lawyer and has made a specialty of obtaining favors for the 'Big Mules.' "[35]

Simpson's campaign was a quiet one. He had made his name and his conservative governmental philosophy known in the 1944 campaign against Hill. In 1946, however, he claimed to be the true "liberal statesman" in the race, testifying to the political climate in Alabama in liberalism's hey-day. Boykin campaigned in his characteristic flamboyant style

—old-fashioned oratory and heightened rhetoric. Something of an America Firster, he lambasted Sparkman as an "internationalist." [36]

Still, the campaign generated little interest. The weather was hot and the crowds were small. The people had spent their political fervor in the gubernatorial contest two months earlier. With no clearly defined or heated issue in the race, voter interest lagged.

Sparkman appeared headed for an easy victory. Folsom announced that he intended to vote for him, and several of his campaign workers went to work for Sparkman. Senator Hill also endorsed Sparkman, as did the Birmingham *News*, thus spurning Birmingham's own Jim Simpson. Not even Boykin's revelation a few days before the election that the dying Bankhead had whispered to him the hope that Boykin would succeed him seemed likely to save the Mobile Congressman's campaign. Simpson raised the spectre of an all-powerful liberal machine dominated by Folsom and Sparkman, and Boykin charged that the C.I.O. was trying to purge him from Congress. The voters responded with indifference.[37]

Perhaps in desperation, Boykin turned to the faithful standby of Southern politicians who think they are losing—the issue of race, with overtones of outside interference by radical agitators. It was a bad rerun of Handy Ellis' charges against Folsom or Simpson's against Hill in 1944. In an unscheduled radio speech from Montgomery four days before the election, Boykin brought to an end what one commentator had called "the gentleman's campaign." Calling Sparkman by name for the first time, Boykin charged that "radical elements in Washington and New York" were behind the Sparkman campaign. He warned that communists linked with the C.I.O. were trying to elect Alabama's Senator and pointed out that the Negro Progressive Council of Birmingham had endorsed Sparkman. The election of such a candidate, Boykin charged, could contribute to the passage of a federal fair employment practices act which would force "the hiring of Negroes to work side by side with white men so long as they were equally qualified to hold the job." [38] To Boykin that was a frightening prospect.

The voters were in no mood for such charges, however. They were in little mood for charges of any kind, but these had been leveled with such little success against the New Deal, against Franklin Roosevelt, against Senator Hill, and recently against Folsom, that one wonders what led Boykin to resurrect them. But it is difficult to judge the quiet desperation any public man must feel when he realizes he is losing. Bigger men than Frank Boykin have succumbed to equal temptations.

With Folsom's endorsement and the backing of Senator Hill and of labor, Sparkman won by a narrow majority of 230 of the 169,638 votes cast. He received 50.1 percent of the vote, Boykin 21.2, and Simpson 27.5. The race issue had failed to salvage the election for Boykin and had divided the conservative support that might otherwise have gone to

Simpson. Ineffective against Hill in 1944 and against Folsom and Sparkman in 1946, the issue of race seemed to be losing its potency. Perhaps
H. C. Nixon's hopes for a "new crop of social Democrats" were not
wholly unjustified. Indeed, race had never been the staple issue of Alabama politics as it had in Mississippi and at times in South Carolina and
Georgia. As the Montgomery *Advertiser* phrased it in 1942, "Alabama
has had incompetent governors, greedy governors, good, bad, and indifferent governors. But it has been spared the shame of having a vicious
governor or one willing to exploit the Negro issue." [39]

The effectiveness of race as a political weapon seemed at a low ebb
in Alabama in the mid-forties. But divorced from personality and from
an engaging candidate acceptable on other issues, it was still a potent
factor. The reaction of the state in late 1946 to the prospect of an expanded Negro electorate demonstrated anew the power of the ancient
nemesis.

Dummy of Truman being hanged in effigy from the balcony of the Tutwiler Hotel during the 1948 Dixiecrat convention in Birmingham. (Courtesy of Associated Press Wirephoto)

Bibb Graves campaigning in 1935 (Governor 1927-31, 1935-39).

Bibb Graves fishing in 1942, a few days before he died campaigning for a third term.

Folsom towers over Chauncey Sparks (Governor, 1943-47).

James E. Folsom in 1946 (Governor, 1947-51).

Gessner McCorvey, Dixiecrat (State Democratic Chairman, 1940s).

Handy Ellis, Dixiecrat leader, tearing up his credentials to the 1948 Democratic convention on his return to Birmingham. Looking on is E. C. "Bud" Boswell, author of the Boswell amendment designed to prevent negro registration.

Dixiecrat Leaders confer in Birmingham before their 1948 Presidential Convention. L to R: Fielding L. Wright, Governor of Mississippi (1946-52); Frank M. Dixon, Governor of Alabama (1939-43); Benjamin T. Laney, Governor of Arkansas (1945-49); Horace Wilkinson, Alabama segregationist.

Frank M. Dixon, Dixiecrat (Governor 1939-43) and Chauncey
Sparks, Loyalist (Governor 1943-47).

Grizzled farmer writes suggestion for Folsom's "Branch-head Hopechest."

Overflow crowd at Folsom rally in a county high school.

Folsom signs Klan anti-masking bill of 1949 (Looking on, L to R, Senator Henry Mize of Tuscaloosa County, Representative John Snodgrass of Jackson County, Representative Earl McGowin of Butler County).

Left to right: Senator Sparkman, Senator Lister Hill, an unidentified man, and Justice Hugo Black.

Cartoons by Brooks
(from The Birmingham News)

The Birmingham News

MAY 10, 1948

It Could Happen Here

The Birmingham News

MARCH 23, 1950

The Race

The Birmingham News — JULY 16, 1948

Making It A Race

The Birmingham News — NOVEMBER 4, 1948

The Surprised Gravedigger

The Birmingham News

It Needs Two Strong Columns

4

RACE, CLASS, PARTY, AND
THE BOSWELL AMENDMENT

In 1944 the Supreme Court held Texas' white primary unconstitutional.[1] In January of 1946, the Executive Committee of the Democratic party in Alabama declared its spring primary open to all voters. Efforts had been underway for two years, however, to tighten Alabama's rather lax registration procedures so as to preclude the possibility of mass registration of Negroes.

After reading the Supreme Court decision outlawing the white primary, former-Governor Frank Dixon, a leader in the conservative faction of the state party, wrote Gessner T. McCorvey, the chairman of the State Democratic Executive Committee, urging a careful study of measures to tighten the web of restrictions that surrounded the ballot box in Alabama. "There should be some definite planning by the best brains in Alabama," Dixon urged, "with the view of setting up a system [to prevent mass registration] which will stand up" in court. If such a system were not devised, not only would the Democratic party's supremacy in the South be endangered but so also would conservative hopes of dominating Southern Democracy. "It is obvious," Dixon wrote, "that the only thing that has held the Democratic Party together in the South for many years past has been the thing which caused its strength in the first place, namely, white supremacy." The Democratic party nationally, "through its titular chieftain [F.D.R.], has repudiated this doctrine," he warned, and "if that repudiation affects our local control, through forced registration of negroes in this State, the Democratic Party will become anathema to the white people in the South." [2]

Alabama's registration laws were enough to give pause to those frightened by the prospect of an enlarged electorate. The Constitution of 1901 exempted anyone who owned taxable property assessed at $300 or more from other qualifying requirements, including literacy. This had been adopted as a constitutionally acceptable means to reassure illiterate but

59

property-owning whites that they would not be disenfranchised along with the masses of largely property-less and often illiterate blacks.[3] But what had been a loophole for whites at the turn of the century might be the doorway to the suffrage for blacks in the 1940's. Custom, fear, poverty, apathy, overt intimidation might forestall the registration of Negroes in the rural counties of the state, but these would have less effect in the urban counties of Jefferson and Mobile. And, if the cumulative poll tax were repealed, what was to keep undesirable whites, particularly in the northern counties, from registering should a political leader incite enough enthusiasm to overcome their traditional lethargy?[4] There was nothing in the law to brake the pace of registration.

Gessner McCorvey needed little prodding from Dixon. His views on the suffrage were even more conservative than Dixon's.[5] In May of 1945, McCorvey submitted to each member of the legislature his proposal to forestall an expanded electorate. McCorvey's letter fulsomely defended the handiwork of the 1901 Constitutional Convention and urged the legislature merely to update the means by which disenfranchisement and a restricted electorate could be ensured.[6]

McCorvey argued for the retention of the cumulative poll tax. One study has concluded that by 1930 more whites than blacks had been disfranchised by the cumulative feature of the state's poll tax and even so conservative a man as Frank Dixon supported its modification.[7] But McCorvey insisted that "some counties have large numbers of thriftless people. Such groups fail to pay a poll tax one year and the next year they again fail to pay. . . . Soon . . . . we have entirely eliminated these people as voters . . . ." The cumulative poll tax, to McCorvey, represented "a lawful and legitimate method of getting rid of a very large number of people who would not cast an intelligent ballot even if they were given the right to vote." This had been done "in a thoroughly legitimate, lawful and constitutional manner . . . without any Reconstruction Days ballot box stuffing." Retention of the cumulative feature was "as little as those of us who live in other sections of the State can do for that splendid group of Alabamians living in the Black Belt." We must "aid them in retaining control of their respective counties and prevent an ignorant and irresponsible group from taking charge."[8]

If sympathy for the citizens of the Black Belt failed to move the legislators, McCorvey also invoked the sanctity of the 1901 constitution. "I do not think that we have the right to undo the work of that great group of Alabama leaders, who . . . had only in mind love of their state and the determination to see to it that no radical and irresponsible group could take charge of our State Government or of any of our County Governments, especially in the Black Belt."[9]

McCorvey could not agree with those who argued that "we can raise the educational and other standards required for voting" and thus more legitimately avoid the difficulties of absolute democracy.[10] The cumulative poll tax was necessary and its repeal "at this time would merely be taking down one more barrier which has stood the test of time . . . ." "Why surrender this additional protection . . . ?" McCorvey asked. Should some federal court undertake to force local boards to register certain applicants, then we would not be so harmed "if these prospective voters had not paid their poll tax." Let us "stick by the laws," McCorvey urged, "as given to us by that group of great Alabamians who wrote the Alabama Constitution of 1901." Indeed, instead of removing hurdles to the effective exercise of the suffrage, McCorvey recommended the erection of additional ones.[11]

McCorvey urged the state legislators to eliminate the clause in the 1901 constitution which exempted from the qualifying requirements of literacy any individual who owned personal property assessed at $300 or more.[12] In a classic, though somewhat earthy, defense of the conservative position on limited suffrage, McCorvey argued that it is "ridiculous to permit a man, whether he be black or white, to become a registered voter—regardless of his lack of other qualifications—merely because he might own some junky automobile . . . ." In 1901, "we had no automobiles, and any person . . . who had $300.00 worth of property assessed to him was a person who had some real interest in his government and some substantial rights to be protected." Now "every Tom, Dick, and Harry has an automobile and this safeguard which the drafters of our Constitution tried to throw around us so as to give us an intelligent electorate are [sic] no longer effective." [13]

To remedy this defect and restore such safeguards, McCorvey recommended the repeal of the provision granting the unqualified right to register to owners of a predetermined amount of property. In its stead he proposed the enactment of a clause to require of a prospective voter not only the ability to read and write any article of the United States Constitution but to demonstrate to a local board of registrars a satisfactory understanding of it as well. After all, McCorvey pointed out, "a smart parrot could be taught to recite a section of our Constitution." [14]

McCorvey's suggestion of an "understanding" clause came inconspicuously at the end of the last substantive paragraph of a two-page letter. But it was the heart of his proposal. The clause exempting those who owned $300 worth of taxable property was not McCorvey's major worry, despite the attention he flourished upon it. Even with the repeal of that clause, the literacy requirement could no longer be depended upon to block registration of large numbers of Negroes.[15] If the courts forced local boards to administer existing requirements equally, the way was already open for registration of great numbers of Negroes, especially in the urban areas, where educational opportunities had been greatest. What was needed was a wide discretionary power lodged in local boards to determine who could or could not register. This was what the "understanding" provision, as well as other provisions that later became part of the Boswell amendment, was designed to do. McCorvey cryptically conceded his purpose when he noted that the adoption of an "understanding" clause, "of course, would give certain discretion to the Board of Registrars and enable them to prevent from registering those elements of our community which have not yet fitted themselves for self-government." [16] In other words, local boards could administer registration requirements in as discriminatory a fashion as they saw fit.

There is of course a responsible argument that can be made for a limited suffrage. It is not one, however, that has met with much electoral success in a society whose political dynamic, lacking the restraints of a feudal past, has ever moved toward majoritarian democracy. Moreover, it is a principled argument which in modern times might have received a better hearing had it, like states' rights, not been sullied by its repeated use to screen motives base and ignoble.

In the privacy of their libraries and among trusted friends, both Gessner McCorvey and Frank Dixon would have made the traditional case for a restricted suffrage, a case which holds good without regard to race or color. But this was not the argument they made for public consumption. For despite the legend of the patrician South, theirs was a society that in the mass was fiercely democratic. A defense of an electorate restricted to Hamilton's rich and well-born could not be sold to the Alabama electorate. It might have great appeal and meet with solid approbation in the country clubs of Mountain Brook and Mobile, but Dixon and McCorvey were public men and they knew that the mass of Alabama voters would reject such arguments out of hand—unless the line of restriction were that of color. McCorvey and Dixon knew in 1946, as again in 1948 in the Dixiecrat revolt, that the race issue was their most telling ally. And, in the end, they were willing to compromise the integrity of their argument by tying the defense of a restricted suffrage to the only factor politically palatable to a majority of white voters—fear of the Negro. Even then, as events of the next few months would show, Alabama voters were torn between their traditional views on race and their commitment to the American ideal of equality before the law.

McCorvey's proposal eventually took form as an amendment to the state constitution. Named for the state senator who introduced it, E. C. (Bud) Boswell, the Boswell amendment was approved almost unanimously by the state legislature. There were only two dissenting votes. It was subject to aproval by the voters in a special election in November, 1946.[17]

The Boswell amendment differed in detail from McCorvey's recommendations, but the essential ingredient of local board discretion and, therefore, the opportunity for discrimination, was preserved and indeed enlarged.[18] As former-Governor Dixon observed, "there is absolutely no way in which the prevention of mass registration can be worked out without leaving discretion in the hands of the registrars. There is no more discretion left in their hands," he maintained, "than is essential to achieve the result we must have." [19]

The contest over the Boswell amendment was another of those compelling clashes in Alabama politics, described by V. O. Key, that divide the state along a reappearing "progressive-conservative cleavage." The historic alignment of the Black Belt and the "big mules," the industrial interests, of Birmingham and Mobile, against the hill-country whites appeared as it had in the Jacksonian era, in the crisis of secession, in the Populist era, and most recently in Folsom's primary victory.[20]

The nomination of Folsom in May made the Boswell amendment all the more crucial for conservative Democrats in Alabama. For Folsom had committed himself to reapportionment, to poll tax repeal, and to the convening of a constitutional convention which could remove the stringent fiscal restrictions placed on state and local government by the conservative framers of the 1901 constitution.[21] And as Handy Ellis had pointed out in the campaign, Folsom could appoint men to local boards of registrars, especially in the urban areas, who would register qualified blacks and work to broaden the suffrage in general.[22] By the summer of 1946, initial doubts that Folsom's promises were little more than campaign blather had evaporated,[23] and leaders of the conservative faction within the state party pushed all the harder for the Boswell amendment.

Frank Dixon of Birmingham and Gessner McCorvey of Mobile, both of them "big mule" lawyers and leaders in the anti-New Deal faction of the party, were joined in the fight for the Boswell proposal by the spokesmen of the conservative agricultural interests of the Black Belt. J. Miller Bonner, former state senator from Wilcox County and legal advisor in the Dixon administration, organized a Black Belt citizens committee to campaign for adoption. Senator Bruce Henderson of Wilcox and former Commissioner of Agriculture Joe Poole of Butler also campaigned for the amendment.[24]

Out-going Governor Chauncey Sparks, the "Bourbon from Barbour," whose administration had surprised many by its progressive cast, supported the amendment,[25] as did old-line segregationist Horace Wilkinson of Birmingham, whom the Florence (Alabama) *Times* once dubbed "Alabama's leading race-baiter." [26] With the exception of Sparks, these same men—Dixon, McCorvey, Bonner, Henderson, Poole, and Wilkinson—were the architects of the 1948 Dixiecrat revolt in Alabama. Then, as in 1946, they were opposed by the liberal faction of Senators Hill and Sparkman and Governor Folsom.[27] The struggle over the Boswell amendment was but a prelude to the larger struggle between States' Righters and Loyalists in 1948.

As in 1948, Gessner McCorvey used his position as state party chairman to great effect. Well before the anti-amendment forces had organized, McCorvey persuaded a majority of the State Democratic Executive Committee to adopt a resolution favoring the amendment and permitting him to expend the Committee's funds in the campaign for adoption.[28]

In an open letter to "THE VOTERS OF ALABAMA," mailed at the expense of the State Committee and printed on its official stationery, McCorvey reassured the voters that "we have done in the past, and we intend to do in the future, everything that can legally be done to preserve white supremacy in our State." We have done this, he wrote, "not with the idea that all white men are good and all Negroes bad, but with the firm conviction that the vast majority of Negroes have not yet fitted themselves to vote intelligently on important governmental matters." [29]

McCorvey reminded the voters that the official emblem of the state party was a crowing rooster with the words "WHITE SUPREMACY" emblazoned on a banner above the proud, white cock. We are at the cross-roads, he warned. The 1944 Supreme Court decision outlawing the white primary "has opened the way to a flood of negro registration and negro domination at the polls of Alabama—especially in our Black Belt Counties." [30]

McCorvey reiterated the arguments he had developed in his letter to the state legislators over a year earlier and raised the spectre of counties in the Black Belt falling prey to "vast hordes of ignorant and illiterate people." Even outside the Black Belt, Negro voters might attain the balance of power and elect "negro Judges, negro City and County Commissioners, negro Legislators and negro Law Enforcement Officers just as we had in the dark days of Reconstruction." [31]

"These things must not come to pass in Alabama, where our fathers fought to break the chains of reconstruction and win back our State to white control," McCorvey admonished, invoking the sanction of illustrious forebears. It would not be difficult to remove the threat, McCorvey maintained. Neither the state nor the Democratic party would defy the national government. But, the state, "acting within the law, can by action of its people surround the exercise of suffrage in Alabama with such legal safeguards as will protect our state from the veritable flood of negro registration and negro domination, which the Supreme Court has released." [32] The state can, in short, adopt the Boswell amendment.

i   Gessner McCorvey waged his campaign in behalf of the Boswell amendment chiefly through the mails and through press releases, while former-Governor Dixon was the leading speech-maker for the amendment. In a major speech to the Athens, Alabama, Rotary Club in mid-October, Dixon maintained that the decision on the Boswell amendment would be the most important one Alabama voters had made since the adoption of the 1901 constitution. "It is my firm belief," he said, "that we face elimination of our segregation laws, of our zoning laws; that we will see our children in mixed schools of white and negroes; our legislature with strong negro minorities, our juries of mixed races; many of our city and county governments either manned by negroes or largely dominated by them, should we fail to pass the Boswell Amendment." [33]

Dixon was not "one of those who believe that negro blood should be an absolute and arbitrary bar to the franchise," however. "Rather, I am one who believes that the members of that race should be given every encouragement, that their economic level should be in every way raised, that as they become qualified for the ballot it should be extended to them, as is now being done and as has been done in the past." There were thousands of Negroes voting in Alabama, he maintained, and though "the percentage is not large—the number qualified is not large, either." [34]

The real question, Dixon argued, was not preventing the registration of qualified Negroes. Rather, "it is one of preventing mass registration of two hundred thousand unqualified electors, capable only of being willing tools in the hands of unscrupulous men." The horrors of Reconstruction were recalled. It was then that "the people of Alabama went through their Gethsemane. The newly enfranchised negroes, utterly incompetent to understand even the meaning of the privilege of voting, were willing tools in the hands of the carpet baggers and scalawags. The elections were scenes of debauchery—recently freed slaves and their white associates dominated the state, stole the public funds, imprisoned those who protested, issued millions in bonds still unpaid, created a reign of terror in which the lives of decent men, women and children were always in danger." [35]

By implication, these same conditions would exist if the Boswell amendment failed to pass. Dixon did not ask why so little had been accomplished since Reconstruction in fitting the Negro population for the suffrage. Indeed, his speech is a curious one. The danger of massive Negro registration was heightened precisely because the Negro had been educated and could now read and write.[36]

The ambiguity in Dixon's speech, the curious shifting of ground, betrays the dilemma Dixon faced. He himself cherished the classic conservative belief in a suffrage restricted to men of substance, those men who by birth and training and position had a genuine stake in society, regardless of race. Yet he was compelled to state his case in such a way that it referred to a group denied the suffrage chiefly because of race. He felt it necessary to repeat his belief that color was not the basis for his opposition to Negro voting. To him "the only argument against the Boswell Amendment which deserves consideration is the feeling held by some that any man or woman of voting age should have, now, the right to vote." That was an argument with which Dixon could differ on principled grounds. But in the same paragraph, it was clear that publicly he would object only to Negro participation in an unrestricted suffrage. It was his belief "that those who are fighting [the Boswell Amendment] . . . believe fundamentally that, whatever the consequences in racial animosities, social revolution, rotten government, outraged feelings, the entire negro population of voting age should vote *now*." [37]

ii   In his letter to the voters, Gessner McCorvey had argued that "the principal opposition to the Amendment comes, of course, from four sources:

> 1. The small but ever active radical-reformer element which has moved into our State, but who are really not of the South, who hold the viewpoint that no distinction whatsoever should be made between the races, and that negroes should associate on equal terms with the whites in all matters. (including supporters of FEPC, etc.).
> 2. The meddling Northern 'uplift reformers' who spend their time berating everything South of the Mason-Dixon line, and who are constantly at work to tear down Southern customs and traditions.
> 3. The Communistic groups, which for their own selfish ends, desire to enfranchise many more thousand negro voters in order to enhance their own power in our State, by increasing the number of voters who will blindly support their un-democratic theories of Government and assist them in breaking down our American institutions.

And certainly the most dangerous:

> 4. The Republican party, which, with understandable confidence, believes that the registration of countless thousands of negro voters will largely increase its voting strength in Alabama and give to it the first opportunity [it] has had since Reconstruction Days to dominate our people.[38]

In the face of this opposition, McCorvey urged the good people of Alabama to keep their "feet on the ground and continue having in Alabama the kind of Government with which we have been blessed, in which intelligent people of this state control our government." Perhaps in fear of being labeled an elitist at best or an intellectual at worst, McCorvey hastened to add that by "intelligent people" he did not mean "any super-educated folks, but just the right kind of people." [39]

If, in September, McCorvey expected the chief opposition to the Boswell amendment to come from alien radical elements, Northern do-gooders, Communists, and Alabama Republicans—politics does indeed make strange bedfellows—by November he was shorn of such delusions. Richard Rives of Montgomery, long active in the progressive wing of the party and a close political associate of Senator Lister Hill, led the fight against the amendment. Senator Hill himself lent his powerful support to the campaign against the proposal, and Governor-nominate Folsom and Senator-nominate Sparkman also campaigned against the amendment. Most of the major newspapers of the state were against the Boswell amendment, as was organized labor, notable civic leaders, and leaders of the state's religious minorities.[40]

Few of those in public life who actively opposed the Boswell amendment did so as advocates of racial equality. Rather they approached the issue obliquely. The Boswell amendment, it was argued, was designed to limit the registration of whites as well as blacks, to prohibit voting by those whom "the Big Mules do not approve," as Senator Hill put it.[41] The discretion it gave local boards was of such latitude as to be arbitrary. Its implementation would violate the minimum canons of fairness, and its powers would be open to abuse.

Opponents of the amendment disparaged the dire predictions of the Boswell supporters, but seldom did they squarely face the racial question. To do so, perhaps, would have been to take on an unnecessary political liability. It is difficult, after the last twenty years, however, not to find fault with the limited and oblique opposition offered by political opponents of the amendment. But it is less a comment on the courage of Southern liberals than upon the engrained racial sentiments that suffused Southern society that to defend so elemental a right as the suffrage and equality before the law was deemed fraught with political danger. The amendment had become part of an ongoing factional struggle and, by a curious process often at work in politics, had taken on a force beyond the merits of the issue at stake. That, no doubt, accounts for the solid liberal phalanx opposing the amendment. Still, in a time when Negro voting strength was negligible, it took no small measure of political courage for public men to take even the dissembling stand of Hill, Sparkman, and Folsom.

The chief complaint of those who opposed the Boswell amendment was the arbitrary and unlimited power it placed in the hands of county registrars. How could anyone expect the members of the board of registrars, much less prospective voters, critics asked, to understand and explain sections of the Constitution whose legal history was long and complex? And by what criteria was good character and an ability to understand the duties of citizenship to be judged? [42] The vagueness of the provisions was intentional and the possibilities for discrimination and abuse of power were open-ended.

In a series of editorials, the Birmingham *News* stated the case for those opposed to the amendment. The *News* argued that the proposal conflicted with the United States Constitution and with the "demands of justice." It is a "flagrant fact," the *News* maintained, that the amendment seeks to "discriminate against a whole group of citizens." Its provisions are contrary to any fair and impartial system, the *News* concluded, since it lacks uniformity of application.[43]

The *News* also argued that the amendment was unnecessary. A literacy requirement, justly and equally applied, was enough to prevent "the indiscriminate registration of unqualified persons." After all, qualified Negroes had voted in Democratic primaries before—though, granted, in limited numbers—and there had been no ill effect. Adoption of the Boswell amendment, the *News* concluded, "would seriously interfere with the orderly and just meeting of the whole problem of racial relations and suffrage requirements." [44]

Passage of the amendment, the *News* warned, might also produce dangers far greater than those which motivated its supporters. "We still have regulations which have worked since 1903 to make the Negro a negligible factor politically." And that system will stand up in court. The Boswell amendment, the *News* argued, will not, and that might well undermine the present safeguards. "Gentlemen who cry for so crude and invalid a proposal as the Boswell Amendment as our only salvation against mass registration by Negroes," the *News* cautioned, "might consider what could happen if the Supreme Court undertook . . . an exploration of all the safeguards which have been set up by us to protect the ballot box." Barring that, and "unless there are extremist efforts to deny fundamental rights to Negro citizens," the *News* held out hope for "an orderly, gradual settlement of the whole problem in time. It will not be settled by sheer repression," the *News* counseled. "That way lies the greatest danger." [45]

iii   Other newspapers across the state echoed the *News'* arguments and embellished them. Some editors contended that the amendment was unconstitutional on its face, others that it represented just another chapter in the long struggle between north and south Alabama for control of state government. A number of letters-to-the-editor maintained that the emphasis on race by those in favor of the amendment smacked of Hitler's tactics. One writer argued that it was simply a matter of Black Belt politicians getting scared about something, "and that something is that they are about through dominating the affairs of the State." The *Hale County News* of Moundville felt that the amendment was "nothing but an attempt of the old line politicians to further handcuff the electorate of Alabama." If adopted, it would bring nothing but unrest and hard feelings. Even the *Progressive Farmer* revived something of its earlier liberalism and argued that the amendment "not only violates the simplest principles of sound government; [but] it could become an extremely vicious weapon to destroy all semblance of good government." [46]

While the newspapers editorialized, those actively opposing the amendment had to go about the business of arousing the public against the measure. Unfortunately, the public is often moved more by fear and exaggeration than by appeals to common sense and the principles of sound government. Certainly Dixon and McCorvey and others who favored the amendment knew this and capitalized upon it. Those opposed to the proposal were not above exaggeration in their campaign to defeat the measure.

Attorney-general nominate Albert A. Carmichael, long a member of the progressive wing of the party, was one of the leading speakers opposing the amendment. The backers of the Boswell amendment, he charged, fear not the Negro so much as "the free and unfettered expression of the white democracy of Alabama." The real purpose behind the amendment was not just to bar Negroes from voting but "to keep the white electorate small and more easily within control." In tones reminiscent of the clash between Populists and Democrats in the 1890's and of the more muted debate over the 1901 constitution, Carmichael charged that the prospect of an enlarged white democracy "throws a dark shadow across the path of the small but powerful reactionary element of the democracy of Alabama." [47]

Despite Carmichael's impassioned rhetoric, it was difficult to counter the advertisements put out by the amendment's backers. Did you know, one asked, that 2000 Negroes in Macon County had marched to the courthouse to demand the right to register, that Governor Sparks had been petitioned to appoint "NEGRO REGISTRARS?" The horror of such a prospect was unspeakable—and this in a county in which over 80% of the population was Negro and in which, because Tuskegee Institute was located there, many were well-educated. The violence done the principles and spirit of democracy was forgotten when the spectre of 200,000 Negro voters was raised and when the ghosts of honored forebears were called upon to bear witness to the horrors of "Reconstruction and Carpetbag rule." [48]

iv   While editors mused and politicans ranted, the most philosophic critique of the amendment came from a wholly unexpected source. It was based on the best of truly conservative convictions. In a letter to the Birmingham *News*, William D. Lanier, Jr., of Jasper, offered a closely-reasoned and pungently-phrased analysis of the amendment and of the consequences of its adoption. The Boswell amendment, to his mind, was both unconstitutional and poor political tactics. But the greatest danger, he argued, was in the potential abuse of the discretionary power to determine who may or may not vote.[49]

Lanier did not oppose the amendment because it might inhibit the growth of an indigenous liberalism. Rather, he opposed it for very "conservative and common sense reasons." After all, as a small town merchant he regarded the C.I.O. "about as fondly as the Egyptians regarded the seven plagues of Moses." He was "about as much of a 'left-winger' as Calvin Coolidge" and he had not agreed with Eleanor Roosevelt about anything "since she said Hitler was a heel." Nor did he favor inter-marriage, social equality, or a revolt of the masses.

Lanier believed that the primary purpose of the amendment was not necessarily the preservation of white supremacy but rather the perpetuation in power of a political machine. But even if the motives of the amendment's backers were simon pure, their proposed remedy could later be put to evil use. This was "one gift horse which it behooves us to look straight in the mouth—its teeth are as false as a dime store diamond."

Lanier was well aware of the profound ambivalence with which the founding fathers had regarded power. Experience had clearly proved that while "government, by its very nature, needs no protection from the individual citizen, the citizen very definitely needs protection from his government." "The Boswellites," he contended, "with a cheery contempt for the facts of life, loudly proclaim that their opponents are 'visionary,' 'theorists,' and 'impractical do-gooders,' while they themselves are practical realists." The truth is, he argued, "that the proposed amendment would require a confidence in the wisdom and probity of a multitude of minor officials that would test the simple faith of a six-year-old child." Could anything be more visionary, he asked, "than the blithe assumption that these backwoods bureaucrats would possess the wisdom of Solomon and the discretion of John Marshall? Is it not a pure case of 'theorism'— this happy hypothesis that these underpaid clerks would be automatically invested with the integrity of Cato and the honesty of Benjamin Franklin. And would it occur to the most 'impractical do-gooder,' as it does to these 'practical' people, to entrust an untrammeled and unrestricted power to those very people who are most interested in abusing that power?" No, the true realists are those "who refuse to submit our future to the unchecked vagaries of human nature—those who insist, regretfully but logically, that there is nothing in our record as a people in general and politicians in particular to justify throwing caution to the winds and trusting an unknown pilot to steer the ship of state on an uncharted course in shoal waters." The issue, in short, was not white supremacy but potential "machine supremacy." It was a bid for "potential tyranny."

v   In the midst of the debate over the Boswell amendment the Southern Historical Association met in Birmingham. There a young and promising Southern historian delivered a paper in which he cited Mississippi's Vardaman as an example of a paradox in Southern progressivism. Those in the South who had led the revolt against the conservative Bourbon machine in behalf of a wider democracy were often more narrow and vehement in their view of the Negro than were their opponents.[50]

The Birmingham *News*, in commenting on C. Vann Woodward's paper, wistfully hoped that time had wrought a change in attitudes throughout the South. More and more, the *News* argued, "Southerners are giving to justice and fair play the place which they formerly granted to a traditional emotion." [51]

Events of the past few years seemed to buttress the optimism the *News* expressed. Race had been rejected by the voters in Alabama as a determining factor in the Senate races of 1944 and 1946 and in the most recent contest for governor. The vote on the Boswell amendment showed once again, however, that the old emotions were not yet extinguished and could be drawn upon for electoral effect. The amendment passed narrowly and with some grumbling that it had been counted in.[52]

The passage of the Boswell amendment was a harbinger of the difficulty that lay ahead for the liberal wing of the party and for Jim Folsom and his program. It was a warning flag that an indigenous Southern liberalism which seemed at its peak in 1946 could be toppled.

5

FOLSOM IN RETREAT:

The Fruits of Victory Denied

The hotels were packed, more crowded than ever in Montgomery's history, veteran hotelmen said.[1] Big Jim had invited all of Alabama to his inaugural and many of them came.

Montgomery had never seen an inauguration such as this. The crowds were larger and the parade longer than those of the past, but it was more than that. Not that the formality and dignity which accompany such affairs of state were absent. Richard Rives of Montgomery presided over the formal ceremonies in front of the stately capitol with aplomb. Chief Justice Lucien Gardner, who had served on the supreme bench since 1915, lent his "solomn mien and felicity of phrase" to the proceedings.[2]

No, the customary formality was not absent. It was just overwhelmed. The inaugural address was followed that evening by one of the strangest inaugural balls ever concocted. Big Jim had invited his campaign audiences to come to his inaugural and come they did. A two-day drizzle that had left the spangled bunting bedraggled failed to dampen the spirits of the plain folk come to town to celebrate. They were there in force, 6000 strong. The Strawberry Pickers, the hill-billy band that had campaigned with Folsom, was there, playing alongside Montgomery's leading society dance band. At first dancing was spasmodic, the floor was too crowded. Later, as the crowd began to thin and as the older celebrants shifted to the chairs along the sides of the auditorium, the floor was abandoned to the young, daring, or inebriated. Folsom promised to dance with every girl there, but he soon had to give it up. Girls had come dateless and were soon dancing with each other. Bobby-soxers, with their "shabby runover shoes, blue denim slacks with blouses," were there in impressive numbers, as well as jitterbug exhibitionists.[3]

There was mass confusion. The Strawberry Pickers tried to organize a square dance, but their efforts foundered. The hall was too crowded, the crowd undisciplined. Cheers and applause filled the hall when the hill-country band picked their way through the "Milkcow Blues." The musicians chanted "cornbread and buttermilk" while the soloist ambled through the lyrics.

Yes, Big Jim had asked them to come and they were all there, all ages, all stations in life, all manner of dress from black-tie and tails to blue jeans. There was even a one-legged jitterbug enthusiast, Peg Parks, to delight the crowd with his "nimble demonstration in the art of terpsichore."

It was an incongruous crew. But there was about it all something of a glorious celebration of the democracy of the mass, something reminiscent of the stories told of Andrew Jackson's inaugurals. The curious character of the occasion was appropriately symbolic of the larger meaning of Folsom's victory. The little people, the rural folk, the blue-collar workers and their teen-aged sons and daughters had come to celebrate their triumph over the well-to-do and properly behaved. Their multiple resentments were flaunted in one night of frenzied glory. They had come to share their hero's triumph.

i   Folsom's inaugural speech was simply phrased, a bit homespun, but powerful. He opened with a look backward to his youth, to the years of the "happiness of growing up in a big family," to the "good lessons" his mother preached to him, and to "the nights in front of the fireplace listening to my papa." He thought of the river that courses through Elba, of the devastating flood of 1929 that ended his college career. That flood "had more to do with the course of [his] life than any other thing that happened," he said. For after it had subsided and the family had weathered the deluge, he left "to catch a boat and see something of the world." [4]

These recollections were but a passing reference, the kind of warm and nostalgic memories Folsom delights in recounting. Quickly he moved on to a statement of his faith in democracy, in the unfettered sovereignty of all the people. Democracy to him was not an abstract system of government to be studied in a theorist's text. It was a living state that should touch the everyday lives of everyday people. "I believe," he said, "in the kind of democracy that touches the home of the average man . . . . that goes back to the branchheads and the brush arbor gathering places." He believed in "the kind of democracy that gives the average man and woman more to say about the way our government is run," and that means "we want to get rid of worn-out restrictions on voting." It means that every section of the state must have a fair and equitable representation in state government.[5]

If democracy is to remain strong, Folsom continued, "it has to have a regeneration every now and then." The prospect of a regenerated democracy might be frightening to some. There are those, he said, who are terrified by real democracy. "They have always worked to trim it down a little here and trim it down a little there." They are the ones who "want to keep power in the hands of a few." He was not one of those "afraid of too much democracy," however. Rather "I am afraid of what happens to people when they have too little democracy." [6]

There followed a transition passage that took Folsom from the generalities of his political faith to the specifics of his program. "If we make our government more democratic, it is going to do a better job in developing our human resources." If government were more representative, then, this would naturally result in wiser and better public policy. It would mean that the schools would operate not eight months of the year but the standard nine. It would mean better-paid teachers, for "a child must not be penalized for being born in Alabama." [7]

More representative government would mean that women would be granted a fuller share in state government, that the old and infirm would be guaranteed security in their declining years, that wage levels and working conditions in Alabama would be raised to the national average. It would mean that state government would play a more active role in developing both the human and natural resources of the state. Good roads would be built "so that the farmer can get what he raises to town" and so that "the products turned out by our factories can be distributed." [8]

A government more responsive to the people's will could broaden opportunity for all by fighting "all forms of monopoly." The threat from monopoly was real, Folsom warned. "If we don't fight monopoly our system of free enterprise is going to be choked to death." Then he announced that as the first act of his administration he would instruct the state attorney-general to join the state of Georgia in an anti-trust suit to force removal of the discriminatory freight rate differentials that kept southern industry subservient to northern industrial interests. [9]

Folsom called for the development of cheap electric power to spur industrialization, and he warned the owners of the state's natural resources—"our iron ore, our coal, our timber, our river valleys"—that they must use their private holdings for the public good. "They can make a fair profit," he said, "but their aim has got [to be] to make the best use of our resource for Alabama. They can't think only of controlling these resources for the benefit of some other section." [10]

Such words were not popular in some quarters and he knew that. Political fights there would be, for "that's the way of democracy." He expected them, and he was accustomed to them. How much would be accomplished in spite of political squabbles "will depend . . . on whether we work together" for the common good. As for himself, he began "this new day in Alabama . . . with malice toward none and good will toward all. I want to be and I am going to be the governor of all the people.

. . . There's opportunity ahead for Alabama," he told his people. But "we've got to have vision to see it. . . . Let's not be frightened by those who are satisfied to live in the past. Let's have faith in Alabama's future." [11]

ii   The major newspapers of the state generally found Folsom's address reassuring. The Birmingham *Age-Herald* thought Folsom's strength lay "in his sincerity, in his devotion to the common good. in his earnestness, in his fine intentions." Though the speech was lacking in concrete measures by which to translate Folsom's "hopes and ideals into action," the new governor nonetheless rightly considered himself, the *Age-Herald* maintained, to have a mandate to press forward on poll tax repeal, increased old age pensions, reapportionment, and higher appropriations for education. The best part of the speech, the Birmingham editor thought, was that containing the governor's "renewal to the principles of democracy." Folsom had "shown himself as a person with considerable highness of spirit. He deserves a cooperative hand from everyone." [12]

Though the *Age-Herald's* comments were warmer than most, they were not atypical. There were some, however, who failed to view the address as conciliatory. Indeed it was thoroughly disquieting to those of more conservative bent. The removal of antiquated restrictions on the suffrage, the prospect of an unfettered democracy, the veiled reminder that property rights were less than absolute and entailed an element of social responsibility—these were not the kind of things they were accustomed to hearing from their governor.

Conservative fears were allayed somewhat, however, by the realization that Folsom's ability to implement his ambitious program would be sharply curtailed by an unsympathetic legislature. In the run-off contest between Folsom and Ellis, many of Ellis' partisans had pointed out that Folsom would have to deal with a hostile legislature if elected.[13] The newly-elected representative from Scottsboro, John Snodgrass, who later became a Folsom legislative leader, had foreseen four years of "fussing and fighting" in the legislature if Folsom were elected. Handy Ellis had also predicted a clash between Folsom and the legislature. "Bitter fighting, deadlock and stagnation" would ensue, Ellis predicted, if Folsom tried to implement his program.[14]

Former-Governor Frank Dixon, who did not view Folsom's election with equanimity, nonetheless felt that "the legislature is predominantly sound" and could serve as a check on Folsom. Joe Poole, out-going commissioner of agriculture and defeated candidate for governor, wrote Dixon two months before Folsom's inauguration about probable sentiment in the Senate. "It looks as if Bruce Henderson [conservative and able senator from the Black Belt county of Wilcox] will be President of the Senate and Robin Swift [vehemently anti-labor senator from a county bordering the Florida panhandle] Chairman of Finance and Taxation." Prospects were bright for retaining conservative control of the Senate and "if we can get the right men [on the proper committees] . . . the State will get along very well." [15]

Poole thought that Folsom would be forced to rely on a contingent of competent conservatives in the legislature, men like the able Earl McGowin of Butler County. "I think Jim will have to do this," Poole wrote, "because he happens to be one Governor . . . that . . . will not be able to control his legislature. . . . He doesn't have the ability to dominate a Legislature." In any case, Poole looked forward to the first few months of the new legislature "with amused curiosity." [16]

iii   Folsom's effectiveness might be curtailed by an unsympathetic legislature. But still a governor with such an immense popular following posed a distinct threat to conservative control of the state's affairs. Efforts had been underway since Folsom's election to neutralize that threat in whatever manner possible.

Since his victory in the May primary, Folsom had been assiduously courted by the established politicians in the liberal wing of the state party. Though his orientation was overtly liberal, Folsom had not come up through the ranks of the old progressive coalition, and there was always some doubt as to where his loyalty lay. Just as Senator Hill and others sought to bind themselves to Folsom, and him to them, so conservatives in the state also sought to come to terms with Folsom in the summer and early fall of 1946, to secure an agreement that Folsom would not carry through on his more disquieting campaign promises. Grover Hall, Jr., reported that some of Folsom's expenses to attend the American Legion's national convention in Los Angeles with a large entourage were paid by representatives of the business and industrial interests seeking concessions from Folsom.[17] The movement of Joe Poole and perhaps of Elbert Boozer to Folsom's support in the run-off primarily represented an attempt by these men and those they represented to come to terms with the inevitable victor on the best possible basis.

Such attempts were not extraordinary in Southern politics. The list of bogus champions of the people who chanted the litany of reform and who covertly protected the interests they damned is long and colorful. But Folsom was not to be a hireling of the "big mules." Either Folsom proved immune to their blandishments or they decided that he could be dealt with more easily and perhaps less expensively by other means. In either case, they soon forced an open clash with the administration that signalled the beginning of a bitter, rancorous feud between Folsom and his conservative foes. It was the first in a series of struggles in which

Folsom's conservative opponents sought to destroy his political clout. Only then could the threat that Folsom represented be neutralized. Then, neither as governor nor as party leader, could Folsom again frustrate conservative hopes for a postwar resurgence.

The issue over which the break first became apparent was an innocent and unexpected one. It is an incoming governor's traditional prerogative to name the president pro tem. of the Senate and the speaker of the House. The president pro tem. of the Senate is largely an honorary position without great power. But the speaker of the House is quite powerful and of vital importance to the success or failure of any administration's program. Not only does he exercise the power of the chair, a power of great latitude in the Alabama House, but he also determines the membership of each standing committee and decides to which committee each bill shall be assigned. There is no rule of relevancy in the Alabama House, and the Speaker can assign a bill which he opposes to a hostile committee regardless of the subject matter of the bill or the proper province of the committee.

Because of his power over legislation, the Speaker exercises great influence with his fellow House members. On the surface, the inherent power of the Speaker's position would seem to permit him to counteract and balance the great power of the governor, to guarantee an aceptable separation and balance between the legislative and executive branches. In practice, except on rare occasions, such has not been the case.

Tradition, respect for the executive's popular mandate and for the levers of power and patronage available to an incoming governor—all have combined to permit the governor to handpick the Speaker, to decide the composition of House committees, and thoroughly to dominate the House. The Speaker generally becomes the administration's chief lobbyist, though he may follow an independent path on a handful of issues. Tradition was one thing usually cherished by conservatives, but when tradition might increase the power of a governor who could not be influenced or moderated, that was another matter. Folsom met a determined and nearly-successful effort to deny him his choice for Speaker.

There had been a curious and, as it happened, crucial delay in making known the administration's choice for Speaker. Folsom had gone into an uncharacteristic retreat immediately after the election. Perhaps it was sheer exhaustion from his grueling campaign pace. Grover Hall, Jr., suggested that it was symptomatic of Folsom's "outlander" outlook, that he viewed himself the foe of every incumbent politician and of most of those who had been elected to the state legislature.[18] Perhaps, unconsciously, the governor-nominate wished to forestall his day of reckoning with them. Or, more likely, he never conceived of anyone's challenging his choice for Speaker—it was just not done. If so, he failed to appreciate the revolution he had worked in Alabama politics. There were many things that were "just not done" that would be: he had misjudged his opponents just as they had misjudged him.

Folsom's opponents had evidently decided that he could not be won by their overtures, that he was serious about reapportionment, constitutional revision, higher taxes and expanded state services.[19] His stand with Hill and Sparkman against the Boswell Amendment undoubtedly confirmed conservative fears. If he could not be controlled, perhaps he could be destroyed. The fight over the speakership was the opening barrage in a campaign to frustrate and embarrass the new administration, to hamstring it at the start, to undercut public confidence in it. Folsom's delay in naming his choice for Speaker provided the opening wedge for opposition forces. Before the second week of the new administration, the Governor and his conservative foes in the legislature were at loggerheads complete and irreconcilable.

Folsom's delay permitted two men to declare for the position of Speaker before he named his choice. Outgoing Speaker Charles Normal of Bullock announced he would be a candidate, as did W. L. Martin of Greene. Though both appealed to the same conservative factions, Martin was the candidate of the Black Belt and of the major corporate interests of the state.[20]

Though there was no doubt of his election, Folsom announced that he would make no move until after the general election in November when he would officially become governor-elect instead of merely governor-nominate. Once the general election had passed, the Governor was forced to move. He could support Martin or Norman, name his own choice and risk an early and embarrassing defeat, or seek a compromise candidate. Even before the general election it had become clear that Folsom's views were closely attuned to those of a third representative who had entered the race for Speaker. Bill Beck, of DeKalb County in the northeastern corner of the state, was young, attractive, and a veteran. Moreover, though not an ardent Folsom supporter, he shared the typical north-Alabama outlook and could be counted on to support most of Folsom's program. Whether his candidacy was prompted by Folsom is unclear, but after November 5, Folsom, now governor-elect, announced that Beck was his choice for Speaker.[21]

There were those in the House who sought to avoid a clash between governor and legislature. Representative Earl McGowin was put forward in early January as a compromise candidate. McGowin was unsympathetic to much of Folsom's program. Yet even though he was a Black Belter he felt that a more equitable legislative apportionment was long overdue. He had made it clear that he would support or oppose Folsom's proposals solely on the basis of merit. He was a man whose integrity was respected by all factions.[22]

Folsom had his dander up, however, and would hear nothing of a compromise candidate. Martin, whom Folsom regarded as the "pet candidate of the Black Belt and the corporate interests," was the more serious threat and claimed to have pledges of support from a majority of the House members. But administration forces were at work rallying support for Folsom's choice. The governor-elect realized that the fight for Speaker was not only "an initial test of his strength but also . . . an indirect determinant of the success or failure of his program." If he lost in this contest, he could not hope to control the legislature. Without the Speaker's great power, his program would be lost. And just as important would be the symbolic dimension of such a loss. To lose on such a vital but traditionally uncontested issue would discredit the new administration and destroy any chance for passage its program might have, regardless of its merit.[23]

Folsom was determined to win. Both his innate stubbornness and his realization of the political implications of defeat forced him to fight for his choice. Legislator after legislator was called to his office. As one reporter put it, he "exhausted every possible trading medium" to win votes for Beck.[24]

The legislature met on January 14, four days before the new governor was to be inaugurated. Folsom was seated in the gallery as the House convened to choose its officers. As the balloting progressed, Folsom's face broke into a grin. Beck had enough votes to win with four to spare.[25]

It was a considerable victory for the administration, but the cost had been great. The prestige of the new administration had been damaged and Folsom's precarious hold on the legislature had been made glaringly public.

The sturggle over the Speakership was a contest of major importance to the new administration. But it was only the opening shot in a feud that would grow in bitterness and intensity. Before the month was out, the clash between Folsom and his conservative foes in the legislature over the office of Speaker would seem but a minor skirmish. The major battles were yet to come. The conservative campaign to undercut Folsom and thus remove a major impediment to the conservative resurgence had begun.

iv   Folsom's challenge to the business and industrial interests in the state was far reaching. He seemed determined to overhaul the state's corporate tax structure, rewrite the state constitution, repeal the poll tax, reapportion the state legislature, and expand the social welfare role of state government.[26]

The narrow margin of Bill Beck's victory in the contest for Speaker had demonstrated the strength of anti-administration forces in the House.

On such a heated issue as an overhaul of the corporate tax structure, where great interests were at stake and where the administration would be denied the moral weight of tradition, it would be impossible for the administration to muster a majority. In the Senate, the conservative forces were even more strongly entrenched. As established politicians in their own right, members of the Senate were generally more independent of the governor's will than were members of the House. In addition, conservatives had an ally in the Senate's presiding officer, Lt. Gov. Clarence Inzor.[27]

Inzor did not openly break with Folsom, but he was not wholly sympathetic with the governor's program and appointed legislators of a decidedly anti-Folsom cast to key positions in the Senate. Robin Swift, for example, was appointed chairman of the powerful rules committee. Swift was an arch-conservative lumberman from Atmore, and a close friend of out-going Governor Sparks. With the anti-administration tenor of the Senate, Folsom could have done little to block Swift's appointment, but he did secure from Swift a perfunctory promise that he would not arbitrarily bottle up administration bills in committee.[28]

In both the House and the Senate, then, anti-administration forces had votes enough to defeat any administration measure they opposed, and almost enough to pass any measure they favored. It would seem unnecessarily risky to force any further confrontation with the new and overwhelmingly elected governor at the beginning of his term. But this was no ordinary governor. Conservative forces were generally the last to engage in public debate, preferring to rely upon their vast but unseen power in the committee structure of the legislature.[29] But when the new governor challenged the unchallengeable, when he sought to destroy the power of the Farm Bureau in state politics, the response was immediate, devastating, and public. Conservatives already had the administration on the defensive and now, when Folsom moved to challenge one of the bastions of their power in state politics while simultaneously moving to revamp the state tax structure, they moved quickly and decisively.

The Farm Bureau had long been an important cog in the conservative alliance that generally controlled the legislature. Through its publications the Bureau exercised considerable sway with many rural voters. But it exerted its real power through its well-financed lobbyists who ensured that bills the Bureau opposed were bottled up in committee and never reached the floor. At times, the Bureau had essayed a wider role. Working in tandem with the state Extension Service, headquartered at Auburn University, the Farm Bureau had led the fight against the efforts of Governor Sparks to divert surplus income tax revenue from property tax reduction to the schools. The federally-financed and supposedly apolitical Extension Service employed paid representatives in each county. It was a convenient and potentially powerful ally for the Farm

Bureau and a ready conduit to the individual farmer for the Bureau's point of view. Usually circumspect with the use of the Extension Service's web of influence, the Farm Bureau had overstepped its bounds in 1944 when an effort was made to oppose the renomination of incumbent Senator Lister Hill.[30]

Folsom did not confront the Bureau frontally but struck at its most vulnerable point. He moved to destroy the Bureau's greatest source of political clout—its domination of the Extension Service and of Auburn University.

When Folsom became governor, there were four vacancies on Auburn's ten-man board. Another appointment would soon be his to fill, and with himself an ex-officio member Folsom could command a majority of the board and effectively remove the Extension Service from politics. At least he could remove it from the conservative politics practiced by the Farm Bureau.

Folsom announced his four appointees in early February, and there began an immediate clamor. He had failed to reappoint the aging Edward O'Neil, a long-time power in the Farm Bureau and a former national president of the organization. Two days later, former agriculture commissioner Joe Poole and Senator Bruce Henderson of Wilcox organized a bloc of Senators pledged to defeat confirmation of Folsom's appointees.[31]

The Farm Bureau was incensed that Folsom had not reappointed O'Neil. Its conservative business allies were equally disturbed that the appointment of Birmingham business leader Frank Samford might be withdrawn by Folsom. Samford was serving under an interim appointment from Governor Sparks. The appointment had not been confirmed by the Senate and the new governor had the option to withdraw it and substitute his own if he chose. Samford was a respected leader of the business and industrial interests of the state, interests which had fought Folsom, which had long been identified with the Farm Bureau, and which would be most directly affected by the overhaul of the corporate tax structure Folsom had proposed. The fear of such an overhaul was scarcely unconnected with the effort to thwart Folsom's attempt to remove the Extension Service and Auburn University from the clutches of the Farm Bureau. The controversy offered another chance to frustrate the administration and to discredit it with the public.[32]

v   There were, to be sure, great interests at stake, both economic and political. But what made Folsom's appointments to the Auburn Board doubly galling to the Farm Bureau was not only the loss of Edward O'Neil but his replacement by Gould Beech of Montgomery.

Beech had been an editorial writer for the Birmingham *News* and the Montgomery *Advertiser*. He had attended the University of Alabama and upon graduation had worked for a time with the Extension Service in a public relations capacity. He had received high praise for his work at Auburn and upon his return from the war had been offered another position at the University. He had chosen instead to accept a position as editor of the *Southern Farmer*, published in Montgomery.[33]

This farm journal had been purchased after World War II by Marshall Field, Chicago-based publisher of the *Sun-Times* and of New York's liberal *PM*. Field envisioned the *Southern Farmer* as a spokesman for the tenant farmer and the small independent farmer, whose interests were neglected by the Farm Bureau and by the *Progressive Farmer*. It was a publication of considerable but largely unrecognized influence. Its national circulation was over 300,000 with over 70,000 subscribers in Alabama alone.[34]

Field had chosen Aubrey Williams, former head of the New Deal's National Youth Administration and a native of Springville, Alabama, to head the operation. Williams had been an outspoken liberal on racial as well as economic issues and was distrusted by the conservatives of the South.[35] He had chosen the young Beech as editor.

Beech was an intense young man, an uncompromising idealist of the first-water. Over a year before the controversy over Beech's appointment to the Auburn Board, Grover Hall, Jr., recalled the first time he had met Beech. It was "on the sweaty August night his papa brought him to see an editor [Hall's father] about a job. He looked like a boy then, he does now, and even if . . . he grows a pumpkin on his wire, he will always look boyish." The only way to assess Beech, Hall thought, "is to look into his eyes, preferably when you have said something which rawhides his own viewpoint about human values. The large hazel eyes widen and whitened [sic] and he has the aspect of an eagle batting his eyes. His lips get thinner, his pronounced drawl speeds up to three-quarter time and you have a cataract of spirit, statistics and historical precedent to cope with." [36]

Hall had never seen "a man with a more earnest and reasoned solicitude for the underdog than Beech." He knew "the history and the meaning of agrarian agony," Hall thought, and "when he talks of tenant farmers, their squalor and miseries, he does so, not because he has done his slumming by seeing or reading *Tobacco Road* but because he has grasped the meaning of [Howard Odum's] *Southern Regions.*" Some think Beech a "radical" or pinkish, Hall conceded. "Maybe he is. But if so, he rarely writes or says anything for which he can't make a jury argument. And if you'll think that over, that's saying something." [37]

Beech had known Senator Hill and had been sought out for advice on farm problems by Governor Sparks. He had won the respect and loyalty of newspaper editors in Birmingham and Montgomery where he had worked. He had taken time from his editorial duties to work in Folsom's behalf. He had written speeches and worked diligently in the run-off campaign. After Folsom's election he had acted as the governor's emissary on a number of occasions.[38] But his friends among the mighty availed him little when administration foes sought to make him a scapegoat to destroy the administration's public confidence. Folsom's appointment of Beech and the close relationship between Beech and the controversial Aubrey Williams gave the governor's conservative opponents an issue with which to discredit Folsom and undercut his political power at the very outset of his administration. Beech became an early victim of the type of character attack that became commonplace in the postwar years.

vi   Senator Henderson and Joe Poole, who led the opposition to Folsom's appointments, began to enlarge on the rumors that Beech, because of his association with Williams, was a dangerous "leftist." It was said that Beech was Folsom's choice to become President of Auburn, a post that was vacant and reportedly desired by the director of the Extension Service, P. O. Davis, ally of the Farm Bureau. Beech's rumored elevation to the presidency of Auburn was seen as part of a concerted move by Folsom to gain control of all institutions of higher education in the state. Ellis Arnall, former governor of Georgia and a man Folsom admired, would be made president of the University of Alabama; the liberal editorial writer for the Montgomery *Advertiser,* Charles G. Dobbins, later executive secretary of the American Council on Education, would assume the presidency of Alabama College in Montevallo, and Folsom would follow through on his announced intention of ending the self-perpetuating feature of the University of Alabama's Board of Trustees.[39]

Determination to block Folsom's appointments to the Auburn board was strengthened after the newly constituted board, with Folsom's unconfirmed appointees voting, adopted a statement sharply critical of the Extension Service.[40] It was the custom for interim appointees to take their seats on the board and participate as full voting members. It was, however, a tactical mistake in this instance. It made more plausible the charge of usurpation already leveled against the Governor and stirred the Farm Bureau to an even higher pitch of opposition.

Still, the resolution had been adopted unanimously; the incumbent members of the board voted for it as well as Folsom's appointees. The board charged that the Extension Service "has not done an effective job . . . promoting the welfare of the farm population of Alabama." Specifically, the Service had failed to cooperate with other agricultural and educational agencies, it had failed to give aid and assistance in developing farmer-owned cooperatives, had been the subject of constant interference in and manipulation of its internal affairs by the Farm Bureau, and had engaged in political activity. The board directed the head of the Extension Service to appear before it to answer the charges included in the resolution.[41]

Folsom added to the pressure for reform. In a speech at Auburn, delivered on the day the Board of Trustees adopted the resolution critical of the Extension Service, the Governor stated emphatically that the "Extension Service has got to get out of politics and stay out of politics. And I mean all kinds of politics—local politics, state politics, national politics, my kind of politics, your kind of politics, governmental politics and farm organization politics." Folsom's speech drew prolonged applause from the 6000 faculty, students, and townspeople assembled there.[42]

In that same speech, Folsom reiterated his determination to increase state revenue and to revamp the tax structure. He charged that those who complained loudest about his economic program were those who had profited most during the war. The "average citizen," Folsom argued, "isn't worried about taxes. He's worrying about whether we in Alabama are going to build a first class state. He's thinking about roads and schools and colleges. He's thinking about the future." On that same day, Folsom's Revenue Commissioner, who was himself suspect among conservative interests in the state,[43] was presenting the administration's tax proposals to the interim committee on finance. It was indeed a program designed to increase governmental revenue drastically.[44]

Folsom was also pressing for a constitutional convention to revise the outmoded and much-amended state constitution. Few denied that the constitution needed an overhaul, but even here Folsom met determined opposition from conservative interests who feared that constitutional limitations on taxation might be revised upward or eliminated altogether.[45]

To call a constitutional convention and to confirm his appointees to the Auburn board, Folsom acted upon the recommendation of an interim committee of the legislature and called a special session for the first week in March. He would seek action on these two matters before presenting his proposals for increased appropriations for education and welfare.[46]

The Farm Bureau and its allies, meanwhile, had not been idle. The Bureau's president, Walter Randolph, filed suit in state court to enjoin Folsom's appointees from sitting on the Auburn board before they received Senate approval.[47] Randolph branded Folsom's action calling a special session of the legislature a "desperate act." "He knows the courts will not sustain him in his usurpation . . . and he is desperately relying on the . . . Senate to back his play to seize control of Auburn so that he may repay his debt to the CIO–PAC and cement his alliance with Aubrey Williams and the Farmer's Union." Randolph urged all farmers to bring pressure upon their legislators to block the Governor's appointees.[48]

The special session of the legislature opened Monday, March 3, and was the scene of an amazingly confused scramble till its inconclusive close two days later. The Governor appeared before a joint session of the legislature, his hulking frame constrained in a dark double-breasted suit. He appealed to the legislature to give him and his program a vote of confidence by confirming his appointees and calling a constitutional convention. His appointees, he maintained, were men and women of the highest integrity, with strong sentiments about democracy, who will serve in the best interests of all the people. "They have my unqualified endorsement," he said, and if "fairly and openly considered would be overwhelmingly approved." [49]

Folsom reiterated his support for a constitutional convention and sought to identify the popular will with his request. Surely, he argued, the legislature is not opposed to permitting the people themselves to decide whether such a convention should be held. "The sovereign power rests with the people," and to fail to let them decide would be an invasion of the legislature's fundamental duty. "Let the people decide if this is the time for changes, if changes are needed." [50]

The legislature was in no mood to consider Folsom's appointments "fairly and openly" or even to discuss the question of a constitutional convention. Even before the Governor had arrived to deliver his address to the joint session, a message from his office withdrawing Governor Sparks' interim appointment of Earl McGowin and Frank Samford had been ignored by the Senate and the appointments confirmed. In the case of McGowin, the Senate's action was a startling display of ill-temper. The term for which McGowin had been named had expired the previous January. The motion to confirm had been offered by Senator Henderson, the president pro tem. of the Senate, and had carried 30-0 after an attempt to table was defeated 24-6. The administration had suffered a devastating defeat.[51]

Still, the day was not wholly lost. Approval of McGowin's interim appointment to a term which had already expired was a meaningless gesture of pique and defiance. The administration had effectively been denied only that place held by Samford. Three other vacancies on the Auburn board remained to be filled, and that number was shortly increased to four by the death of an incumbent trustee.[52]

Folsom and his advisors were "stunned" and "bewildered" by what had happened to them in the Senate. The display of ill-will had indeed been remarkable. The confirmation of McGowin was a gratuitous insult that served only to emphasize "the rebellious mood of the Senate." Even that, however, did not end the surliness of the Senate's anti-administration forces. Wtih Senator Henderson leading "the knifing crew disemboweling the governor's Senate hopes," the Senate added insult to injury. When twenty or so interim appointments made by Sparks were called up by anti-administration forces, Senator Joseph Langan of Mobile urged the Senate to forego its emotional binge and to follow a more reasonable course. He pointed out that Folsom had nominated the same persons to the same positions—ostensibly to "show them that [he] also approves . . . and wants them to be a part of his administration" but also, perhaps, to recapture some of his sinking prestige. The Senate, Langan argued, out of deference to the new governor and out of common courtesy ought to consider Folsom's nominations rather than Sparks'. But anti-administration forces had tasted victory and were in no mood for conciliation. Langan's move failed 5-27. It was, one Folsom floor leader remarked, "just like walking into a deep-freeze." And, according to newspaper reports, "hundreds of Extension Service and Farm Bureau leaders and members were sitting in the galleries," ironic witnesses to proof of the charges Folsom and others had made.[53]

The administration now knew that the appointments could not stand as originally offered. Acting at Beech's request, Folsom withdrew the one nomination that had been most sensitive. Beech issued an impassioned statement decrying the "organized, systematic campaign to destroy me." "The personal attack against me," he argued, "has overshadowed the fundamental issue at Auburn. That issue is whether an educational function shall be corrupted and prostituted for the petty political ambitions of a few men. . . . Auburn lies helpless and bleeding, the morale of its faculty and its students is at the lowest ebb in history. Today the farm services which are supposed to improve the welfare of all farm people are shot through with feuds and powermad political activity." [54]

A mass meeting of over three thousand students and faculty was held at Auburn in support of the Governor's appointments, and on successive days two hundred and then six hundred Auburn students appeared at the state capitol to demonstrate support for Folsom's efforts. But their presence only irritated anti-administration Senators even more. The Senate balked at confirming Folsom's nomination of State Senator V. S. Summerlin to replace Beech on the Auburn board, and action was postponed on a motion to hold public hearings on the nominations.[55]

There followed a complicated series of legislative maneuvers. Senator Henderson had introduced a resolution declaring it to be the sense of the Senate that it had completed its business and was ready to adjourn sine die. Motions to meet as a committee of the whole to dispose of the outstanding nominations, to wait until all executive nominations to the board were forthcoming before acting, and to postpone any action until the regular session in May were offered in rapid succession. Debate was heated, with several senators, including Senator Albert Patterson of Russell, urging a quick end to the controversy. Senator Patterson read a telegram from the president of the Auburn student body urging the Senate "to rid our school of political factions which are hindering its pro-grams," and he quoted a resolution of the Auburn faculty expressing support of Folsom's efforts to make Auburn "the equal of any land grant college in the United States." Finally, in a welter of confusion, the Sen-ate simply recessed until three the following day.[56]

Folsom then withdrew the two other appointments that had been chal-lenged, and his second round of appointees, including Senator Summer-lin, was quickly confirmed. Action on two additional appointments, which had not been subject to challenge, was postponed until the regu-lar session in May. The Senate then promptly adjourned sine die. As if to reinforce their displeasure, they did so without advising the Governor or the House of Representatives. The House informed the Governor of their intentions and, as was customary, asked him to address them in closing. Folsom arrived in the House chamber to a thunderous ovation —though it came chiefly from the Auburn students in the galleries. Fol-som pointedly thanked the House for its courtesy and expressed regret at the legislature's failure to call a constitutional convention.[57]

vii   In its public aspects, the contest between the Governor and the Senate was a struggle by a liberal governor to wrest control of a politically powerful quasi-public agency from his conservative oppo-nents. In that effort he had the support of the other members of the progressive wing of the party, Senators Hill and Sparkman. In the back-ground, though scarcely subtly, were economic interests that might be affected by the Governor's ambitious tax program, men who looked askance at further expansion of social services and governmental ex-penditures. It is this aspect of that clash that is most significant. But that clash of ambitions and interests was also a personal and individual trag-edy. And Gould Beech was its victim.

In an era when those who looked with favor upon unionization of labor were viewed by some as wild-eyed radicals, Gould Beech had early ob-tained a reputation for liberal views on social and economic questions. His association with Aubrey Williams and the *Southern Farmer* rein-forced that reputation. To those who hated the New Deal and Franklin Roosevelt, who were convinced, as was Robin Swift and, in a milder sense, Frank Dixon, that the country was on its way to ruin, such views were scarcely less than subversive.

When great interests were not at stake, the notions of this idealistic and intense young man could be tolerated with a degree of levity.[58] In harsher times, however, such views would make Beech vulnerable. He became both pawn and victim in the contest between the Governor and his foes over control of the Auburn board.

For Folsom, Beech's rejection was a humiliating rebuke, for the pro-gressive faction within the Democratic party it was a temporary defeat, for the Farm Bureau it was a smashing victory, but for Gould Beech it was a personal tragedy. The Birmingham *News* rebuked the Senate for its refusal to correct "the shameful illegality that so long has prevailed" and for rejecting the Governor's nominations without a fair hearing. "An aspiring, able Alabamian, with an excellent record of service to his country and his state, has by plain implication been condemned as a dangerous citizen." He may well hold some ideas that many would disagree with, but that was no crime. "The great majority of the people of Alabama are profoundly opposed to this kind of treatment for courage and independence of conviction and devotion to the public welfare." [59]

Beech was stunned by the affair. He remained in Alabama for a brief while and served as a Folsom appointee to the Alcoholic Beverage Control Board. His service there was commended by the most exacting, and often exasperating, reporter on state politics, Hugh Sparrow of the Birmingham *News*. But the damage done to his reputation and to him personally was not easily repaired. Ultimately he left Alabama and emigrated to Texas. There, in Houston, in association with Judge Roy Hofheinz, promoter, developer, public servant, and a power in Democratic politics in Texas, he made a modest fortune. [60]

The Governor blamed P. O. Davis, the director of the Extension Service, Joe Poole, former commissioner of agriculture, and Walter Randolph, president of the Farm Bureau, for the successful opposition to Beech's appointment. "It's the most disgraceful thing I've ever heard of," he told a press conference the day after Beech's name had been withdrawn. Beech "was tied at the foot of the cross and crucified." [61]

The rebuff the Governor had suffered at the hands of the Senate was devastating. His aides tried to minimize its impact, but Folsom insisted that "they licked me." And then he added laconically, "Maybe I deserve it. It's good for a fellow to get a spanking once in a while. It helps keep his feet on the ground." [62] Folsom would have ample opportunity to savor the advantages of such a position in the next few years.

In mid-March the reconstituted Auburn Board softened its charges against the Extension Service and its personnel. The board praised the Service for much of its good work and condemned, without specification, any political activity on the part of its employees. [63]

Thus ended, on an anti-climactic note, Folsom's initial attempt to undercut one of the mainstays of conservative strength in state politics. Perhaps he tried too much too soon. His attack upon the Extension Service and the introduction of his ambitious tax program brought down upon his administration the unified wrath of those opposed to his political and economic program. And they dealt the administration a stinging defeat.

viii   Folsom's conservative foes in the legislature had succeeded remarkably well in their efforts to undermine the Governor's political appeal. Throughout the remainder of the legislative session, they continued to defeat his proposals and frustrate the mandate for change he thought was his.

Folsom's critics had often charged that though he was full of good intentions, he had seldom proposed specific programs to accomplish his campaign promises. Folsom sought to counter such criticism by turning to respected academic and civic leaders in the state for advice and counsel. But even the imprimatur of men like Roscoe Martin of the University of Alabama and Mark Hodo of Birmingham did little to improve Folsom's fortunes with the legislature.[64]

In his campaign, Folsom had capitalized on a vague desire for change, for something better, that suffused the Alabama electorate in the immediate postwar years. That sentiment, combined with the force of his personality, had been enough to elect him governor but was of little use in taming the legislature. Folsom was not dealing with a mass electorate but with 141 men, some of whom were wily veterans of past legislative battles with reform-minded governors. Here was not the general run of farmers, teachers, laborers, the elderly, but the legislative spokesmen for the Farm Bureau, the Alabama Education Association, the labor unions, and the professional organizations of the aged. Each lobbyist and legislator was interested far more in the portion of Folsom's program that affected him and his constitutency than in any comprehensive reform program.

Folsom's opponents realized the nature of the legislative struggle and took advantage of it. Time and again they out-maneuvered the administration. When Folsom sought to divide the surplus funds in the income tax fund between an expanded program of old-age assistance and the public schools—thus satisfying the advocates of neither and increasing the clamor for further appropriations from both—the legislature coolly earmarked the entire sum for education. By appeasing the educators, the administration's foes could dilute the pressure for reform and hope to hold the line on expenditures for roads and welfare.[65]

Folsom had begun his administration in January with bright hopes of reforming state government, of remaking and revitalizing the liberal faction within Alabama Democracy, and, perhaps, of participating in the national councils of his party. But by fall, with the legislature still in session, Folsom's conservative opponents had forestalled his effort to remove Auburn and the state Extension Service from the influence of the Farm Bureau. They had tarred his administration with the taint of radicalism and had blocked the enactment of his legislative program. The public soon grew weary of continuous strife in Montgomery, and Folsom's political stock plummeted. His poor fortunes were compounded as some who had earlier sought him out sensed impending disaster and began to draw a discreet political distance between themselves and the Governor. Speaker Beck, his own gubernatorial ambitions encouraged by the Governor's opponents, broke with Folsom at least temporarily, and a chill began to develop in the relationship between Folsom and the state's two senators, Hill and Sparkman.[66]

In September, Grover Hall, Jr., who had given Folsom greater latitude than most newsmen in the state, spoke of Folsom's decline to a civic club in the southeast Alabama town of Dothan. Folsom had proved to be a "monumental fraud," Hall declared. He was "washed up" as a political force within the state. With a great deal of truth and, one suspects, a tinge of sadness, Hall spoke of Folsom as a "might have been," a man of "spectacular success and failure." Had Folsom's performance as governor equalled his unorthodox but successful campaign, he could have dominated "Alabama politics for a generation at least. He might even have been a big figure in national politics, even the vice-presidential running mate of President Truman next year." Folsom had "a winsome personality, color, rural background, big size, and a left-wing flair that would have offset some of Truman's lack of appeal." National leaders had evinced an interest in him, and he had been feted at a dinner attended by the President and a host of administration and Democratic party dignitaries. But after Folsom's difficulties in Alabama those national leaders "had not annoyed him" with their invitations.[67]

Folsom had been full of promise. He had received the blessing of Senator Hill, the most powerful figure in Alabama politics in the late 'forties, and Hall found it difficult to understand Folsom's failure. Granted much could be explained by the antagonism of a legislature composed of "solid and successful men who find in Folsom some kind of 'wonder' dangerous to their careers" and inimical to the political and economic interests they represent. But still there was always the haunting thought of what might have been.[68]

The administration was on the defensive now, if not in clear retreat, and Folsom's opponents pressed the attack. In late October, Rep. Walter Givhan of the Black Belt county of Dallas addressed an enthusiastic Farm Bureau convention. Givhan had long been a power in the Farm Bureau and often acted as legislative spokesman for the organization. Folsom's course was "a red course," Givhan charged, and his advisors were "red." Folsom's veto of a measure to establish the machinery by which to revise the state's suffrage and election laws to "take care of any decision the Supreme Court may make" was "a challenge to the white people of Alabama." Representative Beck, whom Folsom had supported for Speaker of the House, echoed Givhan's charges. "Givhan is right . . . ," Beck said. "The white people of Alabama must look to their interests. Gov. Folsom has swung to Aubrey Williams and Gould Beech and that threatens white supremacy and orderly government in Alabama." [69]

It was clear that Givhan feared what others had feared since Folsom's election—that in some manner the franchise might be extended to the masses of blacks and that this would doom any hope of a conservative resurgence. "Every Negro [voter] in Alabama . . . voted for Folsom," declared Givhan. "That is the way Williams and Beech want it and the more Negroes we allow to vote the more Negroes Williams and Beech can count on. It is time for the farmers of Alabama . . . to declare themselves. The extreme leftists, or reds, are going about trying to dominate us and they will, unless the farmers do their part." [70]

The president of the State Chamber of Commerce was more restrained than Givhan but equally harsh in his criticism of Folsom. Speaking to the state organization's tenth annual meeting, he warned his listeners that the state had a governor who is "frankly and openly antagonistic to business" and who has adopted the policy of convincing the public that "the protection and fostering of business and industry is contrary to the best interests of the average citizen." Somehow, he argued, "we must convince the people of Alabama that proprietors of business and industry are not enemies of the average man; that we are not two armies or two classes fighting against each other and competing with each other for possession of the most number of dollars." Far too many people, he warned, "think of us as . . . concerned only with advancing our own selfish interests." Folsom has been successful in portraying the leaders of business and industry as "Mr. Gotrocks from Birmingham . . . interested only in our own well-being and opposed to anything that might add to the health, wealth, comfort or pleasure of those in the lower income brackets." [71]

Folsom's prestige and the effectiveness of his administration were at a low point in the fall of 1947. The State Chamber of Commerce had waged an effective lobbying effort—reportedly funded at $40,000—against his legislative program.[72] But the power of a governor in Alabama, even one who meets the kind of entrenched opposition Folsom met, is not negligible. By executive order, Folsom had greatly increased the ad valorem assessment of the major corporations in the state,[73] and Folsom's foes in the legislature were reluctant to adjourn and leave the governor to his devices for the year and a half before the next legislative session.

Hostile legislators toyed with a number of proposals to limit executive power. Opposition forces in the legislature threatened to remove a number of state agencies from executive control and to subject the governor to a wide variety of new restraints. In an attempt to maintain continuing supervision over executive action, the legislature considered recessing for three to six months, delaying action on a number of pending measures, and reconvening at a later date. A three week recess was tried, but when the legislature reconvened in September it finished its work and adjourned. Not before it had passed a constitutional amendment, however, an amendment to permit the legislature to convene itself without a call by the executive.[74]

The amendment was popularly known as the "self-starter," and was bitterly opposed by Folsom. It offended Folsom's notions of executive supremacy and represented a vote of no confidence in his administration. Folsom had a distinctly modern conception of the executive's role in government. He viewed the chief executive as Andrew Jackson had, and as most strong presidents have, as the tribune of the people, the guardian of the public interest. Somehow, representatives and senators were too tied to local, particular, or special interests. The people expressed their sovereign will more perfectly, more completely in choosing a governor or a president than in choosing a representative or senator. The executive, more than any other elected official, carried a true mandate from the people. He should possess whatever powers necessary to implement that program. The legislature had its proper role to play, and it always stood as a potential check upon too powerful an executive. But it should show proper deference to the executive mandate, to this embodiment of the sovereign will of the people.[75]

Folsom saw the self-starter as but another move by his conservative opponents "to take government out of the hands of the people." It represented further encroachment by the legislature upon the powers of the executive. "I have no objection to taking the issue to the people. . . . It's a good time to let the people decide who is right." He was certain they would reject this legislative maneuver "instigated by special privilege groups who are looking for every chance to checkmate this office." [76]

After the legislature recessed, Folsom undertook a statewide speaking tour to defeat the amendment. As Hugh Sparrow pointed out, the campaign seemed unnecessary. The Governor probably could have defeated the amendment easily without such efforts. He still had a large popular following and the voters are generally dubious of measures which change fundamental governmental relationships. Moreover, even a great success would hold little sway with the hostile legislature. Sparrow could only surmise that the Governor enjoyed campaigning and welcomed another chance to stump the state.[77] The campaign against the self-starter afforded the Governor something other than the pleasures of campaigning, however. It provided him with a relatively certain victory that was sorely needed to enhance his sagging prestige.

Folsom campaigned throughout the state, almost as if he were running again for governor. He pleaded with the people for a reaffirmation of his mandate for better schools, for better roads, and higher old-age pensions. He charged that opposition senators were in the employ of giant corporations alien to the state, and he criticized repeatedly, though somewhat obscurely, the rigid anti-Soviet course of American foreign policy in the postwar years.[78]

There were some who based their arguments over the self-starter on the merits of the proposal, but it became increasingly evident that the contest would be a referendum on Folsom's stewardship. Folsom had done all he could to make it so, sensing that his opponents had handed him an opportunity to vindicate himself despite the reverses of the past year. Folsom's opponents readily took up the challenge—though not without misgivings that they had erred in giving Folsom an easy and much-needed victory.[79]

It was December, but not even the holiday season slowed the pace of the campaign. Folsom's charges became increasingly personal. The issues, he argued in early January, "are the same that were before us when I began my campaign in October . . . whether you are going ahead with our mailbox roads, pensions, and a constitutional convention or whether a little clique of hired corporation lawyers is going to run things . . . ." He replied in kind to what he regarded as attacks upon him personally. "I can call names myself," he said. "I could call the name of a certain North Alabama senator whose clients are listed as the Republic Steel Company, the Alabama Power Company, the Southern Railroad, the Southern Bell Telephone Company, the T.C.I., Goodyear, and about eight big insurance companies." And, he continued, "I could name a South Alabama legislator who represents thirteen corporations owned and operated out of New York. Why don't they tell you who are paying them? Why don't they tell you that they can't even work part time for you because they have to accept fees from those corporations." Yes, "it's the big corporations and the big newspaper boys who are against you and you and you and your children." [80]

Four of Folsom's legislative opponents, including erstwhile ally Speaker Beck, followed Folsom on the radio. Senator Albert Boutwell of Jefferson was particularly critical of Folsom. The Governor, he charged "has been willing to pit class against class and section against section . . . to disturb our people and make for unrest among them. . . . This sectional and class prejudice engendered by the governor will prove very costly to our social and economic status in Alabama." [81]

Other opponents seized upon other subjects with which to discredit the Governor and his opposition to the self-starter. Representative Luther Ingalls of Montgomery objected to Folsom's extravagance and his taste for "one-man rule." He argued that the self-starter was badly needed "in case the U. S. Supreme Court should overthrow Alabama's Boswell amendment—admittedly designed to curb mass Negro registration—and in case Congress should create a fair employment practices commission." Not trusting the Governor's stand on these subjects and fearing that Folsom would refuse to call a special session to deal with such an eventuality, Ingalls argued that "if that should happen some legislation would be needed to protect Alabama, and the Legislature would be powerless." [82]

But all such arguments proved powerless. Folsom ended his first year in office with a vote of confidence from the electorate that had overwhelmingly chosen him governor. The self-starter was defeated.[83]

6

THE ENDURING CLASH:

Race, Class, Party, and the Dixiecrat Revolt

In October of 1947, four of Alabama's leading journalists tried to dissect the nature and prospects of Southern liberalism. Colonel Harry B. Ayers, editor of the Anniston *Star* and a Democrat of progressive views dating back to Woodrow Wilson, argued that the outlook for liberalism in Alabama was auspicious. Dr. D. L. Hunt, editorial writer for the Birmingham *News*, agreed. Liberalism, he thought, was increasing in strength both in the larger cities of the state and in the smaller towns, particularly in north Alabama. Oscar Zuber, editorial writer for the *News* and formerly for the Richmond *Times-Dispatch*, extended the optimistic projections of Hunt and Ayers to the South as a whole, with the lone exception of Virginia. Only Gould Beech of the *Southern Farmer* dissented from the sanguine views of his colleagues.[1]

Beech's recent encounter with conservative forces in the legislature undoubtedly colored his judgment. He was not alone, however, in the pessimism with which he viewed the prospects for Southern liberalism. The Birmingham *News* thought Beech had been "impressive in the picture he drew of oppressive forces at work in the South to crush independence of thought and expression." Still, the *News* felt that "in Alabama, as in the South at large, there are vastly more progressives than is realized by many of us or by critics in other sections of the country." The *News* was optimistic for the future. "If this [liberal] sentiment could be made cohesive, the pace of emancipation from old and unhappy prejudices would become more rapid and more constructive."[2]

The optimism of the *News,* of Ayers and his colleagues would soon be tested in the election year of 1948. The States' Rights revolt in Alabama that year was the successful culmination of a series of attempts by the conservative faction within the Democratic party to wrest control of the state's political life from the adherents of the New Deal and, in more recent days, from the followers of Folsom. Rebuffed in 1944 in their attempt to defeat Lister Hill, defeated by Folsom in 1946, the conservatives had gained the offensive in the closely-fought but successful campaign for the Boswell amendment. Folsom's political fortunes had been dissipated in the byzantine intricacies of the state legislature. The political threat he represented had been deflated. The magic name of Roosevelt would no longer be on the ballot, and the seemingly pedestrian little man from Missouri faced a brewing revolt on the Democratic left and had little appeal. Conservative hopes ran high. The time seemed finally at hand for the long-sought conservative resurgence.

i   Late in 1947, Henry Wallace, the former Vice-President and Cabinet officer, visited Birmingham. Wallace was already the leader of the progressive forces in the country who felt that President Truman was uncommitted to domestic reform and wedded to a rigid and needlessly harsh anti-Soviet foreign policy. Newsmen in Birmingham were as interested in Wallace's assessment of Alabama's governor as in his views of the Truman presidency. "I think Folsom is a right guy," Wallace replied to a reporter's question. "He's the only prominent Democrat that's had nerve enough to introduce me during the last six months. So, of course, I'm for him." [3]

Henry Wallace was the kind of candidate to whom Folsom was naturally drawn. Both shared an agrarian background, an almost mystical solicitude for the common man, a sympathy for the oppressed of whatever color, or religion, or nation. In 1940, Folsom had been one of two Alabama delegates to vote for Wallace's nomination as Vice-President. The remainder of the delegation had favored Alabama's favorite son, Senator John Bankhead.[4] In 1947, both Folsom and Wallace held similar views on United States foreign policy, and both shared with other Democratic liberals an initial distaste for Harry S. Truman.

One of the ironies of Alabama politics in 1948 was the rapidity with which attitudes toward Truman shifted after he endorsed a strong civil rights program. Before that endorsement, Truman was a favorite of many of the conservative leaders in the state. Even the voluble Bull Connor launched his campaign for delegate-at-large to the Democratic convention with a statement of support for the incumbent President.[5]

The President was no champion to the liberal faction of the party in the state. These men had idolized Franklin Roosevelt. Harry Truman was perforce something of a usurper; at best his dedication to Rooseveltian policies was suspect. The state's two liberal senators, Lister Hill and John Sparkman, whose careers and loyalties stretched back into the heady days of Roosevelt's New Deal, shared the suspicions of their fellow liberals throughout the country. Nor was Governor Folsom close to the President. As it became clear that Truman was the likely nominee, however, and as the President came under mounting attack from conservative elements within the state party, the liberal wing of the Democratic party in Alabama shifted to a reluctant defense of the President. Nonetheless, he was accepted as a liability to the Loyalist cause, an obstacle to be overcome by appeals to party loyalty, by a recitation of the benefits Democratic programs had provided Alabama and the South, and by the invocation of the memory of the revered Roosevelt. The Loyalists were, at best, reluctant champions of Harry Truman in 1948. And in Alabama, at least, they were out-maneuvered and out-polled by their conservative opponents.

ii   Conservative elements within the Democratic party in Alabama had been dissatisfied with the national party since the advent of the New Deal. Some conservatives, like former-Governor Dixon, had opposed a third term for F.D.R. in 1940. The ranks of the dissidents had grown by 1944. Though the war tended to quiet domestic criticism of the President, there was renewed talk of a South-wide bolt that year. Nothing came of it in Alabama, though abortive anti-Roosevelt movements did appear in Texas and Mississippi.[6]

Many of the Alabama conservatives were disturbed over the economic and political thrust of the New Deal; many were also perturbed by the administration's equivocal position on questions of race. The administration's penchant for deficit financing, its responsiveness to urban and minority elements within the party, its solicitude for organized labor, the support it lent progressive forces within the state party—all contributed to conservative disillusionment wtih Roosevelt. By and large, these were the same men who had formed the nucleus of opposition to the progressive faction within the state party since the turn of the century. Now they provided the leadership for the Dixiecrats.

Political factions with varying motives ultimately joined the Dixiecrat movement. For many of its advocates, perhaps for most, race was the overriding factor. But among its leaders, at least in Alabama, economics and political strategy were equally important. Nor can one deny a sincere adherence by several States' Rights leaders to the nineteenth-century doctrines of laissez-faire and social Darwinism.

Former-Governor Frank Dixon is an example of the multiple currents of economics, philosophy, race, and history that swirled through the upper ranks of the Dixiecrat revolt. Born in California and educated at Philips Exeter, Columbia, and the University of Virginia, Dixon had long been a leader of anti-New Deal sentiment in the state. A successful corporation lawyer in Birmingham, he had taken an active role in veterans' organizations after World War I and had been elected governor in 1938 on a platform of retrenchment and clean government. His administration was a conservative one, but he took pride in civil service reforms and in the governmental restructuring he had accomplished. He took pride, too, in the successful fight he led as governor to forestall an expanded federal role in state welfare and unemployment programs. His fear of an increasingly powerful central government was eloquently expressed in his valedictory speech delivered in 1942 to the New York City Southern Club.[7]

Dixon had been closely allied with the business and industrial interests of the state. His political outlook was marked by a conservatism both economic and social. His was the classic eighteenth- and nineteenth-century liberalism born of a reaction against the strong mercantilist state of seventeenth-century Europe. To him the greatest threat to human liberty was governmental power, particularly when that power was used to thwart the "natural" workings of a free and unfettered economy.[8]

Dixon's belief in laissez faire, in limited government and states' rights, was paralleled by a belief in a limited franchise. Aware that the American political dynamic had moved ever towards a majoritarian democracy, Dixon nevertheless clung to a belief widespread among the Founding Fathers that government was naturally the business of those qualified by wealth, position, or education, of those who had a genuine stake in society. True liberty could long exist only in a society so ordered. That was an axiom he thought sanctioned by all history.[9]

Dixon recoiled at the solicitude and appeal that men like Franklin Roosevelt and Jim Folsom had for the masses. It was vulgar and dangerous. And though race was not the overriding factor with him, he must have sensed that Folsom, like Graves and Hill, did not fully share his fears of an enlarged electorate. Dixon had supported James Simpson against Lister Hill in 1944 and developed a hearty dislike for the state's senior Senator. In 1947, he had campaigned for the Boswell amendment, and like most men of his station, he had actively opposed Folsom's candidacy for governor.[10]

Dixon realized that the older views of Anglo-Saxon supremacy had been discredited, but his own experience prevented him from adopting the newer environmentalist theories. He could not accept the new egalitarian notions of race. He had expressed his racial views in 1944 in a letter to Grover Hall, Jr. "As a cosmopolitan and a church man I can justify, in theory, racial amalgamation. As a Southern man with the normal human dislike of foreigners both in space and in blood, I doubt my ability to put Christian charity into practice. . . . We are behind the times, I admit. The Huns have wrecked the theories of the master race with which we were so contented so long. Derbies are now being worn by Jackasses and silk purses being made out of sow's ears. Blood lines are out. The progeny of a cornfield ape blackened with the successive suns of Africa and Alabama, mated with a swamp gorilla from the Louisiana rice fields has developed promise as great as the sons of the great American families such as the Adams clan of New England. Henry Wallace is right—anthropology so teaches. But I buy dogs of a certain breed to fight, and I know that the sons of Man-O'-War are going to win races against all comers. The man who is close to the land—who follows blood lines, knows the doctrines in which in my very human weakness, I prefer to keep my faith." [11]

Dixon was knowingly in revolt against the political and economic currents of his time. He was joined in leadership of the Dixiecrats, however, by a man seemingly unaware that he acted in the middle of the twentieth century. Gessner McCorvey, the crusty old chairman of the State Democratic Executive Committee and an appealing and kindly man by all accounts, made a perfect model for the nineteenth-century gentleman statesman. Vaporous, full of pompous rhetoric about the rights of states and the dangers of centralized government, McCorvey spoke for an older age, without bitterness, rancor, or apology—and without an awareness that it had irrevocably passed.

McCorvey's father had been a professor of philosophy, history, and literature at the University of Alabama from 1874 to 1924, and McCorvey had absorbed the attitudes and values common to that generation of tweedy, gentlemanly academics. He had been reared in an atmosphere that permitted a certain unorthodoxy in religious belief but that bred conformity to the conventional economic and social wisdom. An unquestioned belief in white supremacy and in the rightful primacy of the fittest within society—views that were common in many of the most enlightened circles in the America of McCorvey's youth—these lived in happy harmony with a Spencerian belief in the limited role of government. [12]

McCorvey had been chairman of the party since 1939 when he won the post with the support of then-Governor Dixon. In 1947, with the liberal wing of the party in ascendency, McCorvey announced that he would not actively seek renomination as chairman but would willingly serve another term if the committee wished. [13]

Normally an incumbent governor can determine the choice of a chairman, and that might have been the case in 1947 with Folsom. But the Governor, who often tried to conciliate his foes rather than subdue them, [14] put forward no alternative candidate. Perhaps he realized at the outset that he lacked the strength in the committee to overturn McCorvey. Perhaps, too, he thought the prize hardly worth the effort. The chairmanship was a relatively unimportant post in normal times. But McCorvey's use of the office in the fight over the Boswell amendment should have alerted the Governor to the strength inherent in the position. Perhaps the Governor was just too absorbed in the more important struggle over the office of Speaker. For whatever reason, Folsom did not choose to replace McCorvey, and the office remained in conservative hands. Few realized how important that office would become in the factional struggle for control of the state party in the years from 1948 to 1950.

iii   From men like Dixon and McCorvey the conservative faction of the party had traditionally drawn support. There was another identifiable group that lent support to the Dixiecrat movement, however, and that was composed of a remnant of progressive leaders from the 1920's. These man had not followed the route of Bibb Graves and Handy Ellis. They had not become partisans of the New Deal. The personal appeal of Roosevelt and the economic impact of the New Deal could not overcome their social conservatism, their prohibitionist sentiments, their concern for government based on "sound business principles and economy." Racial prejudice and religious fundamentalism ran deep among many of these men and among their followers, and they were in bitter revolt against "modernism" in any form. Particularly were they in revolt against the drift of the Democratic party since the late 1920's. These were the men, like Judge Hugh Locke and Horace Wilkinson, who had bolted the party in 1928 when Al Smith, an Irish Catholic wet from the urban east, was the Democratic nominee. Religious prejudice and social conservatism had swept aside long-standing party loyalty in 1928, and in 1948 racial prejudice and fiscal conservatism would do the same.[15]

There were others, however, who had not bolted in 1928 who joined the States' Righters. The prominent leadership role of the '28 bolters had left the Dixiecrats vulnerable to attack from the Loyalists. (Former-Governor Sparks had already warned that the Loyalists were "not going to turn the party over to the pollywogs and mugwumps" of 1928.) The bolters sought to allay this criticism by attracting prominent Democratic regulars to their cause. Hugh Locke had been named chairman of the anti-Truman campaign committee, but, because of his role in 1928, his party loyalty was already suspect. His opinions on controversial issues had been too often and too vociferously expressed. There was dissatisfaction with his role as campaign committee chairman and a co-chairman was named from the ranks of the party regulars. John D. McQueen, a respected Tuscaloosa lawyer with a "rock-ribbed Democratic background," accepted the co-chairmanship and tersely remarked upon his unaccustomed alliance with Locke: "Political enemies of long-standing have, for the love of our state, buried the hatchet for the time being." [16]

The leaders of the Dixiecrats, whatever their persuasion or chief concern, were generally men who had been outside the dominant faction in state and national politics since Franklin Roosevelt worked his revolution within the Democratic party.[17] The brewing revolt against Harry Truman offered them an opportunity to come to the defense of principles of economy, of limited government and states' rights with a vigor unthinkable so long as F.D.R. lived. It also offered them an opportunity to put their political foes within the state party on the defensive, to re-establish conservative control of the Democratic party in Alabama, control that had largely rested in other hands since the 1930's.

As the Birmingham *News* pointed out, "many of those opposing the civil rights proposals long had opposed the present national administration on other important counts. Many such Democrats saw the Truman civil rights recommendations as presenting a highly fortunate opportunity to take the lead within the party from those who since the election of Franklin Roosevelt had been largely in control." The Mobile *Labor Journal* assessed the Dixiecrats in similar though more colorful terms. "Of course the grounds upon which [this movement ostensibly rests] . . . is the Civil Rights program. . . . But these [reactionaries] have opposed every legislative action, national and statewide, designed to lift the heel of oppression off of the poor whites in this deep Southland. . . . They are insincere men—trying to change the tide. They have lost their grip in Alabama and they are hoping to come back into power for their special privilege clients and friends on the emotional appeal to every prejudice in the minds and hearts of unthinking voters." National commentators also observed the prominence of men who opposed the New Deal on economic grounds among the leadership of the States' Rights movement. Stewart Alsop pointed out that "almost every States' Rights politician speaks as bitter of Franklin Roosevelt, who never really pressed the racial issue, as of Harry Truman, who did." [18]

Some Dixiecrat leaders were sensitive to the charges leveled at them. Talladega Judge D. H. Riddle denied that "this uprising . . . [came] from any so-called political leaders of any faction. It came from the hearts of the people," Riddle contended, people who were "righteously angry at the deliberate attack by Harry Truman on racial segregation." [19]

iv   The leaders of the Dixiecrats, then, were of diverse origin and outlook, though most had been on the fringes of power in state and national politics since the 1930's. Their opponents, the Loyalists, were divided among themselves by personal rivalries, by differences in style and outlook, and by a fundamental disagreement over foreign policy.

The three natural leaders of the Loyalist faction, Senators Hill and Sparkman and Governor Folsom, were united by their common enemies in the conservative faction of the state party. But in foreign affairs they differed sharply. Sparkman and Hill counted themselves among the internationalists in postwar America and staunchly defended the Marshall Plan. They represented a persistent strain of Southern internationalism. Folsom took a position that has often characterized spokesmen for rural constituencies, whether reformer or reactionary: foreign ventures, like foreign wars, only divert the nation's attention and resources from the real tasks at home.[20]

While Hill and Sparkman defended the role of the United States in the postwar years, Folsom sided with the liberal critics of U. S. policy. Like Henry Wallace, Folsom was critical of the increasingly hard line taken towards the Soviet Union, and he was impatient with the support the United States gave to reactionary regimes whose sole virtue, it seemed, was their anti-communism.

In July, 1946, Folsom had announced his opposition to a loan to Great Britain. The money was needed at home, he said. Two months later, after having conferred with Henry Wallace in Washington, Folsom delivered a strong indictment of U. S. policy before a rural audience in Luverne. The greatest mistake F.D.R. ever made, Folsom said, was his refusal to support the Spanish Loyalists in the 1930's. Truman's administration was making similar mistakes. "In Greece . . . we have been using our power to help put a king back on a throne. In Java we gave British soldiers the tanks and guns needed to beat down the people's freedom." It was a speech studded with an old-fashioned rural suspicion of a State Department run by "the rich men and the rich men's sons," "title-worshippers" who toadied to the monarchical British and acquiesced in the suppression of colonial peoples.[21]

Though it was expressed in the rustic vernacular and at times bordered on the demagogic, Folsom's criticism of U. S. foreign policy was of the same essence as that of Henry Wallace. As the controversy over the role of the United States in the postwar world converged on the central issue of the nation's relationship with the Soviet Union, Folsom continued to attack Truman's course.[22]

Folsom's criticism of the administration's foreign policy complicated his relations with the state's two Senators. The close relationship between Hill and Folsom, which Hill had taken pains to foster, had cooled by 1948. Folsom had never been particularly close to Sparkman. He had endorsed him in 1946 for the Senate chiefly because Sparkman was from north Alabama and had a progressive reputation.[23] In 1948, that tenuous relationship foundered on the shoals of rival ambition and differences over the nation's course in foreign affairs.

Sparkman was an independent political figure in his own right, despite the influence Folsom may have exercised on his behalf in the 1946 election. Sparkman was not fully entrenched in the Senate, however, and after his narrow victory in 1946 he might be vulnerable in 1948. Folsom, who had not come up through the ranks of the state' liberal faction and who remained something of a suspicious outsider, even to his liberal colleagues, had little to restrain him from entering a candidate against Sparkman.

Folsom's reform program had been frustrated by a hostile legislature. But if Sparkman's place in the Senate were filled by a trusted Folsom ally, the Governor could still enhance his political position within the state and become the primary spokesman for the state party in national councils. After much maneuvering, Folsom chose to support his close friend Philip Hamm against Sparkman in the 1948 primary. There was bitterness on both sides, and the resultant split in Loyalist forces only weakened their cause. As a result of the split between Folsom and Sparkman, Senator Hill emerged as the most effective Loyalist leader.[24]

Though they were in disarray, the Loyalist faction could agree on one point: the necessity of loyalty to the national party. They could agree on little else, however, and the factional strife, the personal feuds that had their origin here would, over a period of years, weaken the liberal wing of the party that in 1946 had seemed unassailably in control. This internal Loyalist weakness, combined with liberal defensiveness on the issue of race, eased the way for the conservative resurgence that had been in the offing since the death of F.D.R.

v   The struggle between Loyalists and States' Righters for control of the Democratic party in Alabama in 1948 was fought on two fronts. One was the effort by both factions to capture control of the state delegation to the Democratic convention in Philadelphia. The other, and ultimately more important, was the effort by each faction to name the slate of electors that would appear under the official party emblem in the November election. In Alabama, the names of the national party nominees for President and Vice President do not appear on the ballot. Rather the names of individual nominees for elector are listed. These nominees are chosen—for the Democratic party, at least—not by the official party organization but by the voters in the May primary. Thus Dixiecrats and Loyalists worked to win the electoral nominations for their respective adherents.

Since 1944 and before, some disgruntled Southern Democrats had been considering a revolt against the national party. As late as February, 1948, however, the strategy of the Dixiecrats in Alabama was undecided. Ultimately the Dixiecrats fielded candidates in the Democratic primary for both convention delegates and electors, but that at first seemed barred. Since 1945, electors chosen in the Democratic primary had been bound by state law to vote for the national nominees. Former-Governor Dixon thought the provision unfortunate and "unquestionably unconstitutional." Nonetheless, the provision was as yet unchallenged, and Dixon first favored bypassing the primary and fielding an independent slate of electors pledged to vote "for the democratic [sic] nominee unless the party platform contained planks destroying our southern way of life, and pledging themselves to vote for some southern democrat

[sic] if the democratic [sic] party platform did go haywire." The only difficulty with this procedure was that it would mean that the candidates for elector could not run "under the rooster [the state party emblem], and it might be difficult to get the folks to make the race. It ought to be done, however . . . . [for with the present legal provisions in force] it will be impossible, in my opinion, to get eleven men to make the race on the democratic [sic] ticket and then fail to vote for the party nominee. The other route . . . is practicable." [25]

The Dixiecrats eventually decided not to take Dixon's "other route." Control of the official party emblem and ballot position was too important to give up as readily as Dixon suggested. Instead, despite the 1945 act, the Dixiecrats fielded an ample slate for elector in the May primary. Meanwhile, the constitutional validity of the 1945 act was challenged in the state courts. Gessner McCorvey had asked Governor Folsom to request an advisory opinion of the Alabama Supreme Court. Not until that decision was rendered in May, 1945, were the Dixiecrats assured that their chosen strategy could work. [26]

The Dixiecrats greatly benefited from the growing split in liberal ranks and from the lateness with which the Loyalists came into the fray. Even at this early date, battle lines were drawing taut. Gessner McCorvey, the state party chairman, criticized Governor Folsom's rumored plans to lead a liberal delegation to Philadelphia. McCorvey argued that though President Truman might indeed be renominated, a forceful delegation from Alabama and the rest of the South was needed "to make a strong fight to prevent the more radical elements" from attacking the South's interests. He called for delegates "who will stand true to Southern tradition" in the face of the "very radical, unwise and anti-South report of the President's Committee on Civil Rights." Folsom had come under fire for shaking hands with Negroes who attended his rallies in the Black Belt, and it was clear that McCorvey did not include the Governor among those he thought sufficiently dedicated to Southern traditions. [27]

vi   President Truman's attitude toward the Civil Rights Commission report was as yet unclear, and this created considerable confusion within the state party. In late January, Governor Folsom took to the radio and, much to the surprise of many of those close to him, announced that he was himself a candidate for President, at least for favorite son. President Truman, he said, was "a nice man," but he was "hog-tied" by monopolists, Wall Street lawyers, and State Department "fancy-pants boys" and was running neither the Democratic party nor the country. President Truman in reply to questions about Folsom's charges coolly remarked that anyone who wanted a headline could always get one by attacking the President. [28]

Folsom's motive in announcing his favorite son candidacy is unclear. Like other Southern liberals, he may truly have assayed a wider national role. By making himself a focal point for opposition to the unpopular Truman and yet retaining the Southern rebellion within the party, he may have hoped to strengthen his position at home while elevating his importance in national councils as well. Perhaps, as his opponents charged, he was simply hoping Truman's drive for renomination would be stymied and Wallace or another liberal Democrat would then be chosen. More likely, his was the impulsive act of a sometimes erratic man who, when crowded, lunges out in unexpected directions. Too, he may have been deluded by his success against the self-starter into over-estimating his strength within the state and party.[29]

Though Folsom's motives are somewhat cloudy, the reaction of his opponents within the state party was predictable. Bull Connor declared his candidacy for delegate-at-large, a post for which Folsom was also a candidate, in February. He announced his support of Truman's bid for renomination and roundly criticized Folsom. The Governor, he charged, was trying "to help his political buddy, Henry Wallace." Folsom and Wallace and "the goggle-eyed bunch lined up with him" want to split the Democratic party "to the delight of the Communist party." [30]

Whatever Folsom's motivation, the difficulties of his equivocal position were apparent. He continued to pledge support to the national party but openly opposed its probable nominee. Those difficulties increased in ensuing months.

In early February, at the Southern Governors' Conference, Folsom sought support for a Southern favorite-son candidacy—with himself as the probable choice. Along with Governor J. N. McCord of Tennessee, he urged that the disagreements Southerners had with the national administration be fought out within the party rather than take the form of an outright bolt. The conference finally adopted a strongly-worded resolution warning the national administration that unless it ceased attacks upon white supremacy it would face a full-scale revolt in the South. The resolution was sponsored by Gov. Strom Thurmond of South Carolina and passed unanimously, though the conference rejected the proposal of Gov. Fielding Wright of Mississippi to meet March 1 to consider and plan an actual bolt from the party.[31]

By his ploy at the Governor's Conference, Folsom sought to make himself the object around which Southern discontent with the national administration might center and yet remain within the party. This move was paralleled by his effort to become chief arbiter of the position the state party would take toward the national organization. It was increasingly clear, however, that the state's two U. S. Senators did not intend to see the state party become the agency of one man, particularly such a singularly independent and unpredictable man as James E. Folsom.

In early February, the Montgomery *Advertiser* reported that Senators Hill and Sparkman were prepared to break with Folsom and that Folsom and his agents had been scouring the state to raise opposition to Sparkman's bid for a full Senate term. "As we have said before," the *Advertiser* commented, "Hill has been playing a game of footie with Folsom. They had many friends and enemies in common." But, the state's most politically astute paper added, "we knew that Hill could not fail to see Folsom for what he so obviously is."[32]

The break became even clearer as primary day neared. Thus, to the glee of the state's conservative leaders, the progressive wing of the party was split and would remain so. The contest over the future of the Democracy in Alabama was only complicated by such diversionary efforts, and the Loyalist cause only weakened.

vii   Gould Beech had played a leading role in the Folsom administration's search for a viable candidate to run against Sparkman. According to Sparkman, Beech had spoken with the Senator in February and had warned him that unless Sparkman changed his views on foreign policy, he would face opposition in the primary even if Beech himself had to make the race. Efforts to induce former New Deal Congressman Lafayette Patterson to make the race collapsed. The business and industrial interests in Birmingham refused to support Reuben Newton of Jasper, who was allied with the Governor. When these efforts failed, Folsom's close friend and revenue commissioner, Philip Hamm, entered the race.[33]

The chief issue of Hamm's campaign against Sparkman was foreign policy. Folsom also sought to make this the primary issue in his race for delegate-at-large and in his foundering favorite-son candidacy. The Marshall Plan, foreign aid, internationalism, the Truman administration's hardening stance toward the Soviet Union—these were the issues on which Folsom and Hamm made their appeal, with a strong mixture of rustic distrust of Great Britain and of the upper classes. "Why, those very folks our American Revolutionary soldiers and Andy Jackson fought," Folsom bellowed at the Temple Theater in Birmingham in April, "are now being ·bowed and scraped to by the fancy panters in our State Department. What do they know about the problems of the South and of Alabama? Yet they are representing us and are making our foreign policy for us." And he argued, after a reaffirmation of his belief in an absolute separation of church and state and of his opposition to peacetime conscription, that "the Wall Street-Yale-Princeton gotrocks is not a real American."[34]

Hamm echoed Folsom's stand on foreign policy and criticized Sparkman's internationalism, but his campaign never really got off the ground. He drew small crowds and even Governor Folsom's appearances on his behalf failed to awaken voter interest.[35]

In the first flush of victory in the contest over the self-starter amendment, Folsom and his aides had set about to enhance the Governor's position within the state party. Folsom had declared his favorite-son candidacy and his candidacy for delegate-at-large to the Democratic convention. A close political associate, Broughton Lamberth, had run for Democratic National Committeeman and Folsom's close political and personal friend, Philip Hamm, was running for the U. S. Senate against John Sparkman.[36] But in the machine-less personality politics of Alabama, it has always been difficult for a governor to transfer his personal following to other candidates. Folsom did not meet with notable success in 1948. And when a story involving personal scandal broke about him in March, his own candidacy and that of those he had endorsed were quickly deflated. Folsom was publicly accused of fathering an illegitimate son.

Folsom had traveled to Washington to testify before a Congressional committee on the tidelands oil question when news of the paternity suit first broke. A young, attractive blond, Christine Putnam Johnston, who had since married, had filed suit in criminal court in Cullman charging that Folsom had conducted an extended affair with her, had in fact become her common law husband and fathered by her a son, James Douglas, in April of 1946. Mrs. Johnston's suit alleged that Folsom had tried to keep their common law marriage and the birth of their son secret because he was then involved in his successful campaign for governor. Mrs. Johnston claimed that Folsom had promised to acknowledge their relationship and the legitimacy of her son's birth after he was elected but that he had since had a change of heart.[37]

The story was not new. As Ralph McGill of the Atlanta *Constitution* pointed out, it had been "kicking around Alabama for some time." McGill had heard it "more than a year ago, at which time it was said his foes were using the threat of it as a sort of blackjack." [38] Folsom dismissed the suit as a political gimmick aimed at defeating his candidacy for delegate-at-large and embarrassing his favorite-son effort.[39]

Folsom never conceded Mrs. Johnston's charges, and she dropped the case within a few months, reportedly settling out of court. But the damage was done. The newspapers of the state had been filled with pictures of Christine and the boy.[40] The antics of amiable Jim appeared less harmless than they had before, and the image of "Kissin' Jim" was ruefully recalled.

Folsom's campaign, and those of his followers, Hamm and Lamberth, had never quite caught fire, but the paternity suit, whatever its merits,[41] effectively destroyed Folsom's candidacy and made an embarrassing shambles of his campaign.

Despite the paternity suit and the effect it had upon the candidacies of Folsom and those associated with him, Senator Sparkman was increasingly occupied with his campaign against Hamm, and Senator Hill took the lead of the Loyalist forces—at least of those Loyalists not personally allied with the Governor. Hill had surprised many when, in early March, he had declared his continuing support for Truman. In entering the delegate-at-large race, the Senator had emphasized his disagreement with the President on some domestic issues but argued, in an indirect criticism of Folsom, that on the overriding issues of international peace and the Marshall Plan Truman was right.[42]

Still, Truman and the civil rights issue were not popular in the South, and both Hill and Sparkman, as well as Folsom, Congressman Albert Rains, and many of the conservative leaders, kept alive the prospect that someone other than Truman might be the Democratic nominee. General Eisenhower was the figure most often mentioned, and he had appeal for all elements in the party—except Folsom.[43]

Senator Sparkman had suggested General Eisenhower as a possible substitute for Truman, and in late March, he called upon the President to renounce his candidacy as a means of unifying the party. With Eisenhower as the party's candidate, Sparkman argued, the Democrats would be united and assured of success. Senator Hill also expressed the hope that Eisenhower might be the eventual nominee.[44]

Though the popular war hero held great appeal for both incipient States' Righters and Loyalists, the Loyalists had to face the probability that Truman might indeed be the nominee. They had to preserve some ground to retreat to. Senator Hill, speaking to the state on radio in March, made an appeal to party loyalty that became in time the Loyalists' chief argument. The South's only hope, Hill said, lay with the Democratic party. The chief reason he and Senator Sparkman wanted to stay within the Democratic fold was to forestall a Republican victory. He had come to Washington under Coolidge and had served there under Hoover. "I bear witness," this liberal spokesman for the TVA and for progressive health legislation asserted, "that the South received no consideration at the hands of the Republican Party. Tariff impositions, freight-rate discrimination, unjust taxation and financial policies made heavier the South's burdens and riveted even tighter the chains that bound us in economic dependence to the North and to the East." And besides, the Republicans offered nothing better on civil rights.[45]

With the vigorous support of Senator Hill, working in tandem with the national committee,[46] and with the active support of Senator Sparkman, Governor Folsom, and former-Governor Sparks, the Loyalists were in a powerful position. Even the strained relationship between Folsom and the two Senators did not appear an insurmountable barrier. Yet despite their strength in elected office, the Loyalists did not control either the chairman or a majority of the members of the State Democratic Executive Committee. These positions proved to be among States' Righters' greatest assets.

viii   Gessner McCorvey summoned the State Committee into special session in April. The Committee adopted a resolution calling upon each delegate or alternate to the national convention to walk out if any part of Truman's civil right proposals was adopted. A majority of the Committee agreed that "the Democrats of Alabama are entitled to know how each candidate for delegate and alternate stands" and called upon all candidates to make known to the State Chairman whether or not they intended to conform to the Committee's request. The State Chairman was also empowered to use Committee funds to publicize the Committee's stand and, in effect, campaign for candidates who agreed to do the Committee's bidding.[47]

Several county executive committees took issue with the State Committee's actions. The Walker County Committee criticized the move as "undemocratic" and an attempt "to deny the right of the people of Alabama to exercise their franchise at the polls" in November. The Winston County Committee echoed similar charges. Both former-Governor Sparks and Circuit Court Judge Roy Mayhall were sharply critical of the State Committee's actions. Former state Senator B. J. Cowart called the resolution "infamous and undemocratic" and State Senator Langan of Mobile charged that the use of Committee funds on behalf of some candidates in the primary was "discriminatory and unfair." [48]

The Executive Committee's stand seemed to draw the line between opposing forces clearly. But its immediate impact was sheer confusion as candidates first announced for the walkout and then, as public opinion shifted or political pressure mounted, switched and announced their opposition to it. Eventually, however, the confusion was dispelled and rival positions were known.[49]

Candidates for elector were now divided into two groups: those who were pledged to vote for the nominee of the national party and those who were "unpledged," free to vote for whom they pleased if, as likely, the Democratic convention nominated a candidate or adopted a platform considered objectionable to the South. So too were candidates for delegate and alternate divided, roughly, between those who wished to stay within the party and those who wished to bolt the party by walking out if the convention should take an "anti-South" stand. Here was drawn an enduring line between Loyalists and States' Righters. The struggle between these rival factions dominated the state's politics for the next fifteen years and continues to influence political alignments today.

In the race for elector, the results of the May primary represented a clear victory for the States' Righters. Five of the "unpledged" electors won outright. Ten unpledged candidates made the run-off for the remaining five places. Thus the States' Righters were guaranteed a clean sweep in the contest for the state's electoral votes. All ten Democratic electors were certain to oppose the Democratic nominee for President if he were Harry Truman or anyone else running on a pro-civil rights platform.[50]

The major decision had been made, though it was uncertain that the voters clearly realized the anomolous political situation they had created. The race for delegate, however, was wholly indecisive and is perhaps illustrative of the voters' confusion. Of those elected outright, eleven favored a walkout and eleven opposed. Of those in the run-off for the remaining positions, four were in favor and three opposed. Senator Hill, the leader of the anti-walkout faction, had led the ticket. Yet he was followed by three bolters among the top six candidates. In the end, fourteen delegates favored the walkout and twelve opposed.[51]

The results of the primary, then, were mixed. They represented something of a personal triumph for Senator Hill. Considering the lateness with which they entered the fray and the divisions they faced, the state's Loyalists had done rather well in the delegate race. They had not entered their strongest men in the race for elector and had been clearly outmaneuvered.[52] The primary results had been a thorough setback for the Governor. In January, he had hoped to widen his influence through the primary contests. But he had barely made the run-off for delegate-at-large, running tenth. His chosen candidates for Senator and for Democratic National Committeeman had been roundly defeated, and none of the Congressional candidates identified with his point of view, if not with him personally, had succeeded. It was not a happy day on Dexter Avenue.[53]

With the sweep of the races for elector by the bolters, the die was cast. The electors listed under the official emblem of the Democratic party in Alabama would refuse to vote for the national party nominee if that nominee were Truman or any other "anti-South" candidate or if the platform endorsed any advanced position on civil rights. The matter seemed settled. But for politicians on both sides the remaining months before the November election were a time of bitter recrimination that persisted long past Truman's surprise victory.

ix   When the Alabama delegation arrived in Philadelphia in early July for the Democratic National Convention, it was still unclear precisely which faction—Loyalist or States' Righter—held a majority. Fourteen delegates generally thought to be States' Righters had been chosen in the May primary along with twelve Loyalists. But there was always the possibility that Senator Hill's intensive lobbying efforts had swayed one of the fourteen States' Righters, thus giving the Loyalists an even break.[54]

The fears of the States' Rights faction were heightened by the knowledge that one of their fourteen was too ill to attend the convention and that his alternate was a young legislator of the Loyalist persuasion. Those

fears proved unfounded, however. The Alabama National Committeeman, Marion Rushton of Montgomery, a staunch States' Righter, presided over the organizational session of the delegation and ruled that no
alternate could assume a delegate's place until after a chairman was
chosen. Handy Ellis, the former lieutenant governor and Folsom opponent, was then chosen chairman of the delegation over Senator Hill, the
choice of the Loyalists.[55]

That afternoon when the convention opened, the predictable scenario
was enacted. The convention rejected the three versions of a Southern
minority report on the civil rights plank, and then, prodded by the ringing oratory of the newly-nominated Senator from Minnesota, Hubert
Humphrey, proceeded to reject the administration-backed majority report on civil rights and to adopt an even stronger minority report. When
the minority report was adopted by a vote of 651½ to 582½, the chair,
ignoring the frantic efforts of Bull Connor to be recognized, quickly recessed the proceedings until 6:30 p.m.[56]

When the assembly reconvened that evening, the chair moved to the
next order of business, the roll-call of the states for nominations for the
Presidency. When Alabama was called, Handy Ellis asked to speak to a
point of personal privilege. Ellis explained that much of the Alabama
delegation had been elected on a pledge to walk out if a strong civil
rights plank were adopted. "At this time, without fear but with disillusionment," he said, "we are carrying out our pledge to the people of
Alabama. We bid you good by." With that, the bolters among the delegation, with their ranks augmented by some of their colleagues from
Mississippi, marched out of the hall into the summer rain and, spurning
the waiting limousines provided by the convention, returned to their
hotel by cab.[57]

The twelve remaining delegates from Alabama reorganized the delegation with Senator Hill as chairman. They were joined by that Loyalist
legislator who had been prevented from assuming full delegate status
earlier. He was an uncommonly young state representative from Barbour
County who had sponsored a progressive and forward-looking vocational
education program in the House. Small of stature—almost diminutive—
of a rather sallow hue with dark hair slicked down tight against his skull,
Representative George C. Wallace took his stand with the Loyalist wing
of the party and remained in the convention to second the nomination of
Senator Russell of Georgia.[58]

The Loyalists chose to remain within the convention and within the
Democratic party, but they did not choose openly to support Harry
Truman in the balloting for the nomination. Truman did not need their
votes, and, whatever their personal predilections may have been, they
found it expedient to yield to Georgia for the nomination of a respected
Senator from the South, Richard B. Russell.[59] A vote for Russell could

always be cited when opponents attacked the Loyalists for refusing to walk out.

Despite the actions in Philadelphia, the major victory had already been won by the bolters. They had captured the state's electoral vote in the May primary. The initiative had passed now to their hands, at least in Alabama. And there, in Birmingham, States' Righters from throughout the South gathered in July for their national "conference."

x   Birmingham is pre-eminently a city of the New South. In 1948, it was the second largest city in the South. Only New Orleans surpassed it. And it was among the fastest growing.[60] It was a city without a Southern past. Founded in 1871, the product of a postwar invasion of Northern capital, it was a city of railroads and steel mills and labor unions, of skies heavy with industrial haze and suburbs winding up and down the iron-pocked hills of Red Mountain. It was a bustling city, then; local boosters called it the "Magic City—Youngest of the World's Great Cities." Except for the muted accents of its people and the heat of its summers, there was little in the industrial giant sprawling the length of Jones Valley to remind one of the South of Margaret Mitchell. Time had not yet softened either the scarred gashes in its hillsides or the attitudes of its people. There was an edge to life in Birmingham, raw and brooding. It was the rawness of a town still in the making, the dark disquiet of a rural people not yet adjusted to the harshness of the industrial order. Its tranquil suburbs, the often leisurely and mannered way of life of its people, seemed inconsistent with its oft-won distinction of "murder capital U.S.A." That was part of the paradox of this city of perpetual promise.[61]

It was to Birmingham that the dissident Democrats of the South repaired in 1948. The city was hot. It was July. The air was still, but it soon rang with a rhetoric reminiscent of Alabama's fiery secessionist, William Lowndes Yancey. The city was filled with talk as heated as the air.

The municipal auditorium was jammed when the Dixiecrats from throughout the South convened on July 17 for their national conference. From Texas and Louisiana came politicians and laymen concerned about off-shore oil and government paternalism. Judge Leander Perez of Plaquemines Parish added his own brand of peppery oratory to the proceedings. And from Mississippi came the bulk of its Congressional delegation, including Senators Stennis and Eastland.[62]

From throughout the South, and particularly from the lower South, came local and state politicians of all varieties. Men of character and sincere principle mingled freely with representatives of various selfish interests, political and economic. Men of restraint and moderation brushed shoulders with those who, without hesitation, fed upon the worst in an ugly and tragic tradition of racial prejudice. Men of sober mien sat quietly sweating in the heat of summer side-by-side with common rabble rousers and overzealous college students. Perhaps it was to be expected. Politics has never been the preserve of the high-minded alone, and the variegated character of the men present in that high-domed hall could be matched at most large political gatherings throughout the nation's history. Conspicuous by their absence, however, were Southern Congressmen and Senators, save for the state of Mississippi.

xi   Monday night's wrestling ring had been removed from the municipal auditorium and the fans had been oiled. The leaders of the States' Rights revolt thought of their movement as a national one, and the arrangements committee had avoided any hint of sectional identification. The Confederate battle flag, omnipresent at most political rallies in the Deep South, was discreetly absent, and the hall was bedecked with the flags of the forty-eight states, suffused by the Stars and Stripes.[63]

Former-Governor Frank Dixon of Alabama was temporary chairman of the conference and its keynote speaker. The delegates who heard him rap the proceedings to order that warm July Saturday at 11 a.m. were a varied lot. Gessner McCorvey, the state party chairman, had appointed a fifty-two-man delegation to represent Alabama. It consisted of twenty-six delegates and alternates to the Democratic Convention, the eleven unpledged electors, the state's National Committeeman and Committeewoman, the officers of the State Executive Committee and ten others. Mississippi was well-represented by members of her Congressional delegation and by her governor.

Other states were not represented so handsomely. The delegation from the Commonwealth of Virginia consisted of four students from the University of Virginia and a young woman who had stopped off on a cross-country tour. Texas was represented by ten members of the state's delegation to the Democratic Convention, Florida by three nominees for presidential elector. Tennessee, like Virginia, was represented by college students, and Georgia had no official representation. Kentucky's banner was carried aloft by an Alabamian who had formerly lived in Kentucky. North Carolina was not so fortunate. A native Alabamian, with no known connection with the Tarheel state, saw the state's standard standing in its place, grabbed it and plunged into the milling crowd. After all, "somebody's got to carry it."

Three of the South's incumbent governors were present and participated in the conference: Fielding Wright of Mississippi, Strom Thurmond of South Carolina, William Tuck of Virginia. Governor Ben Laney of Arkansas, who had played an active role in Southern maneuvering earlier in the year, had come to Birmingham for the conference but remained inexplicably absent from the hall. Later Governor Folsom appeared briefly to welcome the delegates to the state. Four former Southern governors were present: Hugh White of Mississippi, Sam Jones of Louisiana, William H. (Alfalfa Bill) Murray of Oklahoma, and Frank Dixon of Alabama.

These were not men evil in intent. Many of them had genuine and principled reservations about the course of national policy, politically, socially, and economically. But they were joined in Birmingham by representatives of the hate fringe always present in American politics. Gerald L. K. Smith was there, and J. B. Stoner, founder of the Anti-Jewish Party. The author of *Jews Have Got the Atom Bomb* and the president of the National Patrick Henry Organization of Georgia both graced the proceedings by their presence.

The leaders of the bolt were sensitive to charges that their movement was based on prejudice and sought to divorce themselves from these known purveyors of hate and prejudice. Rev. John Buchanan of Birmingham's Southside Baptist Church, delivered the invocation and implored the Lord God to "purge from our hearts all prejudice." The convention refused to issue credentials to Gerald L. K. Smith.[64]

As the proceedings got under way, Bull Connor came to the rostrum and, with his gravelly boom of a voice—which had been the source of his nickname and which he had used to good advantage in his days as a baseball announcer—called all the representatives who had been national convention delegates to the front of the hall. Cheers filled the hall as the names of Senators James Eastland and John Stennis of Mississippi were called. Rebel yells greeted Representatives Colmer and Williams and Winstead and Whitten and Abernathy—all of Mississippi—as they marched down the long aisles. And when the name of Representative Frank Boykin of Alabama was called, chants of "Where's Lister?" filled the hall.

After the introductions had been completed, the convention elected the Speaker of the Mississippi House, Walter Sillers, its permanent chairman. Former-Governor Dixon was then introduced to deliver the keynote address. Dixon gave a fighting speech to repeated cheers from the crowded hall. For thirty minutes he denounced the national Democratic party and Truman's civil rights proposals. The national Democratic party, he charged, "has sunk so low as to be willing to barter our individual liberties for the votes of minority groups in doubtful states." "We are being sold down the river," he told his frenzied audience, "for a mess of political porridge." Truman and the national party were "trying to force a social revolution in the South." "Do we belong in this kind of Democratic party?" Dixon asked repeatedly. And each time the answer came back a thunderous "No!"[65]

The South would not stand alone, Dixon assured his audience. "Right thinking people everywhere will rally to the cause because the liberties of individuals are at stake in every state—in California, New York, everywhere—not in the South alone." The States' Rights movement would prevent the establishment of a "federal gestapo" and would serve as a defense "against those who would destroy our civilization and mongrelize our people." [66]

Dixon's speech was met by wild enthusiasm. For twenty-five minutes after he finished pandemonium ruled the hall. A group of students from the University of Mississippi, over fifty-strong, formed a cheering section and chanted, "to hell with Truman." The hall was filled with the Confederate battle flag so obviously absent from the official decorations. Students from Birmingham-Southern College carried the picture of Robert E. Lee aloft, and shouts of "We want Dixon" and "Dixie wants Dixon" filled the halls.

After brief remarks by other dignitaries, the convention recessed a half hour after noon to reconvene two hours later. The period of recess was one of uncertainty and confusion. Governor Laney of Arkansas, who had remained in his hotel room during the morning session, issued an unexpected announcement that temporarily cooled the enthusiasm of the morning. Laney called for unity in Democratic ranks. It is not too late to "avoid permanent division of our people," he reminded his fellow Southerners. He urged those present in Birmingham to put aside selfish political ambitions and to work through the party's official organization in each state. And he repudiated the tenor of the morning session: "The spirit of obstinacy and revenge is not the Spirit of the Southland." [67]

The uncertainty and confusion were heightened when the conference reconvened that afternoon. Conflicting reports and vague statements from the chair were compounded by unfounded rumors on the floor. The convention threatened to get out of control as delegates debated the varying strategies of revolt—a set ticket for all the states or simply a slate of unpledged electors in each state. While the delegates debated these and other questions of lesser significance—whether to call the gathering a convention or a conference—a small group of leaders set the movement's real course. Having first offered the Presidential nomination to a reluctant Frank Dixon, the leaders of the States' Rights revolt settled upon a ticket composed of Governor Thurmond of South Carolina and Governor Fielding Wright of Mississippi.

Late in the afternoon, Horace Wilkinson, the Alabama segregationist, rose to nominate both Thurmond and Wright. But though the course was set, confusion was still apparent. Thurmond could not be located, nor could a copy of the resolutions committee's "Declaration of Principles" which was to be acted upon.

While the convention waited for its Presidential nominee to be found, Governor Folsom appeared briefly to extend an official welcome to the delegates. In a short speech, he avoided committing himself to the bolt while attacking the Truman administration.

The rhetoric of Thurmond's acceptance speech was designed to raise the Southern ire. He could not resist dropping the a-sectional image the planners had striven for. An "accidental President" with an overweening desire for support from a minority bloc had "stabbed the South in the back," Thurmond charged. "No true Southerner could fail to answer the call of his people."

Down Truman's road lay a "totalitarian state," and Thurmond flailed both the President's civil rights program and those who supported it. The proposed FEPC is "the nearest thing to communism ever advocated in these United States. If it's passed state lines will be practically wiped out." Northern "do-gooders" were being misled in their opposition to segregation. Segregation could never be abolished by force. Besides, segregation had not held the Negro back. The Negroes of the South had made more progress in the last fifty years than any other race anywhere at any time.

Thurmond closed with an appeal to the manly pride of the South. We must show the nation that the South is not "in the bag." "I can think of nothing worse [than] for the South to tuck its tail and vote for Truman. If we did, we would be nothing worse than cowards." But if we persist we will prevail. "The nation will never forget this fight we're making. We can go on to victory because right is on our side."

xii   When the proceedings ended, the delegates and observers streamed out across the green expanse of Woodrow Wilson Park, back to their hotels and on the nearby bus stations or the more distant railway terminals. Back to their homes to carry their enthusiasm, their hopes and fears raised high by their collective exercise of protest. Spirits had been lifted in Birmingham, and to the committed prospects seemed bright.

But to the more realistic of the leaders, including Frank Dixon of Birmingham, the proceedings portended trouble as well as hope. During the conference, the emotional outbursts of men like Horace Wilkinson, the speeches which flagrantly catered to racial prejudice, had elicited the most fervent response. To Dixon and to others like him these speeches were ungentlemanly and unwise. To men of Dixon's character, background, and persuasions such raw emotional appeals were unpardonable in and of themselves regardless of their content. The frenzy of the demagogue was not Dixon's style; it was not the way respectable men responded.

It was more than just a question of conduct, of manner, that troubled Dixon, however. It was also a question of strategy and even of principle, of what the revolt was all about. It was a question that continued to plague the Dixiecrats, and one which can no more be answered with certainty today than when Frank Dixon pondered it in 1948.

Dixon, like Folsom, had read his history. To him the States' Rights battle was another episode in the eternal struggle against the tyranny of an all-powerful state. The anti-statism of Jefferson, reinforced by the laissez-faire doctrine of the classical economists and the social Darwinism of Herbert Spencer, convinced Dixon that the great issues at question in 1948 were not ephemeral, transient, or sectional. Fundamentally, they were "the ancient issues of a highly centralized . . . state as opposed to local self government" and individual freedom.[68] Unless the drift of national policy under the New Deal were reversed and the New Deal's adherents driven from positions of power in state and national politics, the prospects for the survival of individual liberty and initiative, Dixon had concluded, were dim.

As the campaign wore on, Dixon grew gloomy and foresaw the eventual end of "constitutional government." His rhetoric grew heightened and exaggerated. The States' Rights revolt, he wrote Virginius Dabney, is "an effort to defeat the determination of [the national parties] to create a police state." He reeled off a bill of particulars to prove his charge: "the anti-lynching law is the first step toward shifting police power [69] from the states to the central government. The law abolishing the poll tax is the first step toward federal control of elections. Add these two together and you have the pattern of dictatorship." If added proof were needed, the Fair Employment Practices Commission was an obvious "attempt to revolutionize the social and economic life of the nation, by force and through a federal police." [70]

Dixon's speeches and letters referred with increasing frequency to a "police-state," a "federal Gestapo." He ended a long letter to the Birmingham *News* with a bitter query that, he thought, disposed of all objections to the bolters: "they die hard, don't they—those who would remake these United States into the image of the police states of Eastern Europe." [71]

Despite the strained emotionalism of his speeches, Dixon preferred to keep the campaign on libertarian and principled grounds. Not only did it conform to his view of himself as the high-minded man of principle leading the forces of liberty against the dark and menacing forces of tyranny, but it also had strategic advantages. Such an appeal, divorced from the race issue, would garner support from throughout the nation. "These . . . threats [to liberty and individual freedom] are not sectional," he wrote Dabney. "They are as real as tyranny." Dixon was certain that there were eager legions throughout the country who had looked on with helpless alarm as the New Deal expanded the power of the federal government. Now was the time to seize the initiative from the time-serving minions of the New Deal who had dominated state and national politics since the early thirties. "There isn't any other course for us to pursue," Dixon confided to Donald Comer, scion of a family long identified with its own brand of humanitarian and enlightened business progressivism. "You and I, and all of us, have squirmed under our helplessness in the National political picture. We are adopting the only way out . . . ." [72]

The Dixiecrat movement, as Dixon envisioned it, aimed to reverse the recent and dangerous increase in the power of the federal government. There was, however, another, more immediate and related goal—to restore to the South the influence she had had within the Democratic party, and thus in national affairs, before the repeal of the two-thirds rule in 1936.[73] (In part, the conservative leaders of the South were engaged in the same task that John C. Calhoun had begun over a century earlier—protecting the influence of a minority section and a minority economic interest in a society ever moving, for good or ill, towards majoritarian democracy.)

The effort to restore the South's disproportionate influence in national councils was, of course, tied to the broader aim of curbing the role and power of the federal government and reaffirming the venerable doctrines of states' rights and laissez-faire. The one was but a means to effect the other. Nonetheless, the two goals were distinct and at times in conflict.

For the Dixiecrat strategy to be effective, the South must be united. But as writers, historians, and analysts have been saying for decades— without much apparent impact—the South is not monolithic. There are many Souths. Interests, attitudes, and ways of life vary greatly within the bounds of that supposedly close-knit and homogeneous entity. Still, whether it be its past, the collective unconscious of its people, or whatever, there is an indefinable unity in the area. U. B. Phillips may have been mistaken that the central theme of Southern history revolves around race. But it is true, nonetheless, that at certain crucial moments in Southern history race seems to be the one issue that can unite more white Southerners than any other. It is an issue that unites rich and poor. It is a powerful solvent that can dissolve economic, class, or sectional differences as tensions heighten and emotions rise.

If the success of the States' Rights movement depended first upon uniting the South, it was clear that the race issue, whatever principled desires of men like Dixon, was most likely to insure that unity. Dixon, Comer, John Temple Graves and others might fight to keep the movement on a different plane. And to one correspondent Dixon might proudly announce that "the problem with us is not so much one of the negro race . . . but the maintenance of the republican form of government . . . ." [74] But the Negro question would not down.

An official of the State Chamber of Commerce wrote Frank Dixon that business people in the southern part of the state were anxious "to give support to the States' Rights principles and candidates, but there have been some severe criticisms" of the Birmingham conference and of the immoderate speeches of men like Horace Wilkinson. "A good part of the people I talked with expressed the desire that the speakers that are to present the States' Rights position be cautioned to refrain from the type of talk that would inflame both races." [75]

Dixon and men like Comer became somewhat touchy on the issue and took pains to cite their own personal records when editors and others ranked the Dixiecrats with "sinister movements founded on bigotry." Such blanket charges were indeed unjust, but Dixon's sensitivity to the charges, the lengths to which he went to justify his innocence, perhaps betray an awareness that he was the circumstantial confederate of men of baser motives, men he did not repudiate.

To the editor of the Richmond *Times-Dispatch,* Dixon wrote a letter, that, despite its characteristic restraint, plainly shows his hurt and anger at charges leveled against him and against the movement. As for his "connection with 'sinister movements founded on bigotry,'" which the *Times-Dispatch* had alleged, "my record is completely clear. Continuously throughout its existence as an active force, I fought the Ku Klux Klan, and that in the days when it was not easy to do so. I wish as much could be said for some of our other Alabamians, who used the mask and robe of the Klan to climb into high public office, and who are now vigorously engaged in the effort to kill local self-government and substitute a police state." Moreover, Dixon argued, he had stumped the state in 1928 for Al Smith—"and that was not easy either. The same forces of intolerance," he said in a revealing slip, "were on the other side then." "Am I 'using States' Rights as a mere smokescreen,' as you say? . . . The record is so clear, so long and so well known that you could easily have found the truth." [76]

But would the truth, even if easily found, completely absolve Dixon as he so confidently assumed? The issue of race was never far below the surface of the Dixiecrat revolt, even for Dixon. "It may be that the time has come for us to see established in the South a great big mongrel brotherhood of mixed races, but I don't think so," he wrote to a local circuit judge in Jefferson County. He added, however, that "deeper than the race question, affecting all parts of this country alike, is the question of whether we are to have a police state with a federal gestapo trailing the average American citizen in his daily life." [77]

Despite such disclaimers, however, the necessity of uniting the South behind the States' Rights ticket led men like Dixon to acquiesce in blatant appeals to race prejudice. He may have been uncomfortable with such appeals but he did not renounce them. Gessner McCorvey had come into possession of a photograph of a Negro lawyer from St. Louis addressing the Democratic convention in Philadelphia and calling for the expulsion of the Mississippi delegation. McCorvey was quick to recognize the value of such a picture. "Many of our people don't understand what we are confronted with," he wrote. Publication of the picture throughout the

South would alert the people to the danger. The photograph was uniquely suited to such uses, McCorvey thought. "I don't think I ever saw a human being whose picture more resembled a gorilla." [78]

It was indeed, as McCorvey wrote, "a corking good glossy picture." But McCorvey realized the dangers of an appeal to prejudice. He wrote Frank Dixon that it would be a good idea to have the photograph reproduced and sent throughout the state, but he doubted "very much if it would be well for me to send this out as being sponsored by the state Executive Committee." His dilemma was plain. "I appreciate how much we want to keep the States' Rights Movement off the Negro proposition but on the other hand this picture will make any white Southern man or woman boil over with indignation." It "would make many a vote." [79]

Dixon and other Dixiecrat leaders were largely untouched by such appeals. Yet occasionally, Dixon himself revealed that under the exterior of principle lay a residue of prejudice, restrained though ever-present. "Some . . . have criticized me for bringing the negro question into it, but I fail to see how it is possible to discuss that problem so long as it is the meat in the coconut." [80]

xiii   The Alabama ballot in November 1948 was unlike any other in the nation. Nowhere among the names listed was there a slate of electors who would vote for the incumbent President of the United States. Those who wished to vote for Mr. Truman—though they may have been few—could not do so.

The Dixiecrats had seized the regular party's ballot position in four states—Louisiana, South Carolina, Mississippi, and Alabama. These were the only states Thurmond carried. But in each of the states other than Alabama, electors pledged to Truman appeared on the ballot.[81]

The muddled state of electoral affairs in Alabama was at root the result of the curious vagaries of the federal political system by which this nation is governed. Except in presidential elections, the national parties are largely shadow organizations. They resemble less a truly national party than a variegated confederation of fifty independent state parties, each one oriented to the issues and personalities of state rather than national politics. Initially, the confusion in Alabama was the accidental and inadvertent product of faulty state law and clumsy political timing by the state's Loyalists. In the end, however, that confusion represented conscious design in a situation that, for the Loyalists, was hopeless.

When the States' Righters captured all eleven electors in the primary on May 5, it was already too late for the Loyalists to secure independent ballot position under existing state law. That deadline had passed in March.[82] Why had the Loyalists not foreseen this foreclosure and left open an alternate course?

The explanations are several and, at the time, were perfectly plausible. First, it was not until February of 1948, when President Truman endorsed the limited requests of his Civil Rights Commission, that a full-scale Southern revolt against the national party became probable. Until that endorsement, conservative Democrats in Alabama had been almost unanimous in their support of Truman. Even after the first rumbles of serious revolt in Southern ranks, there was still the expectation that a spirit of compromise would prevail. Moreover, the Loyalists were unwilling to bolt the state party. The basis of their appeal was party loyalty, and it would undermine the logic of their argument to be the first to bolt. Nor was it at all clear by the March deadline that there would be a full-scale conservative revolt in the May primary. Even if there were, the Loyalists stood a good chance of turning back any challenge from their conservative opponents. If they failed, however, there was a state law enacted in 1945 to fall back on. That act bound electors to vote for the nominees of the party under whose auspices they sought election.[83]

With revolt not yet apparent, with the outlook for victory encouraging even if one appeared, and with the comforting knowledge that state law seemingly assured that electors chosen under the Democratic column would vote for the Democratic nominee, the Loyalists were not yet worried. Their main concern was a bolt of dissident elements at the national convention, and they focused their interest and energy on the races for convention delegate. The March 1 deadline for an independent slate came and went and nobody seemed to notice.

The size and success of the Dixiecrat revolt soon shattered the Loyalists' complacency. In May, 1948, they received another jolt when the Supreme Court of Alabama declared unconstitutional the 1945 act binding electors to vote for the nominee of their party. Electors were "free agents," the Court argued, and could not be bound by state law, party directives, or any other means. Electors chosen in a party primary might have a moral obligation to support the nominees of that party, but there was no legal remedy by which to compel them to do so.[84]

After the May primary and the invalidation of the 1945 act, there were still a number of options open to the Loyalists. Governor Folsom could call the legislature into special session to seek ballot position for a slate of Truman electors. Or through further legal action and moral suasion, the Loyalists could try to compel the dissident electors to vote for the national nominee.

Should they fail, however, the Loyalists faced an unwelcome dilemma. The basis of their argument in the intra-party struggle had been an appeal to party loyalty. Yet now the nominees for elector chosen in the regular party primary were pledged to vote for someone other than the national Democratic nominee. The position of the Loyalists was made more difficult by the stance of the state party chairman. Gessner McCor-

vey had made it clear that any member of the Loyalist faction who failed
to support the duly chosen nominees for elector would be barred from
the party primary in 1950.[85] This posed a particularly difficult problem
for Senator Hill, who was up for reelection in 1950. Though protesting
continued loyalty to the national party, Hill and other Loyalist leaders
decided to accept the primary verdict.[86] Public leadership of the irreconcilable Loyalist forces, who were determined to place a slate pledged to
Truman on the November ballot, then passed to other hands.

State senator Joseph N. Langan of Mobile, a New Deal partisan and
one of the handful of supporters of Folsom's legislative program, presided over a meeting of pro-Truman Democrats in Montgomery in mid-
August. Langan had earlier held out hope that, with the seriousness of
the Southern revolt beyond question and with the lack of enthusiasm for
Truman's candidacy in liberal ranks still apparent, the President would
withdraw. By August it was clear that Truman entertained no such
plans. Langan now sought to persuade the Dixiecrat electors to resign
in favor of electors loyal to the national party.[87]

The Montgomery meeting was dominated by the leaders of organized
labor. The state director of the C.I.O., the President of the United Mine
Workers in Alabama, the chairman of the state A.F.L. League of Political
Education, as well as other labor leaders, were present. Senator Langan
set the tone for the meeting, citing the benefits provided to Alabama by
past Democratic administrations and charging that "those most critical
of the Democratic Party now are those who were most bitter in their
criticisms of Franklin Roosevelt. They are really Republicans at heart."
He decried the use of racial prejudice by the Dixiecrats and compared
their conceptions of race to those prevalent in Hitler's Germany. Truman's civil rights program did not receive his endorsement, however. He
thought the poll tax and other measures should be left to the states. But
"these are not enough—are not important enough—to make us desert the
Democratic Party which has done so much for Alabama and the South.
. . . They are not so terrible and not so important as to destroy the Democratic Party." It was clear, however, that he was not hostile to the cause
of civil rights. A devout Catholic infused with a Christian commitment
to the brotherhood of all mankind, Langan argued that ". . . when we
[in the South] make some 15,000,000 persons nothing but slaves . . . .
when we degrade and hold down a segment of our population," we only
create fertile ground for communism.[88]

At later meetings in Birmingham and elsewhere, Langan continued to
charge that the Dixiecrats were supported by "big oil interests who are
working for the election of a Republican President" and that civil rights
"is merely a smokescreen being used to hide the selfish interests of a
party dominated by big business." By late August, Langan and the
leaders of organized labor in the state had decided to seek a writ of

mandamus against the Dixiecrat electors compelling them to vote for Truman.[89]

In support of the strategy worked out by the Langan forces, Governor Folsom filed suit against the Dixiecrat electors in October. In the press release announcing his action, Folsom reaffirmed his support of Truman and the national party. "The President is the titular head of the Democratic Party. He belongs on the ticket as a Democrat. I will vote the straight Democratic ticket in November and I hope it will be counted for President Truman." Folsom bypassed lower state and federal courts and brought suit before the United States Supreme Court, "in the name of the sovereign state of Alabama." "A handful of slickers have tried to take the vote away from 3,000,000 people in the state . . . ." But, he vowed, "they won't get away with it." [90]

Folsom's move was turned down by the Court on technical grounds, but he continued to hold out the hope that further court action after the election would ensure that Alabama's electoral vote would be cast for Truman.[91]

The Loyalists had exhausted their legal avenues, at least temporarily. But they had always had available the course taken in Georgia and Louisiana. The Governor could call a special session to place a separate Loyalist slate on the ballot. Though the legislature was hostile to Folsom, a bill to place Truman electors on the ballot still might pass. The leaders of the Dixiecrat revolt in Alabama had publicly proclaimed their eagerness to see a slate pledged to Truman. They hoped, they said, to show how small the Loyalist following was.[92]

The Loyalists decided against a special session of the legislature to secure ballot position for a slate of Truman electors. The probability of defeat undoubtedly shaped Loyalist strategy. The Democratic National Committee had assigned Alabama and the tangle of problems it represented to one of its staff members, William J. Primm, Jr., a native of the state.[93] Primm, in consultation with Senators Hill and Sparkman, with Governor Folsom and other Loyalists, advised the Loyalists to forego the attempt to secure ballot position through legislative action.[94] Thus the Loyalists could avoid the embarrassment of probable defeat, relieve Senator Sparkman of an unpleasant and perhaps damaging diversion of loyalties, as well as appropriate an effective issue to use against the bolters in 1950 when the two factions would again struggle for control of the state party. Loyalists could not be charged with deserting the state party and thus could not be barred from running in the 1950 primary. They could argue that the Dixiecrats had denied the people of Alabama their right to vote for—or against—an incumbent President of the United States. It proved to be a telling argument, as Grover Hall, the perceptive editor of the Montgomery *Advertiser*, had foreseen.[95]

The Loyalists, then, accepted their temporary political limbo and prepared for the battle ahead. The Governor and other Loyalist leaders urged their supporters to go the polls and vote "under the rooster," fulfilling their obligation to support the Democratic ticket.

Even after the election, legal hassles dragged on in a series of interminable anti-climaxes. Folsom filed suit in a lower court asking for an injunction restraining the Alabama electors from voting for anyone but Truman and for a writ of mandamus to compel them to vote for Truman. In mid-November the Governor sent each elector a telegram asking them to reconsider the vote for the President. They indignantly refused. One of the electors, Horace Wilkinson, replied with a 700-word blast of his customary rhetoric. He accused Folsom of spreading "unfumigated falsehoods," called him a "disgrace" to the state, and urged him to "resign and leave the state." He charged that Folsom had turned against the States' Righters only when they "snubbed you and did not make you [their] standard bearer or use you in the campaign because you were regarded as a liability." He accused the Governor of supporting President Truman in order to better his chances for a federal job and pointed out, correctly, that Folsom shared responsibility for the absence from the ballot of an independent slate of Truman electors. The Governor could have called a special session but failed to do so, Wilkinson charged, because he feared he would be impeached.[96]

Wilkinson's heated charges were but prelude to the years of protracted struggle waged by States' Righters and Loyalists for control of the state party. Alabama would not be the same for over two decades.

7

STALEMATE:
Alabama Politics 1948-1950

The election of 1948 meant vastly more than simply counting the state's eleven electoral votes for Strom Thurmond. It was also a signal that without the magnetic personality of F.D.R., the traditional bonds of party loyalty were not enough to keep the Deep South aligned with the national party when the Negro was an issue. With the urgency of depression gone, the race issue re-emerged and overshadowed the economic issues that had been the mainstay of progressive Democrats of national orientation in Alabama. Conservative forces that had been in retreat since the 1930's had once again found an issue on which to garner the public backing that had been denied on other issues. And just as in the days of Redemption and of the troubled decade of the 1890's, that issue was race.

The historic conservatism of the mass on social issues once again was used by conservative leaders to counter the appeal of economic liberalism. Conservative leaders within the state party were motivated by a genuine adherence to the principles of laissez-faire and of nineteenth-century liberalism. They wished to reverse the national trend toward centralization and economic liberalism. They were, in varying degrees, also motivated by notions of race. But equally important and more immediate and tangible was the desire to defeat their traditional rivals within the state party, to seize control of the state's political affairs from the adherents of the New Deal who had held sway since the 1930's.

The rivalry of long-standing factions within Alabama Democracy, the jockeying for factional advantage in the contest of 1948, points up once again the importance of local factors in national elections. Historians must perforce generalize about the great political movements that sweep the country and that culminate in the election of a President. We speak, albeit a bit glibly, of the Jacksonian movement, of the Populists, of the Progressives. And, of course, these movements do take on a character and a momentum that transcend the peculiar vagaries of local and state politics. But there is always at hand an enterprising scholar to remind us of what we are apt to forget. And that is the enduring federal character of our politics. Local factions maneuvering for advantage attach themselves to a national or sectional candidate. Factional leaders may be motivated by philosophic agreement, self-interest, or a mixture of both. But often the prime motivating factor in the minds of local and state politicians is the desire to gain political advantage over competing factions within the state or party. So it was in the era of Jackson; so it was in the days of Woodrow Wilson; and so it was in Alabama in 1948.

The election of 1948 also served as a warning flag to progressive Democrats in the South. They had beckoned the South on to a new and brighter future, free of the ancient prejudices of section and race. But already Ellis Arnall and his adherents had been defeated in Georgia, and within two years both Claude Pepper of Florida and Frank Porter Graham of North Carolina were ousted from the U. S. Senate by opponents whose campaigns relied heavily on the inflammatory issue of race.[1] In Alabama, the liberal faction of the Democratic party had seemed in complete control in 1946. Now it was in retreat. Weakened by internal division and unable to counter the rising tide of racial sentiment, the Loyalists were on the defensive.

By cutting their losses, however, by accepting the Dixiecrat *fait accompli* and refusing to desert the state party, the Alabama Loyalists insured that they would be free to fight for control of the state party in 1950 when a new State Executive Committee would be elected. States' Righters, who controlled the existing committee and who would lay the ground rules for the 1950 primary, could not claim that the Loyalists had failed to support the chosen nominees of the state party—that is, the unpledged electors—and thus should be barred from the primary.

For Jim Folsom, 1948 also held a lesson. The high hopes of the new year had soured by November. In January, just after the successful "self-starter" fight, the Governor had felt cock-sure. Despite the defeats he had suffered at the hands of his conservative opponents in the legislature, he faced the new year with renewed confidence. He set about to make himself the chief mainstay of Loyalist forces in Alabama. To do so he had challenged his liberal allies, Hill and Sparkman, for leadership of the Loyalist faction. But Folsom and his followers had been rebuffed by the voters. His favorite-son candidacy became an embarrassment to him, as was the personal scandal that broke about him in April. He failed to win a place on the state's delegation to the Democratic convention, and his later legal maneuvers against the Dixiecrats were decidedly anti-climactic. Just as his hopes of enacting an ambitious program of reform had been stymied by conservative opposition in the legislature the year before, his hopes of extending his influence within the state party, hopes that had run high in January, had ebbed in failure by year's end. They had met defeat not only by Folsom's conservative opponents, the States' Righters, but within the liberal faction itself.

Folsom ended the year as he had begun his political career—as a politician of immense but unrealized potential, a man with an incredible hold upon the loyalty of his people, a man who had achieved the highest office within his state, but an outsider still. With a streak of truculent independence, of obstinacy and suspicion and perhaps an inner uncertainty, he was still as much an outsider to the liberal faction, which should have been his natural ally, as to the conservatives who were his perennial and self-chosen enemies.

Folsom had been in office almost two years at the end of the November campaign. It had been two years of triumph and frustration. The prospects for the remainder of his term were equally checkered. The regular session of the legislature—a headache for any governor and certainly so for one whose relations with the legislature were as ragged as Folsom's—convened in May. The contest between the administration and its legislative foes that had characterized the previous sessions was renewed. The struggle between States' Righters and Loyalists for control of the state party continued, spilling over into the elections of 1950. Conservative efforts to restrict the suffrage and to put the progressive forces within the party on the defensive once again raised difficult and sensitive problems of race and class.

i   "The legislature will meet next May," Horace Wilkinson had written to Gessner McCorvey shortly before the November election. "In my judgment we are going to need some constitutional and statutory enactment to head off the movement now under way to enroll fifty thousand negro voters." The immediate goal was clear, "to insure the preservation of white supremacy in Alabama and to rid the Democratic party of the negro." "I am convinced," Wilkinson added, "that there is a lawful way of accomplishing this result." [2]

Not all Dixiecrats were so rabid on the race issue. But the leaders of the conservative wing of the party shared Wilkinson's concern for the future. Those motivated by sincere doubt about untrammeled democracy—for the white man as well as for the black—joined the Negrophobes in their determination to prevent a further loosening of the suffrage.

Given their conservative outlook, their concern was justified. For in January of 1949 the federal court in Mobile declared the Boswell amendment unconstitutional. The court held that it "clearly appears" that the amendment "was intended to be and is being used for the purpose of discriminating against applicants for the franchise on the basis of race or color." [3]

Governor Folsom greeted the decision calmly and with approval. He had opposed the amendment when it was before the people and had not changed his mind about its merits. It was a dead letter now and appeal, in his opinion, would be useless. To settle the matter, however, he announced that the state would appeal to a higher court. The Governor clearly hoped that the court's decision, if upheld on appeal, would end the controversy. Agitation over Negro voting would cease, he told the press, when barriers to the suffrage were removed.[4]

It was precisely the removal of those barriers that conservatives feared. Diminution of political influence and consequent loss of control over the taxing and social policies of state and local government was the prospect that frightened conservative leaders. "We must do something," wrote a south Alabama legislator who was a large landowner and long a leader in the Farm Bureau. "We must do something to protect Alabama from the mass registration of negroes which is about to take place; and which, if allowed to happen, will destroy democracy in Alabama government as you and I have always known it." [5]

The Negro was only the most immediate and obvious threat to conservative control. He was but the convenient symbol of the "uneducated masses" who threatened control of state government by responsible men. "Unqualified" whites were equally feared by this Black Belt legislator, though the Negro made the most immediate target. A month later, in a letter to the state Democratic chairman, this same legislator expressed in more explicit terms his fears for the future of state government. "The trend in Alabama at the present time is towards turning our government over to the masses, and in my opinion if we do not place restrictions and qualifications on a voter at this session of the legislature, we will have seen our last election in Alabama where the people who carry the burden of taxation would have any voice in our State government." He issued a call for action to "the thinking people of Alabama to rally together and get behind a movement that will protect the interest of the people who made Alabama great." Time was short and the need was great. "This is our last chance if we turn the ballot box over to the uneducated masses in this State we can expect nothing but chaos in the future [sic]." [6]

ii   The lower court's decision declaring the Boswell amendment unconstitutional was upheld by the Supreme Court in late March. Governor Folsom declared himself "cheered" by the decision. "I opposed the Boswell amendment in the election and I think the Supreme Court decided right." [7]

The decision may have cheered Folsom, but it brought further dismay and a greater sense of urgency to the conservatives. Negro leaders in Mobile, who had brought the original suit against the Boswell amendment, reported that 1200 Negroes had registered to vote in Mobile alone in the two months since the lower court decision. In the previous two years only 104 had been registered.[8]

Impressed by the fact that "on yesterday alone" sixty-eight Negroes had registered in his native Mobile, Gessner McCorvey had written former-Governor Dixon in January to stress "the real seriousness of the situation." McCorvey had harbored doubts about the constitutionality of the Boswell amendment from the beginning. As early as 1947 he had proposed a substitute amendment with altered wording. In a desultory way, he and others had discussed the steps to take if, as he feared, it were eventually struck down. But no course of action had been agreed upon, and a variety of remedies were advanced in late 1948 and early 1949.[9]

In October, 1948, Horace Wilkinson had written, in vague and general terms, about the need for "constitutional and statutory enactment to insure the preservation of white supremacy in Alabama and to rid the Democratic party of the negro." By January the outlines of Wilkinson's notion had been fleshed in with concrete proposals. They were similar to efforts in South Carolina. Wilkinson proposed that the State party completely divorce itself and its primaries from any regulation by the State, that it become in effect a private, voluntary organization open to all, black or white, who would subscribe to the party's statement of principles. These principles would include belief in states' rights, dedication to the repeal of the Fifteenth Amendment, to "white responsibility for government," and to the right of any candidate to reject any ballot cast for him. (This last, rather curious provision was included to ensure that even if a "negro, . . . republican, . . . communist, . . . [or] socialist" subscribed to the statement his vote could still be rejected.)[10]

Despite doubts expressed by McCorvey, Wilkinson argued forcefully for his plan and enlisted the initial support of Frank Dixon. Wilkinson was convinced that his plan "would pass muster before the Supreme Court in spite of the predelictions of some justices which are sufficient to cause any careful lawyer to wonder whether it is possible to save civilization by law." He pointed out "that race is not made the basis of membership in the democratic party in Alabama. . . . A negro is as free to register as a democrat as is a white man"—if he can subscribe to the party's principles.[11]

Wilkinson's plan was direct and to the point, and this, he thought, was its virtue. "Our trouble, as I see it, is that we have been trying to exclude the negro . . . by subterfuge and as a result we have fallen into disfavor with the federal courts. Why not adopt a direct, positive method, based on sound principles . . . ? As long as we treat the negro exactly like we treat the Republican, the Socialist, the Progressive, and all other minority groups in Alabama he has no cause for complaint. . . . Under the proposed plan, if a voter did not believe in states' rights, white responsibility, and the right to reject a ballot, he would not be a democrat in Alabama, no matter what else he might be. He might be an exemplary citizen, as some republicans are. He might be as white as driven snow, as pure as Ivory soap, and equal to the Master himself in honor, virtue and integrity; but if he did not believe in those three things, he would not be a democrat." [12]

Wilkinson agreed that "the attitude of the Supreme Court is enough in itself to give rise to doubts as to the validity of legislation of this kind," but he argued that "there can be no doubt about this being the only way we can keep the negro from becoming the balance of power in the Democratic Party in Alabama. Registration and poll tax will not adequately control it. If we cannot prevent it this way then we must make up our minds to accept a fate worse than death itself." [13]

Gessner McCorvey had grave misgivings about Wilkinson's proposal. He was "very fearful that we cannot get anywhere with this plan. These Federal Courts . . . are simply *not* going to permit us to get by with any kind of law which discriminates too much against negroes." It would be "almost impossible," he argued, "to create a political party for nominating candidates . . . and have the Supreme Court of the United States hold that such a party is not, to a certain extent, an agency of the State." Moreover, the cost of holding primaries under such a plan would be prohibitive. Rather, McCorvey proposed to resubmit a constitutional amendment, without the defects of the Boswell proposal, to tighten the requirements for registration and "above all else, fight to the last ditch any effort to monkey with our poll tax law." McCorvey had reluctantly concluded that Wilkinson's proposal was impossible. "I'm just afraid we are going to have to 'face the music' and recognize that we will simply *have* to permit negroes to vote in our primaries." Still, the revised Boswell amendment and the cumulative poll tax should "fill the bill" and prevent any significant number of Negroes from voting.[14]

McCorvey also favored revision of the pledge subscribed to by candidates in the Democratic primary. He would make clear the distinction between the state Democratic party and the national party by having the State Executive Committee repeal "everything which could give anyone the right to claim that we were part of any National Democratic Party" and designate "the official title of our party as 'The Democratic Party *of Alabama.*' " Candidates would be pledged to support only the nominees of the state party.[15]

Other proposals were advanced.[16] But it was McCorvey's that were eventually acted upon. The constitutional amendment would have to be submitted to the Legislature in May. The proposed change in the name of the state party and in the pledge taken by candidates would await action by the new State Executive Committee to be elected in 1950. The immediate goal was action by the Legislature.

iii   Governor Folsom was also preparing for the coming legislative session. He had hoped the inflamed emotions of the past year might
die down. But the efforts of his conservative opponents to forestall an
expanded electorate kept the temperature of Alabama politics at fever
pitch. In the face of certain opposition from an intransigent bloc of anti-
administration senators, Folsom sought to rally public opinion behind the
administration's program. He also sought support from city and county
office holders as well as from the educators of the state. In each case, he
met with some success. But in the end it was to no avail.[17]

The Governor was intent upon pressing for enactment of the program
that had been blocked by conservative forces in the legislature two years
earlier. He stumped the state in March and April to rekindle public support for higher old-age pensions, an expanded road-building program,
reapportionment, increased appropriations for education, and the convening of a constitutional convention.[18] With his strong sense of economic
realism, Folsom sought to turn the attention of his people away from the
explosive issue of race and toward what to him were the "real" and
fundamental problems of economics.

Folsom had been impressed by President Truman's success in 1948
in running against the "do-nothing" Eightieth Congress, and he emulated
Truman's tactic. He sought to rally the people behind his program by
denouncing his legislative opponents. The anti-administration bloc in the
Senate were "cowards," he said, and he challenged them to "stand on
their hind legs and be men enough to acept their responsibility to the
people." His program had been blocked in 1947 by "selfish interests represented in the Senate by carpetbaggers." But he promised he would put
his program through or defeat that "little narrow-minded carpet-bag led
clique" at the next election. "Pappy ain't scared of none of 'em." [19]

On the stump, Folsom still spoke of his program in generalities. He did
explain that the expanded old-age pension plan was specifically designed
to cover farmers, who were not included under Social Security. And he
proposed a "little TVA" to develop Alabama's waterways and watersheds.
Still, the details were brushed aside as he sketched in broad strokes and
simple terms what his program would mean for "you and you and you"
and for "your children." [20]

While the Governor toured the state, the specifics of his program
gradually began to circulate out from Montgomery: a $40 million road
bond issue, a renewed attempt to reapportion the legislature, $45 per
month minimum old-age pension, and an unspecified boost in the appropriation for public education. These extensions of state services
would require increased taxes, and the administration had a variety of
proposals under consideration: increased ad valorem levies on utilities, a
one-cent increase in the tax on gasoline, a possible boost in the state sales
tax or in the graduated income tax.[21]

The prospect of increased taxes brought vocal opposition from a number of organizations, including the Alabama Motorists' Association and the Alabama Cotton Manufacturers' Association. Opposition to the administration among some members of the legislature was bitter, and renewed rumors of impeachment were heard in Montgomery.[22]

Opposition to the administration centered in the Senate. Here an "economy bloc," a revival of a similar group that had opposed the progressive Graves administration of the 1930's,[23] was determined to block passage of the administration's program and to stand firm against any tax increases. The "economy bloc" declared open warfare on the administration at the very outset of the legislative session. All executive appointments were blocked and a host of "economy bills," some sixty in all, were introduced, each one aimed at further hamstringing the current executive.[24]

The legislative session wore on from May to September with neither side able to work its will. The anti-administration forces were in a majority, but through parliamentary maneuver, executive amendment, and an occasional filibuster, administration forces were able to forestall hostile measures. In the end, the session degenerated into shambles. The Governor's program was largely scuttled, though the appropriations for the general fund and for education were salvaged. Administration forces, clearly on the defensive and at times reduced to seven in the thirty-five man Senate, resorted to filibuster in the closing hours of the session to block passage of unfriendly measures.[25]

The legislative session of 1949 was reminiscent of that of 1947. The fighting was more bitter, the opposition on both sides more intransigent, but the issues were in general quite the same. Yet new issues were also at stake. The experience of 1948 inevitably colored the proceedings. Not only was there a struggle between forces loyal to the administration and those opposed—a struggle that divided the Senate along liberal-conservative lines on economic issues—but also a complementary contest between progressive and conservative forces within the state party that transcended (but closely paralleled) the division on economic issues.

Conservative forces in the Democratic Party and in the Legislature supported Gessner McCorvey's proposal for the submission of a revised Boswell amendment. The administration sought to defeat the amendment while placing the onus of defeat upon the amendment's supporters. Administration forces had introduced a measure to reapportion the legislature, and they threatened to oppose the revised Boswell amendment in the legislature or at the polls if the Boswell supporters failed to deliver the votes necessary to reapportion the legislature. It was brilliant legislative strategy. The administration knew that Black Belters viewed reapportionment as a fate equal in distaste to mass registration of blacks. (Representative Walter Givhan of Dallas County [Selma] admitted that "we certainly want a sound voter-registration amendment. . . . But I can't think of any legislation worse for us than reapportionment.")[26]

If the amendment's backers failed to support reapportionment, they could be blamed for defeat of the revised Boswell amendment, and they would alienate themselves from populous north Alabama where reapportionment was popular. Moreover, the version of reapportionment before the legislature threatened to fracture the "economy bloc," some of whose members greatly favored this particular reapportionment plan. The administration could only profit from the resulting acrimony in the ranks of its foes.[27]

It was a bitter choice handed the anti-administration forces. In the House, pro-reapportionment forces thought they had secured an agreement from those supporting the revised Boswell amendment and voted for it. Those supporting the Boswell substitute failed to deliver the promised twenty votes when the reapportionment measure came before the House, thus angering those who favored reapportionment in both House and Senate. In the closing hours of the session, when the Boswell substitute was before the Senate, pro-administration forces prevented its passage by filibuster even though to do so meant defeat for reapportionment.[28]

Though the administration had been denied its program, its appointees, and reapportionment, its foes had failed to pass the revised Boswell measure. Because of the protracted wrangling, the session was unproductive for either side, except in a negative fashion. A minor though significant exception was the passage of a measure unmasking the revived Ku Klux Klan.[29] An indication of the growing anti-Communist sentiment in the country was evident when the legislature passed a loyalty oath for public employees. Similar legislation was enacted that year in at least eleven states, including Oregon, Massachusetts, and New York, but in Alabama it met with a veto by the Governor, just as it had in 1947.[30] To Folsom such measures were unreasonable infringements upon first amendment freedoms and grossly disproportionate to the real danger. Moreover, they singled out one class of citizens and required of them special tests of their loyalty which others did not have to meet.[31]

iv   During the legislative session, several opponents of Folsom cast doubt upon the Governor's motives in pushing so hard for his legislative program. It had been decisively defeated in the previous session, and it was again without hope of passage. Sen. Albert Boutwell of Jefferson County (Birmingham) denounced Folsom's "fantastic, multimillion dollar big-taxing and free-spending program." It had "all the financial soundness of a Pyramid Club," he charged.[32]

Boutwell contended that Folsom realized his program had no chance of passage and that the Governor was interested more in creating campaign issues for a reelection effort in 1954 than in solving immediate governmental problems. "Governor Folsom has demonstrated time and again," Boutwell declared, that "he does not want to work with the Legislature. He has failed to offer any program that is practical or possible of accomplishment." [33]

Others echoed Boutwell's sentiments.[34] And in a fundamental sense the Senator from Jefferson was right. Folsom represented, in reality and in his own mind, such a serious and basic threat to the established political order that he was not content with ameliorative measures, with minor concessions from his conservative foes. "What you and I do and how we are remembered," he told a joint session of the legislature in June of 1949, "is not going to be measured in terms of money. It is going to be measured by what we do on the fundamentals of government," by building schools, roads, and promoting the welfare of the people, to be sure, but more important by what is done with the suffrage and reapportionment.[35]

Folsom agreed with de Tocqueville that the nation had historically been divided between two opinions "which are as old as the world and which are perpetually to be met with, under different forms and various names, in all free communities, the one tending to limit, the other to extend indefinitely, the power of the people." [36] He was always tempted to view a given measure in this universal and timeless context. The complexities of legislative policy were always reduced to this issue of principle, were always cast as if they were part of the eternal struggle between democracy and oligarchy.

When issues were so phrased, there was only one side on which Folsom could come down and remain true to his image of himself. This tendency, combined as it was with a strain of native stubbornness, especially if he felt the prerogatives of his office were being challenged, made it difficult to compromise with his legislative foes. He had seen other governors, initially committed to reapportionment, barter away that fundamental goal in order to obtain passage of this or that appropriation or tax measure.[37] But he would not be diverted. It is evidence of his genuinely radical nature that he would not accept compromise on immediate issues if that meant deflecting public attention from the cause of fundamental reform. Rather suffer defeat on immediate issues and keep before the public the intransigence of the opposition in the hope that a groundswell of democratic opposition would one day overwhelm the forces of entrenched privilege.

Folsom was not, of course, oblivious to the political advantage that accrues to a champion of "the people" against "the interests." He was not unaware of his people's romantic tendency to identify with the underdog who struggles, without success but without compromise, against overwhelming odds. He was, like most successful politicians, something of an actor. He relished the minor incidents that lend color to a political figure and confirm him in the public's mind as an authentic hero of the plain folk. He was conscious of the role-playing, the posing, the sham that is part of politics. And yet those who saw only that, only the role-playing, overlooked how deeply the role was embedded in the reality of Folsom's personality, how much Folsom was the character he played.

v   The conservative attempt to undercut Folsom's political effectiveness had largely succeeded by 1948. Folsom had failed in his efforts to push his reform program through the legislature. He had played only a secondary role in the struggle between the Loyalists and States' Righters in the spring of 1948. In the legislative session of 1949, it was his supporters, reduced at times to seven of the thirty-five state senators, who prevented the passage of the revised Boswell amendment. But in the struggle for control of the state party that was renewed in 1950, Folsom again played only a small role in the Loyalist victory. Leadership of the progressive forces in the state rested firmly in the hands of Senators Hill and Sparkman. Nonetheless, in the closing two years of his term, Folsom continued to harass his conservative opponents within the state party.

Despite the aroused public sentiment that enveloped the issue of race and suffrage, Folsom persisted in championing his liberal views. In late 1949, the Governor's legal advisor warned the registrars of Jefferson County (Birmingham) of the legal penalties for discriminating against Negroes. He pointed out that the rate of rejection for Negro applicants was significantly higher than that for whites—only 10 of 1217 white applicants had been rejected between July and October, 1949, while 124 of 254 Negro applicants failed to satisfy the Board. "It is rather difficult to believe," the Governor's legal advisor wrote, that "such a vast discrepancy [in qualifications] exists" and he outlined the civil and criminal penalties that could be levied against board members if a suit alleging discrimination were successful.[38]

The controversy over the Jefferson Board and over similar boards in other counties continued throughout 1949 and on into 1950. The chairman of the Jefferson County board, a Folsom appointee, charged his two associate members with adopting delaying tactics to slow the rate of registration for qualified Negro applicants. With the threat of a grand jury investigation and with the appointment by the Governor of a special advisory committee to investigate such allegations, the pace of registration accelerated in Jefferson.[39]

In other ways as well, Folsom continued to defend his progressive stance on race. In December, 1949, Folsom wrote a strong letter to the circuit solicitor of Elmore County commending him for prosecuting and securing the conviction of two white men accused of attacking a Negro woman. In that same month, Folsom delivered a Christmas message to the people of Alabama. "It is good at Christmas for us to turn our thoughts to the neglected, because Christmas is a time to think of others and not of ourselves. It is a time to ask questions of our inner self. . . . Our Negroes who constitute 35% of our population in Alabama—are they getting 35% of the fair share of living? Are they getting adequate medical care . . . ? Are they provided with sufficient professional training . . . ? Are the Negroes being given their share of democracy, the same opportunity of having a voice in the government under which they live? As long as the Negroes are held down by deprivation and lack of opportunity, the other poor people will be held down alongside them." [40]

vi   After administration forces had blocked the revised Boswell amendment in the legislature, conservatives within the state party were forced to look elsewhere in their efforts to forestall a broadened suffrage. As Gessner McCorvey had suggested the preceding year,[41] they turned to the State Democratic Executive Committee.

McCorvey had proposed that the Committee change the oath required of candidates in the Democratic primary to make clear that by running in the primary they incurred an obligation to support only the nominees of the Democratic Party *of Alabama*. No one could then claim that candidates chosen in the primary were in any way obligated to support nominees of the national party. Any suggestion of a necessary relationship between state and national parties would be deleted from the Committee's rules, and the official name of the party would be changed to add the words "of Alabama" after "Democratic Party."

For McCorvey's proposal to work, however, the States' Rights faction had to retain control of the State Executive Committee. If the Loyalists gained control, they could turn McCorvey's proposal around and change the oath clearly to bind nominees of the state party to the support of the national party. The State Executive Committee was up for reelection in 1950, and a renewed struggle for control between Loyalists and States' Righters was in the offing. The election of 1950 would also determine the extent to which Governor Folsom's hold on the popular imagination had slipped in the past years of intra-party strife and scandal.

In December of 1948, Folsom had written Democratic National Chairman, Senator Howard McGrath, of his optimism in the Loyalists' effort to gain control of the state party. "At the present writing, I believe the reactionaries controlling the Party in Alabama do not have the confidence of the people of this state. Sometime in the future, I believe we will be able to take control from them by one means or another." [42] The National Committee was eager to aid the Loyalist effort. In February, 1949, Chairman McGrath, bypassing the official state organization headed by McCorvey, appointed Herbert J. Meigham, the mayor of Gadsden, finance director for the national party in Alabama. The major fund-raising effort was the Jefferson-Jackson dinner to be held in Birmingham on April 12. The national administration signaled the seriousness of its efforts to bring Alabama back into the party by sending Vice-President Alben Barkley to speak. Barkley's noted geniality and his ties to the South might aid the Loyalists' cause.[43]

The Birmingham dinner quickly became a source of contention between the rival factions in Alabama. Mellifluous words, even from the Vice-President of the United States, were not enough to mollify the States' Righters. J. Miller Bonner, a former legislator and States' Rights leader from the Black Belt, could not see "how any Southern white man" could consider attending "the Barkley-anti-Southern white man dinner . . . ." Still, "some will go—more is the pity. But they may err grievously," for "the sword that was drawn in 1948 will flash again in 1950. And no man will be elected . . . who is ashamed to be called a States' Rights Democrat." [44]

The States' Righters boycotted the Barkley dinner and planned one of their own. It was held in Dothan on April 8, presided over by a young lawyer, Richmond Flowers, who had been active in the Republican campaign in 1948. Indeed, many of those attending had contributed to both the Republican and Dixiecrat campaigns, indicating both their mixed allegiance and their economic conservatism. The crowd was large, but, just as in Birmingham in 1948, there were no major office-holders from the state. Only fifteen of the 141 members of the state legislature appeared.[45]

Four days later, the Loyalists held their banquet in Birmingham. Despite the boycott by the States' Righters, over 1000 party regulars attended. The evening was a success, but in its larger purpose it had failed to quell the States' Rights revolt. On the eve of the Birmingham banquet, the States' Righters issued a statement declaring that there is "no armistice between the vast majority of Democrats of Alabama and those who currently control the party [nationally] . . . ." When Gessner McCorvey was asked a few months later if he would rejoin the national party, he replied testily, "Rejoin what? That Socialist party?" [46]

This kind of sparring between the rival factions persisted throughout 1949. But it was overshadowed by the struggle between the Governor and his opponents in the legislature. Everyone knew that the issue between Loyalist and States' Righter would not be settled until the elections of 1950. Still, the Dixiecrats were at work throughout the year laying the groundwork for their campaign.

vii   Immediately after the election of 1948, the leaders of the Dixiecrat movement in Alabama had met in Mobile to plan their future course. They realized, as Frank Dixon put it, that they must "continue the battle vigorously [on the national level], assuming that both political parties unite in . . . establishment of a police state in this country." But "the first move . . . is to be absolutely certain that we continue to build locally . . . ." Our fight, Dixon wrote, "will be to preserve our hold on the state Democratic Executive Committee and to establish the validity of our thinking so widely that any candidate for public office will have to render more than lip service to it." [47]

The need for concerted action was great. "We simply can't sit still," Dixon wrote, "and let the civilization of this region be sacrificed." It may be that "during the next four years . . . there will be an adequate presentation of our point of view . . . and the formation of a nucleus of people who believe as we believe, capable at any time of becoming a separate and independent nationwide political party." But ". . . the opinion of those of us in Alabama who have been through this fight is that, for the time at least, all operations must be through the straight regular democratic organization." The States' Righters had to retain control of the State Executive Committee if they were to be free in 1952 to follow the course of '48. "We will face the lick-log next May in the election of the state Democratic Executive Committee," Dixon wrote to Wallace Wright of Mississippi, ". . . and at the same time comes the election for Governor and U. S. Senator. We will be busy." [48]

Conservatives within the state party were indeed busy. And initially their attention was focused on more than just the State Executive Committee. They hankered for someone more attuned to their sentiments in the state capitol. And they had long been opposed to Senator Hill. The incumbent Senator had been a target of conservative forces within the state for some time, and his actions in 1948 had further embittered his conservative foes.[49]

There were those among the States' Righters who wanted to run a coordinated campaign for candidates for Governor and Senator as well as for the State Executive Committee. But the persistent fractiousness of Alabama politics prevailed, and no concerted effort was made.[50]

The States' Rights forces focused their efforts upon retaining control of the State Executive Committee. Tom Abernethy of Talladega, a newspaper publisher who later switched to the Republican Party and ran for Governor, was chosen by the States' Righters to head a committee seeking the election of States' Rights candidates to the State Committee. In March, Horace Wilkinson suggested to Abernethy that a strategy similar to that of 1948 be followed. Abernethy should write each candidate who filed for the State Committee and request that the candidate sign a pledge to leave the electors chosen in 1952 unbound to the national party. The names of those who signed and those who refused would be made public. Thus, Wilkinson wrote, "we will effectively smoke the opposition out and require them to take a stand in a way that will be disadvantageous to them." [51]

Abernethy followed the course suggested by Wilkinson, but both public opinion and geography worked against the States' Righters. The fact that the name of an incumbent President of the United States had not been on the ballot in Alabama soured much of the public on the States' Righters. Not that Harry Truman was immensely popular in the state. No, but the public sensed something was wrong and tended, rightly or wrongly, to blame the Dixiecrats. As the Montgomery *Advertiser* had commented in October of 1948, "what has sunk in is that Alabama is the only state in the Union where it is physically impossible for a citizen to vote for Truman." And the *Advertiser* had predicted then that "it may be that [the Loyalists] will be able to exploit this unwholesome circumstance in the future." [52]

Grover Hall, Jr., was convinced that public opinion had shifted against the Dixiecrats. Though a critic of the States' Rights movement, he refused to join other critics in painting the Dixiecrats as usurpers who thwarted the will of the people. Rather he argued that "at the time the electors were pledged to *coitus interruptus* with respect to Truman they were carrying out the inflamed will of a great majority of the people of this state. . . . Unfortunately the people never at the time understood [the anomalous situation they were creating] any more than they understood the original purpose for the electoral college and it goes hard with the movement that Truman's name did not appear." But though he admitted that the Dixiecrats were not usurpers, as some critics charged, Hall thought "that there has been a massive swing of opinion" against the Dixiecrats. Similarly, in October, 1949, a correspondent of former-Governor Dixon discovered "here in Montgomery a great amount of antipathy against the States' Righters." [53]

If a changing public opinion was a handicap to the States' Righters in their effort to retain control of the State Executive Committee, so too was geography. The publicly-known leadership of the States' Rights movement was centered in the Black Belt, in industrial Jefferson, and in the port of Mobile. Outside these areas and particularly in the populous counties of north Alabama, there were few leaders among the States' Righters who were widely known. The members of the State Executive Committee were elected by Congressional Districts, and in several of the districts the States' Righters had a difficult time fielding a viable ticket against the Loyalists. [54] Even in the industrial areas, where the States' Righters had influential supporters, they met with stiff resistance, particularly from organized labor.

The Dixiecrats also faced strong opposition from incumbent office holders. Both Senators Hill and Sparkman, as well as Governor Folsom, campaigned for the Loyalists. So did three of the state's ten Representatives in the U. S. House. A fourth Representative favored the Loyalists but was not active in the campaign; three were neutral; and two actively favored the States' Righters.[55]

With public opinion, geography, and the power of incumbency on their side, the Loyalists were in high spirits. The support of the national party further buoyed their hopes. The significance of this primary contest in an off-year in Alabama was not overlooked in the councils of the national party or in the national press. Stewart Alsop wrote that "it is not inconceivable that the outcome of this apparently obscure Alabama contest could have a far reaching effect on the whole national political future." And Jack Bell of the Associated Press maintained that administration officials "regard Alabama as a test case in their drive to wipe out the revolt that started [in the South] . . . over President Truman's civil rights proposals." [56]

In the campaign of 1950, the issues of 1948 were refurbished. Loyalists appealed to the traditional identification of the South with the Democratic Party, invoked the name of F.D.R., and cited the economic benefits the South had enjoyed under Democratic administrations. The States' Righters, they contended, were but Republicans in disguise. Senator Hill, in a speech to a Loyalist rally in Birmingham in late April, hit upon the major points in the Loyalist argument. The States' Righters, he charged to the cheers of his partisan audience, were "hired agents of the absent landlords, who are Republicans." The 1948 revolt was "part of a campaign to break up the Democratic Party in Alabama so the Republicans could win the presidential election." Hill charged that the States' Righters opposed TVA, the federal farm program, and social security. And he closed in a peroration to Franklin Roosevelt. Roosevelt, he said, had "lifted the level of the age in which you and I and the people of Alabama live." [57]

The States' Righters also had recourse to the arguments they had advanced in 1948. The influence of the South in national councils could be reestablished, they said, only if the South were independent of either party and could not be taken for granted by the Democrats. Once again race was a primary issue for the States' Righters. Tom Abernethy, who headed the conservative effort, told the voters that in the election of 1950 the Democrats of Alabama had to choose "whether they will continue to protect the time-tested system of racial segregation or turn the state over to Trumanism . . . and become one of the principal proving grounds of the national Democratic Party's experiment in racial social equality." Abernethy, who campaigned for Eisenhower in 1952 and who ran for governor as a Republican in 1954, went to great lengths to deny the Loyalist charge that the States' Righters were Republicans in disguise. He repudiated the Republican party and castigated it as the party that brought "the black shame of the First Reconstruction upon us." Abernethy also sought to counter the Loyalists' appeals on behalf of "the party of our forefathers." Our forefathers, Abernethy said, "were men who marched with Lee and Jackson and not with the likes of President Harry Truman, Senator Humphrey, Walter White and the other powers of the Truman-Wallace political axis." They "died for states' rights and framed the slogan 'white supremacy.'" Characteristically, Horace Wilkinson was cruder but to the point. He would "rather die fighting for states' rights than live on Truman Boulevard in a nigger heaven." [58]

The economic conservatism of the States' Righters was muted, but at times it clearly showed. A Loyalist victory, Tom Abernethy warned, "would put us on record as accepting and approving the other phases (besides civil rights) of the socialist nightmare now spurning the Constitution with arrogant feet. Alabamians who vote for Trumanism will be endorsing the tax gougers," Abernethey said, "who regard the thrifty hardworking American as an object of contempt who is permitted to exist only that the fruit of his labor may be confiscated by Washington and squandered in new experiments in socialism." [59]

Though the issues on both sides were similar to those of 1948, the outcome was vastly different. With advantages of geography and incumbency combined with a shift in public opinion that made resentment of the muddled state of electoral affairs in 1948 a greater issue than Truman and civil rights (at least temporarily), the Loyalists gained control of the State Committee. The Loyalists won a lop-sided majority, taking at least forty-three of the seventy-two seats on the committee. [60]

The Loyalist victory, said Arthur Krock of the New York *Times*, was "a victory of national significance" for the Truman administration. The Birmingham *World*, a Negro paper, was cheered by the results. "Alabama liberalism, let's call it, gets a new lease on life. A new kind of politics has triumphed." [61] That was perhaps overstatement. But the progressive faction which had been dominant at least since the New Deal, which had seemed so secure at the zenith of its power in 1946 and yet had been put so quickly on the defensive in 1948, had captured the major source of institutional strength of their conservative foes. Still, the events of 1948 and since had clearly served notice upon liberals within the state party that they were vulnerable on the issue of race.

In May of 1950, after the primary, the Huntsville *Times* wrote that "the Dixiecrat movement is washed up, unless something else comes along in the next few years to revive it." That something else did come along, of course, in the form of *Brown v. Board* in 1954, which, as one writer has put it, ushered in a "decade of demagoguery" and revived in full flourish the States' Rights movement. [62] Much of the tinge of populist liberalism that had colored Alabama politics for decades was muted as progressives within the party felt pressured on the race issue and as the memories of the Depression were dulled by the prosperity of the 'fifties.

In the political vocabulary of the South, "conservative" became the label politicians of all persuasions aspired to. No one in the 1960's would have to explain to an audience of junior high students in Alabama, as a textbook writer felt compelled to do as late as 1957, how it was possible for men labeled "conservative" to be elected in the South.[63]

viii   The Loyalists had recouped much of the ground lost in 1948. They had taken the States' Righters' only source of institutional strength. On the defensive since '48, the Loyalists felt secure enough in 1952 to push through loyalty oaths strictly binding candidates in the Democratic primary to support the national party and its nominees. Their hold on the State Executive Committee was strengthened in 1954, when once again they captured a comfortable majority of Committee seats.[64] With but slight variation in the four years from 1958 to 1962, the Loyalists retained control of the State Executive Committee down to the present time. They have been able to accomplish this despite the defection from Loyalist ranks of a man who dominated the state's politics in the 1960's as much as Jim Folsom had in the 'forties and 'fifties. George Wallace, a former Loyalist himself, adopted the rhetoric and strategy of the States' Righters—though not their economic conservatism—and dominated the state's political life throughout much of the 'sixties. But in the same primaries in which Wallace was nominated, Loyalist majorities retained control of the official state party machinery.

The ascendancy of the Loyalists sent the leaders of the States' Rights revolt into despair and disarray. Some, like Tom Abernethy, publicly switched to the Republican party. Others, like Gessner McCorvey, refused to sign the loyalty oath and were thus barred from running in the Democratic primary. They quietly moved into Republican ranks. Some, like Horace Wilkinson, swallowed their disgust with the national party and retained their party regularity. Some were taken with the notion of a national party of conservative orientation composed of conservative Republicans and conservative Southern Democrats. Many, like Frank Dixon, wavered. Dixon looked with favor upon the Republican successes at the national level in the fifties but he did not publicly commit himself to the Republican cause. By 1958, he was reluctantly recommending that young men who hoped for a political career retain their party regularity and fight for the conservative cause within party ranks.[65]

Dixon's mood was distinctly gloomy after the defeat of the States' Rights faction in 1950. The forces of liberty, he felt, were on the defensive as more and more power was concentrated in the central government. The mindless degradation of the democratic dogma and of all western culture proceeded apace.[66]

Dixon's foreboding for the future was absent from the Loyalist camp. After the 1950 primary, the Loyalists seemed once again, as in 1946, in firm control. Not only were the Governor and the two U. S. Senators of the Loyalist persuasion, but Loyalists now had a majority on the State Democratic Executive Committee. With a Loyalist succeeding Folsom in 1950 and with Folsom reelected in 1954, along with a Loyalist majority to the State Executive Committee, the state and party seemed to rest safely in the hands of the progressive forces. "The pattern of good humor," of liberal politics, still prevailed, wrote Grover Hall in 1954. "Alabama may appear a conservative state, but the Populists and Fair Dealers are enjoying a degree of dominance." All in all, the course of Alabama politics since 1948 and particularly the elections of 1954 amounted, Hall lamented, to a "crop failure for us Plantation Whigs." [67]

But not all Loyalists had fared equally well in the intraparty struggles since 1948. Senator Hill's position had been strengthened. He led the ticket among candidates for the state delegation to the Democratic convention in 1946 and spearheaded the successful Loyalist campaign of 1950 while easily winning reelection to the Senate over a relatively unknown opponent. (Despite the hearty dislike, politically and oft-times personally, that many conservatives harbored for Hill, they could not field a serious candidate against him.) He ran successfully for reelection in 1956 and again in 1962. The 1962 race against Republican James Martin was quite close, and with the health of his wife failing, Hill retired from public life in 1968 after the longest career in Congress of any Alabamian.

Senator Sparkman fared equally well. Having won a special election for a short term in 1946, Sparkman easily won a full term in 1948. The necessities of his own campaign in 1948 prevented him from playing the active role in the Loyalist cause that Hill had played. He ably assisted the Loyalist campaign in 1950, however. Winning reelection in 1954, 1960, 1966, and 1972, Sparkman established a progressive record in many areas of economic policy in the Senate. In 1952 he was the Democratic nominee for Vice-President on the ticket with Adlai Stevenson. His presence there was continuing evidence of the national party's effort to keep the South within the Democratic fold.

Governor Folsom fared less handsomely in some respects. He had been on the defensive from the moment his term began, at the mercy of a hostile legislature, and given to quarreling with his progressive colleagues within the party. His political fortunes in his four years as Governor rose and fell with all the rapidity and violent wrenches in direction that characterize an unsettling ride on a roller coaster.

Folsom's liberal position on race and on the suffrage had damaged his political popularity with some voters. His appeal was further weakened by a scandal in the state prison and parole system in the closing months of his administration.[68] Folsom's political fortunes were clearly on the wane as his administration ended. In 1950, he campaigned for the Loyalists but was secondary at best in his effect. Barred by the state constitution from seeking reelection, he supported his friend Philip Hamm for governor. Despite Folsom's support, Hamm ran a distant second, losing to a fellow Loyalist, Gordon Persons.[69] Folsom left office disparaged by many. He was, many muttered, a disgrace to the state. Four years in office had not been kind to Jim Folsom.

Still, Folsom's ability to rally popular enthusiasm, his ability, like that of a kindly but inveterate alcoholic, to elicit forgiveness from a dewy-eyed and hopeful public, was not to be underestimated. After four years of the quiet, competent administration of Gordon Persons, the voters of Alabama returned Folsom to the governor's chair. Folsom's campaign for reelection in 1954 stressed his maturity and held out hope that he recanted the misdeeds of his first administration and had reformed his administrative ways. Amidst the softened asperities of the 1950's, there was less open baiting of the interests. Indeed, Folsom had been won over to a modern version of the New South Creed, to the notion that the social programs he favored could be financed only by attracting industry to the South. His slogan, "Y'all Come," was addressed as much to the northern industrialist as it was an invitation, in good rural fashion, for the voters of Alabama to attend his inaugural.[70]

Nonetheless, the 1954 campaign was but a refined and updated version of that of '46. Folsom still championed a program of expanded state services that would require increased tax revenue. He still hoped to make good his promise of fundamental reform through poll tax repeal, reapportionment, and constitutional revision. To the surprise of most observers, Folsom defeated seven opponents in the Democratic primary without a run-off. In the general election in November, he easily defeated his Republican opponent, the converted Dixiecrat, Tom Abernethy of Talladega.[71]

Folsom's triumph was complete. A majority of the legislative candidates nominated in the May primary were friendly to the incoming governor.[72] He would not face again the unremitting hostility of an implacable legislative majority, at least not at the outset. There was, however, one jarring note. Nine days after the close of the primary campaign, the U. S. Supreme Court delivered its decision in *Brown v. Board*. Here at the moment of triumph, here was a nagging reminder that the issue of race, the ancient nemesis of Southern liberals, would not down.

Folsom was one of a number of moderate-to-liberal governors in the South in the years immediately following the 1954 school desegregation decision. Initial reaction to the Court's decree was mild. But by 1956 the full fury of segregationist reaction was vented against these Southern moderates.[73] Despite rising public sentiment, Folsom resisted an increasingly aroused legislature. He refused to sign a pupil placement bill designed to circumvent the Brown decision. He refused to sign an interposition resolution and called it "hogwash," having all the effect of a hound "baying at the moon." [74] He vetoed a measure banning the NAACP from recruiting in a Black Belt county and was roundly criticized for entertaining Adam Clayton Powell, the Negro Congressman from New York, at the governor's mansion.[75] While publicly attacking "nullicrats and mobocrats," the Governor privately went well beyond his public rhetoric and encouraged a young Montgomery minister, Martin Luther King, to broaden his demands of the bus boycott that had been launched in the capital city.[76]

Folsom refused to desert his liberal position on race. But he did so only at great cost politically. In the first year of his second administration, before the reaction to the Brown decision mounted, Folsom enjoyed a minor triumph. With a friendly legislature, his program of expanded state services was enacted, with only minor changes. He even succeeded in pushing through a controversial reapportionment amendment and left the capital in triumph for a vacation. He had achieved, in his mind, the fundamental reform on which his political career had been based.[77]

The reapportionment triumph was short-lived, however. For while Folsom was absent from the capital, mob violence in Tuscaloosa frustrated the attempt to integrate the University of Alabama peacefully.[78] The constitutional amendment to reapportion the state legislature had been only a half-way measure.[79] Overshadowed by the raging controversy over segregation, it was soundly defeated by the voters in November.[80]

By 1956, the Governor's moderate stand on the race issue had cost him the support of the legislature. Once again, news stories of extravagant spending and recurrent scandal in the administration cut into the Governor's political support. Perhaps in frustration, Folsom was frequently absent from the capital for extended periods and took increasingly to drink. Once again the issue of race had marred the initial promise of a Folsom administration. Defeated by a segregationist opponent in a 1958 race for Democratic National Committeeman, Folsom left office in January, 1959, under a political cloud even darker than that of 1951.[81]

Since that time, Folsom's repeated attempts at a political come-back have met with defeat. After losing a run-off berth against George Wallace in 1962 by a narrow margin, Folsom has been defeated for the U. S. Senate, twice again for governor, and for a place on the Public Service Commission.[82] In ill-health and in disrepute among those who recall only the image of reckless spending and incompetent administration, Folsom remains today a man who skirted "the narrow edge of political greatness." [83]

Greatness was denied him. A concerted band of opponents had destroyed the threat he posed to conservative resurgence in the post-war years. Lacking either the ruthlessness or the power of a Huey Long, Folsom had failed to subdue his opponents. By the late 1950's, the man who had represented a "fresh green breeze" [84] in Alabama politics already had taken on the image of a political anachronism. His rustic rhetoric had entertained a rural folk from the steps of county courthouses. But in a society increasingly prosperous and urban, he became a relic of a rural past, something to be cast aside, something not quite respectable. The recurrent issue of race, the changing character of the political medium in which he moved, his own flaws of personality and character—all had conspired to deny Folsom the greatness that might have been his.

Defeat and disappointment did not narrow him, however. He refused to desert the liberal principles of race and economics he began with. Amidst the larger failure, that was the minor triumph, the tragic triumph of Jim Folsom.

Folsom failed to subdue the issue of race. He failed to secure the fundamental reforms he sought. With the demand for public services soaring in the 1950's, he did preside over a rapid expansion of state programs in education, welfare, and highways. But all that was incidental, as he himself would maintain, to the larger reforms he sought. He failed, too, in his efforts to become the arbiter of the Loyalist faction. But his liberal legacy endures. "My leadership may have been wrong," he confessed in 1962. But "if so, I have left a heritage." [85]

So too did the factional lines crystallized in the Dixiecrat revolt of 1948 endure. With roots in long-standing factional rivalries and in historic class and sectional divisions, those lines had taken on a clarity and rigidity in 1948 that have persisted. The issue of national party loyalty, tied as it is to questions of race and economics, has persisted in Alabama politics. Though clouded by the emergence of George Wallace in the politics of the 1960's and early '70's, the factional lines drawn in the struggle for party dominance, for control of the state party machinery, remain today basically the same as those of 1948.

The election of 1948 served not only to crystallize factional lines within the Democratic party in Alabama but also to warn progressive Democrats in Alabama and throughout the South that an indigenous Southern liberalism, if suspect on the issue of race, was vulnerable. It could not survive the emotional turmoil of rapid social change in the 1950's and '60's. Most political leaders in the South were indeed engaged, as George Tindall has written of the early 'forties, in a retreat "back within the parapets of the embattled South, where they stood fast against the incursions of social change." [86] The efforts of men like Folsom could not hold back the forces of reaction.

APPENDIX

I. Geographic Divisions of Alabama

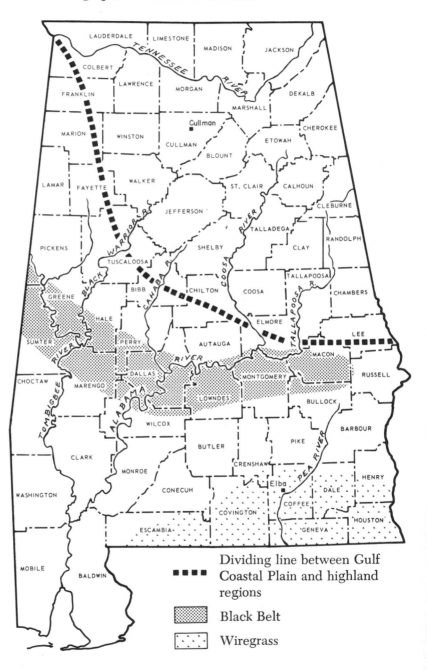

Dividing line between Gulf
Coastal Plain and highland
regions

Black Belt

Wiregrass

II. 1942 Gubernatorial Election

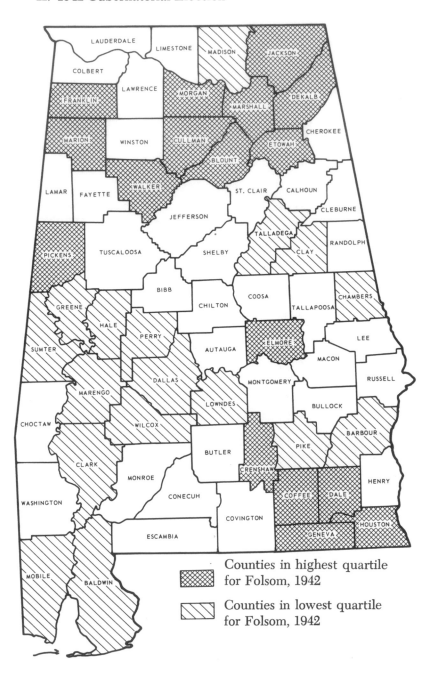

Counties in highest quartile
for Folsom, 1942

Counties in lowest quartile
for Folsom, 1942

III. Negro Population in Alabama, 1940

Counties with over 50%
Negro population, 1940

TABLE I

1942 Gubernatorial Race

FOLSOM RUNS WELL IN AREAS OF LOW NEGRO POPULATION
AND OF RELATIVELY HIGH REPUBLICAN STRENGTH

	Median % Negro Population 1940	Median % Voting Republican in 1940 Presidential Election	% of Total Republican Vote in 1940 Presidential Election	% of Total Vote in 1940 Presidential Election
Counties in Highest Quartile for Folsom in 1942	13.8	15.33	40.70	28.46
Counties in Lowest Quartile for Folsom in 1942	55.5	3.72	12.47	19.76
Alabama (67 counties)	32.0	8.36		

Source: *Sixteenth Census of the US: 1940, Population: Vol. II, Characteristics of the Population, Part I*, 236-239; *Alabama Official and Statistical Register 1943* (Wetumpka, Ala., 1943), 673-684.

IV. 1946 Gubernatorial Run-off

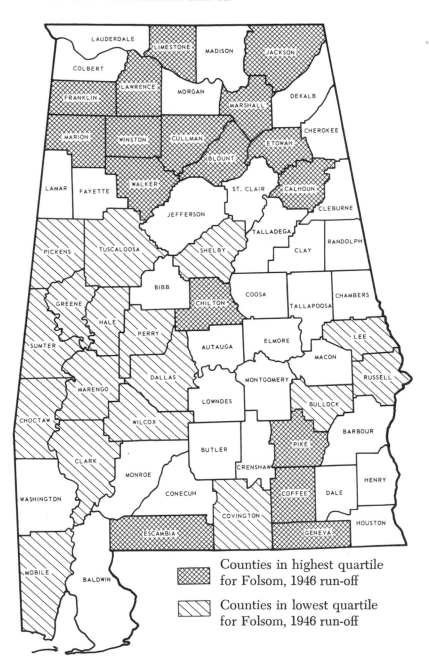

Counties in highest quartile for Folsom, 1946 run-off

Counties in lowest quartile for Folsom, 1946 run-off

V. Vote on the Boswell Amendment, 1946

Counties in highest quartile for Boswell Amendment

Counties in lowest quartile for Boswell Amendment

TABLE II

VOTE FOR BOSWELL AMENDMENT RELATED
TO CONCENTRATION OF NEGROES BY COUNTY

Five Counties Giving Greatest   Five Counties Giving Least
Support for Boswell Amendment   Support for Boswell Amendment

	% For	% Negro, 1940		% For	% Negro, 1940
Sumter	94.4	79.4	Jackson	16.7	6.3
Wilcox	94.3	78.3	Winston	22.7	0.6
Russell	92.0	59.0	Etowah	25.1	14.6
Greene	91.6	83.8	Blount	28.7	4.3
Choctaw	90.8	53.1	Madison	29.1	27.7

median % Negro 78.3   median % Negro 6.3
average % Negro 70.7   average % Negro 10.7

1948 RACE FOR ELECTOR

EXPLANATORY NOTE

There were twenty-eight candidates for the eleven positions of elector. They ran at large, and there was no official or agreed-upon slate either of States' Righters or of Loyalists. Though the States' Righters' victory was overwhelming, the long, confusing, and cumbersome ballot fractured the results.

The returns defy systematic analysis. Name recognition proved most valuable, and most candidates ran well in their home areas. Despite the magnitude of the States' Righters' victory, the enduring sectional cleavages within the state are visible. Of the eight counties in which one of the fifteen leading States' Righters did not run first, five are in north Alabama (Colbert, Cullman, Marion, Walker, and Winston) and two are in the Wiregrass (Coffee and Geneva). The eighth county is Macon in the Black Belt. In all but Colbert and Macon, identified Loyalists ran first.

VI. Vote on the Self-Starter

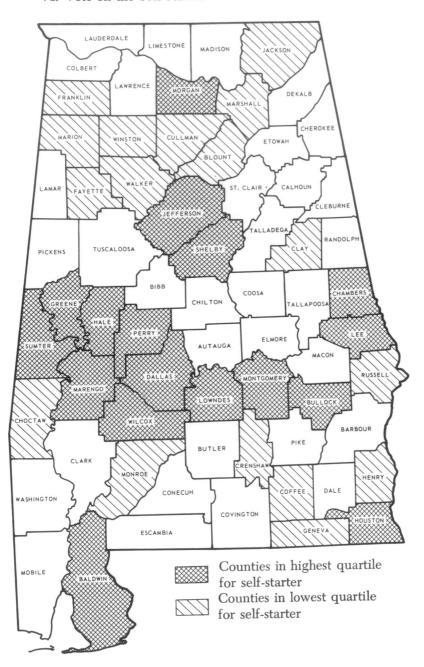

Counties in highest quartile for self-starter

Counties in lowest quartile for self-starter

VII. Loyalist v. States' Righter, 1950

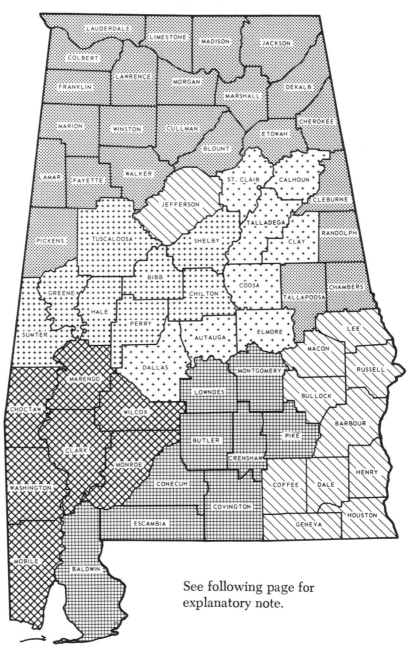

See following page for
explanatory note.

LOYALIST V. STATES' RIGHTER, 1950

In the 1950 contest between States' Righters and Loyalists for control of the State Democratic Executive Committee, candidates ran at large from the nine Congressional districts. Eight members were elected from each district. Congressional district lines seldom coincided with the geographic divisions within the state. Nonetheless, the traditional cleavage within the state can be seen in rudimentary form in the returns. (See Illustration VII on the preceding page. Compare, for example, Illustration VII with Illustration II).

KEY FOR ILLUSTRATION VII:

District 1: Eight States' Righters Elected

District 2: Six States' Righters, Two Loyalists

Districts 3 and 9: Four States' Righters, Four Loyalists Each

District 4: Three States' Righters, Four Loyalists, One Uncommitted

District 6: Three States' Righters, Five Loyalists

Districts 5, 7, 8: Eight Loyalists Each

NOTES

Introduction

1. George B. Tindall, *The Emergence of the New South 1913–1945*, Vol. X in Wendell Holmes Stephenson and E. Merton Coulter, eds., *A History of the South* ([Baton Rouge], 1967), 731.

2. Dixon's sentiments were expressed in a speech before the Southern Society of New York, December 11, 1942. The subsequent quotations are taken from the version of this speech, "Crossroads Democracy," contained in *Vital Speeches of the Day*, Vol. 9 (February 1, 1943), 236–240. For an expression of similar sentiments, see another of Dixon's speeches, "The Dangers of Centralization in Government," *ibid.*, Vol. 8 (August 1, 1942), 621–624. See also, Tindall, *Emergence of the New South*, 724, for a brief account of the speech to the Southern Society.

3. The following account of the 1944 Hill-Simpson contest and of its importance as a test of anti-administration sentiment in the South is taken from the New York *Times*, December 17, 1943; April 15, May 3, 1944; and the Mobile *Press*, December 16, 19, 1943. The course of the campaign from a conservative anti-Hill and anti-New Deal point of view, can be followed in the Mobile *Press*, April 19 through May 4, 1944.

4. Hill received 126,372 votes (55.5%), Simpson 101,176 (44.5%). *Alabama Official and Statistical Register 1947* (Montgomery, n. d.), 428–429. Despite the closeness of the contest, Hill's primary victory in a deep South state over a conservative, anti-New Deal opponent was a source of satisfaction to the Roosevelt administration. Two days after the primary, General Edwin M. ("Pa") Watson, FDR's military aide and appointment secretary, wrote Stephen T. Early, the President's press secretary, that "the Boss asks without using his name that you convey to Hill and [Sen. Claude] Pepper [of Florida, who was involved in a similar race] how much the results have rejoiced him." Memorandum from General Watson to Mr. Early, May 4, 1944. Official File 300, Box 16, Franklin D. Roosevelt Library, Hyde Park, N. Y.

5. A. G. Mezerik, "Dixie in Black and White," *The Nation*, Vol. CLXIV (April 19, 1947), 449.

Chapter 1

1. Birmingham *News*, March 31, 1946. The following discussion of Nixon's views is based on this citation. Later in 1946, Nixon presented his views in his *Lower Piedmont Country* (New York, 1946); see especially the chapter "Piedmont Politics," 178–193.

2. V. O. Key, Jr., *Southern Politics in State and Nation* (New York, 1949); C. Vann Woodward, *Origins of the New South 1877–1913*, Vol. IX in Wen-

dell Holmes Stephenson and E. Merton Coulter, eds., *A History of the South* ([Baton Rouge], 1951).

3. Key, *Southern Politics*, 41–46. Key was also impressed by the importance a candidate's home area played in Alabama elections, regardless of issues. Folsom was uniquely qualified to reestablish the historic political union between north Alabama and the Wiregrass. Not only was his program tailored to appeal to the interests of the two areas, but he had been born in the Wiregrass and made his home in north Alabama.

4. Kolb had been the Jeffersonian-Populist candidate for governor in 1892 and 1894. Manning was a fiery young orator for the Populists. Unlike some Populists he never wavered from his enlightened views on race. Jones and Oates were leaders of the conservative faction within the Democratic party. Both served as governor. A. B. Moore, *History of Alabama* (Tuscaloosa, 1934), 603–679; Woodward, *Origins of the New South*, 244–245, 262, 266–267, 277–278. The standard work on the Populist revolt in Alabama is John B. Clark, *Populism in Alabama* (Auburn, Ala., 1927). Recently the period has been reexamined by William Warren Rogers, *One-Gallused Rebellion: Agrarianism in Alabama 1865–1896* (Baton Rouge, 1970) and Sheldon Hackney, *Populism to Progressivisim in Alabama* (Princeton, 1969). See also, Jerrell H. Shofner and William Warren Rogers, "Joseph C. Manning: Militant Agrarian, Enduring Populist," *Alabama Historical Quarterly*, XXIX, Nos. 1 and 2 (Spring and Summer, 1967), 7–37; John Sparkman, "The Kolb-Oates Election," unpublished M.A. thesis, University of Alabama, 1924; and Charles G. Summersell, "A Life of Reuben F. Kolb," unpublished M.A. thesis, University of Alabama, 1930.

5. See, for example, Moore, *History of Alabama*, 88, 93, 108, 114; Theodore H. Jack, *Sectionalism in Party Politics in Alabama 1819–1842* (Menasha, Wisconsin, 1919), 85; Lewy Dorman, *Party Politics in Alabama from 1850 through 1860* (Wetumpka, Ala., 1935), 7.

6. Dorman, *Party Politics in Alabama*, 14–15; Thomas Perkins Abernethy, *The Formative Period in Alabama, 1815–1828* (University, Ala., 1965), 38–43, 175; Moore, *History of Alabama*, 87.

7. So-called because of a tough and wiry grass once common to the area.

8. Moore, *History of Alabama*, 87–88, 160–161; Dorman, *Party Politics in Alabama*, 7, 11–13. See also Illustration I, p. 148, in the appendix.

9. Moore, *History of Alabama*, 639; Key, *Southern Politics*, 41–46; Clark, *Populism in Alabama*, 173, 181. See also Robert David Ward and William Warren Rogers, *Labor Revolt in Alabama: The Great Strike of 1894* (University, Ala., 1965), 118–119, 137–138; Rogers, *One-Gallused Rebellion*, 222–224; Malcolm C. McMillan, *Constitutional Development in Alabama, 1798–1901: A Study in Politics, the Negro and Sectionalism* (Chapel Hill, N.C., 1955), 44–45, 55–63, 77–80, 98–108, 228–229, 250–255, 296–298, 306–309, 317–318, 350–352, 362–369.

10. Moore, *History of Alabama*, 650–651. McMillan, *The Land Called Alabama* (Austin, Texas, 1968), 352. See Dewey W. Grantham, *The Democratic South* (Athens, Ga., 1963), for a discussion of this bifactionalism as a general characteristic of Southern politics. Sheldon Hackney's *Populism to Progressivism in Alabama*, 278, 309–310, disputes the degree of continuity often presumed between the Populists and the Progressives.

11. Hackney, *Populism to Progressivisim in Alabama*, 210; McMillan, *Land Called Alabama*, 254–268. See also Allan J. Going, *Bourbon Democracy in Alabama 1874–1890* (University, Ala., 1951), for a detailed history of this

period. As Going makes clear, the paragraph presented here is a much simplified view of a very complex era.

12. Moore, *History of Alabama*, 650–656; McMillan *Land Called Alabama*, 342–343, 352.

13. Moore, *History of Alabama*, 663–672, 767–777. It is difficult to sort out the many facets of a movement as complex and all-encompassing as progressivism. Though the impression is based on a cursory look at the evidence, there seems to be a distinct difference in both tone and content between the 1906 progressivism of Comer and Graves' version of 1926. Comer represents that side of progressivism that sought to deal with the economic problems of a modern industrial society through governmental action. Regulation of railroads and a kind of high-minded, middle-class humanitarianism were the staples of his political appeal. Graves represents a step further toward the social service state. A conglomeration of groups which stood to benefit from the positive acts of the state in welfare, education, road building, and a host of other fields was the backbone of Graves' support. They were joined by men who represented the best of the progressive impulse gone rancid. The admirable morality of the progressives, the bent toward social betterment, toward social control in a society whose bonds of cohesion were sorely frayed by the triple impact of industrialization, urbanization, and immigration—these were manifest in their more sour and sometimes ominous forms in support for the Klan, for prohibition, and for fundamentalist attacks upon free thinking. Graves, like many other Southern progressives in the 1920's, consorted with the Klan for a time. By so doing, and by his seeming unconcern for "good government"—that is, economy and civil service—Graves lost the support of some high-minded reformers of the earlier progressive period. They began their trek towards conservatism that ended in vehement opposition to the New Deal. Graves, meanwhile, easily made the transition to ardent New Dealer in the 1930's, though some of his followers did not.

14. McMillan, *Land Called Alabama*, 340–341, 352, 377. Even during the 1930's, when identification with Franklin Roosevelt and the New Deal greatly strengthened the liberal faction of Bibb Graves, Hugo Black, and Lister Hill, conservative forces remained entrenched in the state legislature and were able to prevent reapportionment and to modify Graves' programs. See, for example, Chauncey Sparks to Jeff Beeland, June 20, 1936; W. D. Malone to Sparks, June 23, 1936; Sparks to A. B. Aldridge, June 25, 1936; and Victor Hanson to G. R. Swift, December 24, 1936, in the papers of Chauncey Sparks, Alabama Department of Archives and History, Montgomery, Alabama (hereinafter referred to as Sparks Papers) for an indication of the workings of the "economy bloc" in Graves' second administration.

15. Unless otherwise indicated, biographical details in this chapter can be found in a special inaugural edition of the Gadsden *Times*, January 18, 1955.

16. The population of Elba in 1910 was 1,079, having grown from 285 in 1890. *Alabama Official and Statistical Register 1910* (Montgomery, 1912), 214. This was the era of the small town in the rural South. Small crossroad towns sprang up to service the new agricultural order. See, for example, Avery Craven, *Reconstruction: The Ending of the Civil War* (New York, 1969), 247–251. Moreover, in the late 1800's the pace of migration to the Wiregrass quickened. McMillan, *Land Called Alabama*, 6–7; Moore, *History of Alabama*, 521–523, 677–688.

17. Folsom tried to account for his political ideas to a reporter in 1947. "People are always askin' me," he said, "where I got my political ideas. . . .

Hell, I've always had those ideas. My daddy was a county office holder. We lived in the county seat along the rail line. People was [sic] always stoppin' in on us on the way to the capital. I used to sit by the fire when I was a boy and hear them talk about state politics and elections. Naturally they was [sic] talkin' democracy and I just grew up believin' in democracy and majority rule." Paul E. Deutschmann, "Outsize Governor," *Life*, XXIII (September 15, 1947), 59.

18. Interview with James E. Folsom, Cullman, Ala., June 29, 1968. Thus, Folsom will explain, he has a natural bias against the Catholic Church, not Catholics, but the Church. The Dunnavants, his mother's people, were persecuted in the 1690's by the Cardinal of Lyons. And the Folsoms in England were "on the wrong side, whichever one that was, about the time of the Mayflower." Evidently, the Folsom's have a long history of political insurgency. "Yes, my ancestors met the Cardinal's chopping block in France and the hangman's noose in England and Ireland." The accuracy of detail in this family history is less important than the tendency to view the past in immediate and personal terms.

19. See Birmingham *Post,* July 9, September 3, 20, 1946; Birmingham *Age-Herald,* August 30, 1946; and Atlanta *Journal,* September 4, 1946, clippings in the files of the Birmingham Public Library's Southern Collection (hereinafter referred to as BPL Files), for indications of Folsom's views on foreign policy, particularly his sentiments toward the British, in the post-war period. For indications of his position on race see below, 128, 135–136, 184 n.68, 144–145.

20. Interview with James E. Folsom, Cullman, Ala., June 29, 1968.

21. See below, 92.

22. Folsom Interview, June 29, 1968.

23. The Populist heritage on race is a tangled one, as C. Vann Woodward has made clear in his biography of Tom Watson and in other works. The ambiguity of the Populist legacy on race has appeared time and again in the course of Southern history since the 1890's. Champions of the people who chanted all the Populist complaints against the bankers, the East, the interests, have arisen in most Southern states. Some were frauds, using the technique to mask programs that served not the people they championed, but the interests they damned. Others used the Populist incantations simply as a vehicle to power. The most flamboyant of them persisted in the progressive economic program of the Populists but coupled it with a virulent racism. Some went through a metamorphosis similar to Watson's, moving from a position of racial tolerance to one of vehement bigotry. (A similar charge has been made against George C. Wallace. It has been said that after he lost the gubernatorial race of 1958 as a moderate he became the most ardent of segregationists. There are those who are familiar with the politics of the state who dispute this popular but perhaps simplistic interpretation. See, for example, Marshall Frady, "George Wallace: The Angry Man's Candidate," *Saturday Evening Post,* Vol. 241 (June 29, 1968), 35; and Charles Morgan, *A Time to Speak* (New York, 1964), 34–37, 52, 137.) Some champions of the Southern masses, however, retained and never abandoned the Populist liberalism on race, including Huey Long and his brother Earl, Estes Kefauver, Hugo Black, and "Big Jim" Folsom.

24. Folsom Interview, June 29, 1968. See, for example, the brief account

of Folsom's role in the 1950's in Numan V. Bartley, *The Rise of Massive Re-sistance* (Baton Rouge, 1969), 279–286.

25. For an account of Folsom's campaign, see the Elba *Clipper,* April 9, 16, 23, 30, May 7, 1936; and the Montgomery *Advertiser,* April 20, 29, 30, 1936. This account of Folsom's 1936 campaign is drawn from these sources.

26. Percentage computed from figures in *Alabama Official and Statistical Register 1939* (Wetumpka, Ala., 1940), 592. Two weeks before election day, the ailing Steagall released a "Dear Henry" letter from Roosevelt expressing his concern for Steagall's health, urging him to rest, wishing him a speedy re-covery, and thanking him for the part he had played in the progress of the past few years. Steagall ran as "the true liberal" in the race. He deplored Fol-som's flirtation with the unsound schemes of the Townsendites and firmly at-tached himself to the New Deal's record of liberal accomplishments. Elba *Clipper,* April 23, 30, 1936; Opelika *Daily News,* quoted in Montgomery *Ad-vertiser,* April 20, 1936.

In a letter to Roosevelt after the election, Steagall credited his victory to Roosevelt's endorsement. Steagall to Franklin D. Roosevelt, May 6, 1936. Of-ficial File 300, Box 16, Franklin D. Roosevelt Library, Hyde Park, New York.

It is startling to be reminded how quickly the political climate, or at least the terminology, has changed in Alabama and the South. Politicians in the 1930's and '40's actively vied for the label "liberal." See below, 56. As late as 1954, Arthur Krock of the New York Times could write that "the day of the party conservative is now ending and . . . southern Democracy is about to join the northern on the left side of the American political scene." Quoted in Rob-ert Sherrill, *Gothic Politics in the Deep South: Stars of the New Confederacy,* rev. ed. (New York, 1969), 369. And the able author of the officially adopted high school history of the State of Alabama felt, as late as 1957, that he had to explain to his readers how it was that "conservative" Bourbons could be elected in the late nineteenth century. "The term Bourbon," he wrote, "means that Conservatives ruled the state, and most of the political leaders of this period liked to refer to themselves as Conservatives. The label 'Conservative,'" he continued, "would be a political liability today, but such was not the case during the Bourbon period." Charles Grayson Summersell, *Alabama History for Schools* (Birmingham, 1957), 347.

27. Elba *Clipper,* April 14, 28, 1938. Percentage computed from figures in *Alabama Official and Statistical Register 1939,* 622. In December of 1937, Folsom wrote a penciled note to FDR pointing out Steagall's record of opposi-tion to the administration and the closeness of the 1936 race. Folsom urged Roosevelt to remain neutral in the 1938 race if he could not support Folsom. "If you can't help me," he wrote, "don't help that bear." Folsom to Roosevelt, December 28, 1937. Official File 300, Box 78. Roosevelt Library. There is no evidence that Roosevelt intervened in the 1938 election.

28. Moore, *History of Alabama,* 769–777; McMillan, *Land Called Alabama,* 366–371.

29. Moore, *History of Alabama,* 767–777.

30. *Ibid.,* 771–774.

31. See, for example, the criticism leveled at Graves by Chauncey Sparks and his followers early in the campaign of 1942. Birmingham *News,* January 9, 30; February 1, 15, 1942; *Alabama: News Magazine of the Deep South,* Vol. VII, No. 5 (January 30, 1942), 7.

32. Robin Swift to Chauncey Sparks, October 24, 1940; Emmett Hildreth to Sparks, February 6, 1941; W. D. Malone to Sparks, June 23, 1936, in

Sparks Papers. See also, Sparks to Jeff Beeland, June 20, 1936; to A. B. Aldridge, June 25, 1936. Sparks Papers.

33. Chauncey Sparks to Robin Swift, April 1, 1939; Swift to Sparks, October 24, 1940; Emmett Hildreth to Sparks, February 6, 1941; Robin Swift to Sparks, April 24, 1941; Sparks to Swift, February 28, 1941. Sparks Papers.

34. Montgomery *Advertiser,* April 9, 1942. Sherlock later told Sparks that Dixon had urged him to declare his candidacy. Memorandum by Sparks on a conversation with Sherlock, June 5, 1942. Sparks Papers. "Ain't it hell!!!" Robin Swift had written Sparks earlier, "all this crossing and double crossing." Swift to Sparks, November 9, 1941. Sparks Papers.

35. Birmingham *News,* November 6, 1941; January 24, 26, March 14, 1942.

36. *Ibid.,* March 14, 15, 1942; *Alabama: The News Magazine of the Deep South,* Vol. 7, No. 12 (March 20, 1942), 6.

37. Birmingham *News,* March 22, 1942.

38. See below, 35–37, for the reaction of a perceptive Alabama journalist, Grover Hall, Jr., to Folsom's campaign style as he had refined it by 1946.

39. Atlanta *Journal,* June 9, 1946; Birmingham *Post,* August 27, 1946, clippings in BPL Files. One of Folsom's political rivals tried to account for the response to Folsom. "Jim appeals to the popular imagination," he said. "He's like a big awkward puppy. People love him on sight and, for no apparent reason, feel kindly toward him. It doesn't seem to matter what he says or does, or even if he says or does anything. They just vote for him regardless. To them he's not a politician." Birmingham *Post,* August 20, 1945, clipping in BPL Files.

40. Folsom Interview, Cullman, Ala., July 1, 1968; interview with John Stiefelmeyer, Folsom campaign worker, July 1, 1968, in Cullman, Alabama.

41. Birmingham *News,* May 3, 1942.

42. *Ibid.,* May 4, April 12, 1942; *Alabama: The News Magazine of the Deep South,* Vol. VII, No. 13 (March 27, 1942), 6; No. 16 (April 17, 1942), 6; No. 18 (May 1, 1942), 4.

43. Birmingham *News,* May 3, 1942.

44. *Ibid.,* April 19, 26, May 9, 11, 1942. The vote stood: Sparks 145,798; Folsom 73,306; Sherlock 53,448; and two minor candidates, approximately 7,000. *Alabama Official and Statistical Register 1943* (Wetumpka, Ala., 1943), 754–755.

45. See, for example, the surprise of Grover Hall, Jr., the astute columnist for the Alabama *Journal,* at "the authentic, but Johnnie-come-lately liberalism of Governor Sparks." Alabama *Journal,* November 27, 1945, clipping in Sparks Scrapbooks, Sparks Papers.

46. See Illustration II and Table I in the Appendix for graphic illustration of the sectional nature of Folsom's strength and of its relation to the concentration of Negro population and the tendency to vote Republican in Presidential elections. These maps also serve as the basis for the following analysis of the 1942 vote.

47. These were the same areas, the Black Belt and the Gulf Coast, that were the source of strength for the States' Rights movement in 1948. That movement was the culmination of a long series of moves by the conservative wing of the party to dislodge the liberal adherents of the New Deal. See below, Ch. 6, 95–124.

48. *Alabama: The News Magazine of the Deep South,* Vol. VII, No. 15 (April 10, 1942), 6.

Chapter 2

1. Birmingham *News,* March 24, April 3, 4, 14, 1946; "Hallmarks," [Montgomery] *Alabama Journal,* November 27, 1945, and May 8, 1946; Frank M. Dixon to Floyd W. Jefferson, June 11, 1946, Frank M. Dixon Papers, Alabama Department of Archives and History, Montgomery, Alabama (hereinafter referred to as Dixon Papers); *Alabama: The News Magazine of the Deep South,* Vol. II, No. 12 (March 22, 1946), 12–13.

2. Birmingham *News,* December 16, 1945; January 20, March 3, 1946.

3. *Ibid.,* June 2, March 17, 31, 1946.

4. Key, *Southern Politics,* 40; McMillan, *The Land Called Alabama,* 378–379.

5. See, for example, Birmingham *News,* March 31, 1946.

6. Grover C. Hall, Jr., "Hallmarks," [Montgomery] *Alabama Journal,* February 26, 1946, clipping in Sparks Scrapbooks, Sparks Papers. Unless otherwise designated, subsequent references to Hall's "Hallmarks" column were located in the Sparks Scrapbooks in the Sparks Papers.

7. Birmingham *News,* December 30, 1945; January 20, 1946. Grover Hall, Jr., "Hallmarks," December 23, 1945.

8. Birmingham *News,* January 20, 1946.

9. Birmingham *News,* November 11, 18, December 2, 1945. The conservative business community and the Farm Bureau were particularly eager to elect a governor favorable to their views. They had been disappointed by Governor Sparks. In particular, they had been angered by his advocacy of a constitutional amendment to permit the use of income tax revenue for education. When the state income tax had been adopted in the 1930's, a provision had been written in whereby the ad valorem tax on land would be reduced once the revenue from the income tax reached a specified level. That level had been reached under Governor Sparks and a surplus had accumulated in the state treasury. Governor Sparks sponsored an amendment to permit the use of such funds for education and other social services provided by the state. The amendment was bitterly opposed by the Farm Bureau and by the state's business and industrial interests. It failed to pass. The disposition of the state surplus was still unsettled, and the next governor would have considerable influence on the state's action in the matter. Hence, the great interest by the Farm Bureau and the conservative business interests in the election. Birmingham *News,* September 23, 30, October 21, 1945; February 24, April 7, 1946.

10. Dewey W. Grantham, Jr., *The Democratic South,* 56.

11. *Ibid.*

12. Birmingham *News,* March 31, April 4, 28, 1946.

13. *Ibid.,* December 2, 1945; January 13, 20, 1946.

14. Ellis received support from A. H. Carmichael, former member of Congress and author of Alabama's first prohibition measure, from Vernon St. John, a state senator and leading dry, and from Donald Comer, son of B. B. Comer, the state's progressive governor, 1907–1911. *Ibid.,* April 14, 24, 1946.

15. Grover Hall, Jr., "Hallmarks," March 8, 1946, Sparks Scrapbook; Birmingham *News,* April 14, 1946.

16. Birmingham *News,* December 9, 1945; April 25, May 1, 3, 1946.

17. *Ibid.,* April 21, 26, 1946.

18. *Ibid.,* May 2, April 7, 1946.

19. *Ibid.,* March 31, April 8, 1946.

20. Grover Hall, Jr., "Hallmarks," January 17, 1946, Sparks Scrapbook; Birmingham *News,* May 13, April 26, 1946.

21. Birmingham *News,* April 14, 1946.

22. *Ibid.,* March 10, 17, 1946; Grover Hall, Jr., "Hallmarks," March 7, 11, 14, 1946, Sparks Scrapbook.

23. Grover Hall, Jr., "Hallmarks," March 19, 1946, Sparks Scrapbook.

24. *Ibid.,* November 27, 1945; June 5, 1946.

25. Hall to Frank M. Dixon, February 17, 1945. Dixon Papers.

26. Birmingham *News,* March 17, 1946.

27. *Ibid.,* November 18, 1945; April 21, 26, 1946.

28. *Ibid.,* March 31, April 4, May 1, 1946.

29. See Atlanta *Journal,* June 9, 1946, and *Christian Science Monitor,* June 12, 1946, clippings in BPL Files; Birmingham *News,* May 12, December 29, 1946, for comments concerning the impact of returned veterans on Alabama politics.

30. Birmingham *News,* May 12, December 29, 1946; July 17, 1949.

31. Men close to Joe Poole had spread the rumor back in January that the C.I.O.'s Political Action Committee would spend a million dollars in Alabama to elect a pro-labor governor. The C.I.O. supposedly wanted repeal of the state's right-to-work law and a veto over labor legislation. Poole's camp wanted to frighten the "big mules," the business leaders of the state, in order to secure their unified and generous support. *Ibid.,* January 13, 1946.

32. "Hallmarks," February 2, April 30, 1946, Sparks Scrapbook.

33. *Ibid.,* March 19, 1946.

34. Birmingham *News,* May 5, April 27, May 2, 1946.

35. Grover Hall, Jr., "Hallmarks," January 17, 1946, Sparks Scrapbook; Birmingham *News,* April 26, 1946.

36. Birmingham *News,* March 3, 21, 1946.

37. Deutschmann, "Outsize Governor," 59.

38. Folsom's respect for civil liberties produced in him a respect for the American judiciary unusual in the populistic liberalism of which he was a part. In his own time he had seen the judiciary become the staunchest guardian of civil liberty and the insistent guarantor of equality before the law. For one example of his defense of the Supreme Court, see New York *Times,* December 25, 1967.

39. Birmingham *News,* May 6, 1946.

40. Grover Hall, Jr., "Hallmarks," May 19, 1946, Sparks Scrapbook; Birmingham *News,* May 23, 25, 30, 1946; John Temple Graves, "This Morning," Birmingham *Post,* May 31, 1946, Sparks Scrapbook.

41. See, for example, Birmingham *Age-Herald,* June 6, 1946, clipping in BPL File.

42. "Hallmarks," June 10, 1946; Graves, "This Morning," Birmingham *Post,* May 28, 1946. Sparks Scrapbook; Birmingham *News,* June 2, 1946.

43. V. O. Key, Jr., writes with perception of the power of Alabama's probate judges, and its limits, in his *Southern Politics,* 53–54. Grover Hall, Jr., was impressed by the limits of their power, at least when, as in 1946, the voters have been captivated by a candidate of great personality and magnetism. "Hallmarks," June 10, 1946, Sparks Scrapbook.

44. Grover Hall, Jr., "Hallmarks," March 21, 22, 1946, Sparks Scrapbook.

45. Interview with Roland Johnson, original member of the "Strawberry Pickers," Cullman, Ala., July 30, 1968; Grover Hall, Jr., "Hallmarks," March 24, 1946, Sparks Scrapbook. Folsom did not reveal his "secret method" to Hall at that time—actually it was very simple: multitudes of handbills sent to every mail box along an R.F.D. route—and Hall concluded that "one is left to make

a simple explanation—Folsom is so big that on a clear day they can see him coming two or three counties away."

46. Grover Hall, Jr., "Hallmarks," February 26, 1946, Sparks Scrapbook.

47. *Ibid.*, March 3, 4, 1946.

48. *Ibid.*

49. *Ibid.*, March 27, 1946.

50. *Ibid.*, April 26, 1946. It is from this source that the following account of Folsom's Montgomery appearance is drawn.

51. Birmingham *News*, April 7, 1946.

52. Grover Hall, Jr., "Hallmarks," March 26, 1946. Sparks Scrapbook.

53. *Ibid.*, May 8, 1946.

54. *Alabama Official and Statistical Register 1947* (Montgomery, n.d.) 481–483.

55. See, for example, below, 48. See, also, *Alabama: News Magazine of the Deep South,* Vol. XII, No. 4 (January 24, 1947), 5, and Birmingham *News*, May 23, 1946.

56. Dixon to Horace Hall, May 18, 1946; Dixon to Winston R. Withers, May 21, 1946. Dixon Papers.

57. Ellis' discomfort and defensiveness are apparent in his letter thanking Dixon for his support in the run-off. Ellis to Dixon, June 21, 1946. Dixon Papers.

58. Birmingham *Post,* May 10, 1946. Sparks Scrapbook.

59. Birmingham *News*, May 17, 1946; Montgomery *Advertiser*, May 30, 1946, clipping in BPL File.

60. Birmingham *News*, May 12, 16, 17, 19, 1946. Gordon Persons endorsed Ellis, commenting that "Jim Folsom is a nice boy, but in my opinion he doesn't have the experience to operate a $100,000,000 business." *Ibid.*, May 11, 1946. The concession to Poole and Boozer was seized upon by some anti-Folsom commentators as further evidence of Folsom's incompetence. They charged that he was so deficient in his knowledge of state government that he willingly submitted to such a humiliating agreement. Handy Ellis remarked that Folsom "traded his britches off" in the days following the first primary. But Ellis and the critics had misread their man. With the possible exception of Henderson's appointment as Senate president pro tem, the concessions were meaningless. As Grover Hall, Jr., pointed out, Folsom was "by nature independent." Once governor he would be free to disregard such an advisory committee. That committee was less a concession by which Folsom sought the support of his recent foes than a face-saving device by which Boozer and Poole could cast their support behind the certain winner. It was they who had had to come to Folsom to make the best arrangement possible. Birmingham *News*, May 16, 1946; [Montgomery] Alabama *Journal*, May 30, 1946; Grover Hall, Jr., "Hallmarks," June 5, 1946, Sparks Scrapbook.

61. The conservative challenge by James A. Simpson to Lister Hill in 1944 had been based, in large measure, on the race issue—"as it had to be," former governor Dixon, a Simpson supporter, assured Grover Hall, Jr. Dixon to Hall, August 2, 1944, Dixon Papers.

62. Birmingham *News*, May 13, 1946.

63. Montgomery *Advertiser*, May 26, 1946, Sparks Scrapbook.

64. Birmingham *News*, May 21, 13, 1946.

65. The appeal to "unity" is a powerful one in the South. The illusion of *a* South, *a* Southerner, *a* Southern point of view seems immune to critical analysis. As T. Harry Williams has pointed out, "the mystique of unity" has joined

the Lost Cause and the Old South in the romantic Southern legend. T. Harry Williams, *Romance and Realism in Southern Politics* (Athens, Ga., 1961), 59.

66. Birmingham *News*, May 13, 1946.
67. *Ibid.*, May 26, 28, 1946; Montgomery *Advertiser*, May 26, 1946.
68. Birmingham *News*, May 21, 1946.
69. *Ibid.*, May 29, 1946.
70. "Hallmarks," June 5, 1946, Sparks Scrapbook.
71. Birmingham *News*, May 26, 30, June 2, 1946. The description of Davis is that of Charles Feidelson, an editorial writer for the *News*.
72. Birmingham *Age-Herald*, May 17, 10, 1944; February 5, 1946; January 4, 1945; June 17, 1944. Sparks Scrapbook.
73. *Ibid.*, July 7, 1946; Birmingham *Post*, April 29, 1946. Sparks Scrapbook.
74. Birmingham *Post*, May 10, 1946, Sparks Scrapbook.
75. *Ibid.*, May 11, 13, 1946.
76. *Ibid.*, May 23, 1946.
77. *Ibid.*, May 27, 28, 1946.
78. *Ibid.*, May 28, 1946.
79. *Ibid.* Folsom had been a delegate to the 1944 Democratic convention and, along with Ellis Arnall of Georgia, had supported Henry Wallace's bid for renomination for Vice-President. Others in the Alabama delegation had supported the favorite-son candidacy of Senator John Bankhead, Jr. *Ibid.*, May 21, 1946.
80. *Ibid.*, May 31, 1946.
81. *Ibid.*, June 3, 1946.
82. The historic sectional cleavages apparent in Folsom's 1942 race reappeared in 1946. See Illustration IV in the Appendix for graphic depiction of the returns.

Chapter 3

1. Birmingham *News*, June 5, 6, May 8, 9, June 2, 1946.
2. Quoted in *ibid.*, June 2, 1946.
3. "Hallmarks," May 8, 1946, Sparks Scrapbook.
4. John Temple Graves, "This Morning," Birmingham *Post*, June 18, 1946; Grover Hall, Jr., "Hallmarks," June 5, 1946. Sparks Scrapbook. Former governor Dixon also denied the importance of the C.I.O. in Folsom's victory. The C.I.O.'s role "has been greatly exaggerated," he wrote to the president of a South Carolina textile mill. "There is no question but that they put some money and put some workers into the state. But in the parts of the state in which they have strength they made an absolute failure. In the Governor's race a candidate by name Folsom, a man 6'8" tall and not regarded as particularly intelligent, took advantage of the hill-billy music technique developed by Davis in Louisiana, adopted a platform consisting largely of cleaning up the capitol, and polled a considerable plurality. . . . His nearest opponent [Ellis] was an old-time politician, surrounded in large part by the sorriest element of the old line political forces in the state. The other candidates pretty well succeeded in tearing Ellis . . . to pieces in the first primary, and in the excitement Folsom went ahead." But, Dixon explained, Folsom's greatest vote came from rural people. Other C.I.O.-endorsed candidates were generally defeated. In short, the C.I.O. "did not deliver in those parts where it is supposed to be strongest." There was simply "a sort of people's revolution against old-line politicians. [And] the only one that had any political effect appeal [sic]" was

Folsom. Dixon to B. B. Gossett, May 16, 1946. See also Dixon to Barrett Shelton, June 7, 1946; Dixon to Floyd W. Jefferson, June 11, 1946. Dixon Papers.

5. "Hallmarks," June 10, 1946, Sparks Scrapbook.

6. *Ibid.*, June 18, 1946.

7. This was the revealing phrase which the political correspondent for the Birmingham *News*, Hugh Sparrow, used in reporting Folsom's first primary lead. For Sparrow, Folsom's win had indeed been "upsetting." Birmingham *News*, May 12, 1946.

8. "Hallmarks," March 21, 1946, Sparks Scrapbook.

9. Undated memorandum [late 1946?], Dixon Papers.

10. Dixon to Floyd W. Jefferson, June 11, 1946; McCorvey to Dixon, March 28, 1947. Dixon Papers.

11. Graves' failure to carry through on his commitment to reapportionment was one of the factors that led Folsom to enter the race for governor in 1942. Folsom Interview, Cullman, Alabama, July 30, 1968.

12. Birmingham *News*, February 24, 1946.

13. "Hallmarks," June 16, 15, 1946, Sparks Scrapbook.

14. *Ibid.*, August 29, September 8, 1946. Today Folsom maintains that he got into politics for one reason and one alone—to secure reapportionment, to guarantee each man an equal voice in his government. "They call it 'one man, one vote' now," he recently told a reporter. "But that was what I was working for when I tried in both terms to get reapportionment through the Legislature. And that's why I wanted the poll tax abolished and color restrictions removed as requirements for voting." (Folsom Interview, Cullman, Alabama, July 30, 1968; Birmingham *Post-Herald*, August 11, 1969.) Undoubtedly, Folsom is in part speaking for the record, aware that he may in some way influence history's judgment. But he is also speaking from the core of his political being.

15. McCorvey to Dixon, March 28, 1947, Dixon Papers.

16. Barrett Shelton to Dixon, October 24, 1947, Dixon Papers.

17. Birmingham *News*, May 16, 19, 26, 1946.

18. *Ibid.*, May 23, 19, 1946; Grover Hall, Jr., "Hallmarks," July 15, 1946, Sparks Scrapbook; Birmingham *News*, May 19, June 16, 1946. Folsom Interview, Cullman, Alabama, July 30, 1968. Hammond Interview, Arab, Alabama, May 17, 1968.

19. Grover Hall, Jr., "Hallmarks," June 5, 1946; John Temple Graves, "This Morning", Birmingham *Post*, May 23, 1946. Sparks Scrapbook.

20. "Hallmarks," June 16, July 17, 1946, Sparks Scrapbook.

21. Birmingham *News*, June 6, 1946. The remainder of this section is drawn from this source.

22. "Hallmarks," August 16, 1946, Sparks Scrapbook.

23. *Ibid.*

24. *Ibid.*, August 18, 1946.

25. *Ibid.*

26. *Ibid.*

27. *Ibid.*

28. "This Morning," Birmingham *Post*, July 1, 11, and n.d. [November?], 1946, Sparks Scrapbook.

29. "Hallmarks," July 24, 1946, Sparks Scrapbook.

30. Biographical data drawn from *Congressional Directory, 90th Congress, First Session* (Washington, 1967), 4; New York *Times*, July 27, 1952. The quotation concerning the cow is from Grover Hall, Jr., "Hallmarks," July 14,

1946, Sparks Scrapbook. See also "Hallmarks," July 29, 1946, in re Sparkman's political outlook.

31. *Biographical Directory of the American Congress, 1774–1961* (Washington, 1961), 584; New York *Times*, March 13, 1969; Grover Hall, Jr., "Hallmarks," July 29, 1946, Sparks Scrapbook; Mobile *Press*, March 12–15, 1969; Mobile *Register*, March 13–15, 1969.

32. New York *Times*, December 17, 1943; Mobile *Register*, December 16, 1943; April 20, 22, 30, May 3, 1944.

33. Otis K. Rice, Review of Alen W. Moger's *Virginia: Bourbonism to Byrd 1870–1925, Journal of Southern History*, Vol. XXXV, No. 3 (August 1969), 432.

34. Birmingham *News*, June 15, July 7, 14, 1946; "Hallmarks," June 17, 1946, Sparks Scrapbook.

35. Birmingham *News*, July 7, 1946.

36. *Ibid.*, July 28, 7, 14, 21, 1946.

37. *Ibid.*, July 28, 1946; Grover Hall, Jr., "Hallmarks," July 23, 1946, Sparks Scrapbook; Birmingham *News*, July 14, 21, 28, 1946.

38. Birmingham *News*, July 28, 27, 1946.

39. Figures based on official returns as reported in Mobile *Register*, August 9, 1946; quotation from Montgomery *Advertiser*, July 25, 1942, clipping in Sparks Papers.

Chapter 4

1. *Smith v. Allwright*, 321 U.S. 649 (144).

2. Frank M. Dixon to Gessner T. McCorvey, October 12, 1944, Dixon Papers.

3. Moore, *History of Alabama*, 654–655; McMillan, *Constitutional Development in Alabama*, 275–309, 344–345, 363–364.

4. Dixon was as worried about the wrong sort of whites voting as about the extension of suffrage to blacks. See, for example, Gessner McCorvey's comments in McCorvey to Dixon, March 14, 1947, Dixon Papers.

5. Dixon, unlike McCorvey, felt the cumulative feature of Alabama's poll tax could not be justified and should be modified. Dixon to McCorvey, May 14, 1945, Dixon Papers.

6. McCorvey to MEMBERS OF THE ALABAMA LEGISLATURE, May 10, 1945, Dixon Papers.

7. *Report of the Thirteenth Annual [Alabama] Policy Conference on Democracy and the Constitution, Alabama Policy Bulletin No. 14*, 46–47, cited in McMillan, *Constitutional Development in Alabama*, 354. The suffrage provisions of the 1901 Constitution were considered by one authority as "the most elaborate . . . that have ever been in force in the United States." Kirk H. Porter, *A History of Suffrage in the United States* (Chicago, 1918), 213, cited in *ibid.*, 306.

8. McCorvey to MEMBERS OF THE ALABAMA LEGISLATURE, May 10, 1945, Dixon Papers.

9. *Ibid.*

10. This proposal had been advanced by a number of Alabama moderates and liberals who believed that the minimum required of the state was equal application of suffrage requirements, whatever they might be. Birmingham *News*, December 26, 1948.

11. McCorvey to MEMBERS OF THE ALABAMA LEGISLATURE, May 10, 1945, Dixon Papers.

12. Those portions of the 1901 Constitution which operated to retard the registration of Negroes and poorer whites were evidently sacrosanct to McCorvey but those which did not were less so and were subject to repeal.

13. McCorvey to MEMBERS OF THE ALABAMA LEGISLATURE, May 10, 1945, Dixon Papers.

14. *Ibid.*

15. The ambiguity in the position of men like McCorvey and Dixon is apparent in their arguments for the Boswell amendment. The poll tax and other restrictive measures are designed, so the argument goes, to ensure an intelligent, educated electorate. Yet the threat of "mass registration" had increased precisely because illiteracy no longer acted as a barrier to Negro voting. "Under our compulsory education statutes," McCorvey argued, "there are only a few hundred negroes of voting age in Alabama who cannot read and write." Registrars, in effect, are "required to register practically everyone, both black and white, who are [sic] over twenty-one, regardless of their ability to vote intelligently." (Birmingham *News*, September 18, 1946, quoted in Key, *Southern Politics*, 633. Key disputes McCorvey's sanguine view of Negro literacy in the 1940's, but McCorvey's basic point, whatever his exaggeration, is valid. See also Frank Dixon's speech in support of the Boswell amendment, below, 64–66, for elements of the same ambiguity.) One suspects that the ability to vote "intelligently," as McCorvey and his conservative supporters defined it, was peculiarly entrusted to those elements of the population who could be expected to vote as McCorvey thought best.

16. McCorvey to MEMBERS OF THE ALABAMA LEGISLATURE, May 10, 1945, Dixon Papers.

17. *Alabama: News Magazine of the Deep South*, Vol. II, No. 17 (April 26, 1946), 3.

18. A prospective voter, in addition to displaying an adequate "understanding" of the U. S. Constitution, would also have to satisfy the local board of registrars that he was of "good character" and had a proper understanding of "the duties and obligations of good citizenship under a republican form of government." *Alabama Official and Statistical Register, 1947* (Montgomery, n.d.), 533.

19. Speech by Frank M. Dixon to Athens, Alabama, Rotary Club, October 17, 1946, Dixon Papers.

20. Key, *Southern Politics*, 37, 42, 45–46, 634–635.

21. See above, 33, 48–49.

22. See above, 41.

23. See above, 49.

24. Birmingham *News*, October 6, 27, 1946.

25. *Ibid.*, October 20, 1946.

26. Florence *Times*, July 17, 1948.

27. See below, 97–102.

28. McCorvey to THE VOTERS OF ALABAMA, September, 1946, Dixon Papers; New York *Times*, January 13, 1946.

29. McCorvey to THE VOTERS OF ALABAMA, September, 1946, Dixon Papers.

30. *Ibid.*

31. *Ibid.*

32. *Ibid.*

33. Speech of Frank M. Dixon to Athens, Alabama, Rotary Club, October 17, 1946, Dixon Papers.

34. *Ibid.*

35. *Ibid.*

36. *Ibid.*

37. *Ibid.*

38. McCorvey to THE VOTERS OF ALABAMA, September, 1946, Dixon Papers.

39. *Ibid.*

40. Gessner McCorvey was right in identifying one source of opposition to the Boswell amendment, the Republican party in Alabama. It is doubtful, however, that the lone Republican in the state legislature, Rep. J. B. Weaver of "the free state of Winston," exercised much influence with the electorate at large. Birmingham *News*, October 6, 27, 20, 1946.

41. Senator Hill is quoted in Key, *Southern Politics*, 634.

42. The wife of a noted civic leader in Birmingham voiced similar objections in a letter to former-Governor Frank Dixon. "For years I have been proud of you and your administration," she wrote. "While in Washington working with the League of Women Voters, the American Association of University Women, I frequently discussed the progressive change in our State government, the fine way you prepared yourself for office, the splendid studies you authorized and the intelligent method you used to interest and win the Legislature. It was with great dis-appointment, therefore, that I read of your meeting with Horace Wilkinson and others to form a committee to urge the adoption of the Boswell Amendment." She was certain that Dixon did not share "Mr. Wilkinson's shocking [anti-Negro] views, and you must realize the danger of broadcasting such views over the State." She too believed "in an intelligent, informed electorate but I think this result lies not in passage of the Boswell Amendment but in vastly improved schools and enlightened, well educated teachers." She herself had a college degree and had taken courses in government, "but I should hate to be called on to interpret the Constitution. I doubt if I—or any of my friends—should ever be asked to do so." (Those of lesser position or of the wrong color might not be so lucky.) The Boswell amendment "is a vicious, narrow backward endeavor to arouse prejudice and to grant tremendous power to a few who may certainly misuse it." Mrs. Mervyn H. Sterne to Dixon, September 28, 1946, Dixon Papers.

43. Birmingham *News*, November 3, 1946.

44. *Ibid.*, September 15, 1946.

45. *Ibid.*, October 20, November 3, 1946.

46. Quoted in *ibid.*, October 27, November 3, 1946.

47. *Ibid.*, November 3, 1946.

48. *Ibid.*

49. *Ibid.*, September 22, 1946. The remainder of this section is drawn from this source.

50. *Ibid.*, November 3, 1946.

51. *Ibid.*

52. *Ibid.*, November 24, 1946. The amendment carried 89,163 to 76,843, or 53.7% to 46.3%. *Alabama Official and Statistical Register, 1947* (Montgomery, n.d.), 537–539. In 1949 the amendment was declared unconstitutional. See below, 127–128. The vote on the Boswell amendment once again brought forth the traditional sectional divisions within the state. See Illustration V and Table II in the Appendix.

Chapter 5

1. Birmingham *Tab*, January 19, 1947, BPL File.
2. Unidentified clipping [Montgomery *Advertiser?*] January 5, 1947, BPL File.
3. Birmingham *News*, January 19, 1947; Birmingham *Age-Herald*, January 22, 1947, BPL File. The following description of the inaugural celebration is based upon these sources.
4. *Speeches of Gov. James E. Folsom, 1947–1950* (Wetumpka, Ala., n.d.), 3.
5. *Ibid.*, 5.
6. *Ibid.*, 5–6.
7. *Ibid.*, 6.
8. *Ibid.*, 5–7.
9. *Ibid.*, 6.
10. *Ibid.*
11. *Ibid.*, 7.
12. Birmingham *Age-Herald*, January 21, 1947, BPL File.
13. Birmingham *News*, June 2, 1946.
14. *Ibid.*, May 25, 1946.
15. Dixon to Floyd W. Jefferson, June 11, 1946; Joe Poole to Dixon, November 27, 1946. Dixon Papers.
16. Poole to Dixon, November 27, 1946, Dixon Papers.
17. "Hallmarks," August 18, 1946, Sparks Scrapbook.
18. *Ibid.*, July 17, 1946, Sparks Scrapbook; Montgomery *Advertiser*, June 16, 1946.
19. Grover Hall, Jr., the astute Montgomery editor, overcame his initial skepticism and was convinced of Folsom's seriousness. See above, 49.
20. Birmingham *News*, November 3, December 15, 1946. Martin also moved to insure the support of the Farm Bureau for his candidacy. In November, 1946, he wrote to Walter L. Randolph, president of the Alabama Farm Bureau, promising favorable treatment of the Farm Bureau legislative program if he were elected. He made such a promise, he wrote, "without any understanding from you or the Farm Bureau for your support in my race for Speaker." W. L. Martin to Walter L. Randolph, November 13, 1946. Walter L. Randolph Papers, Alabama Department of Archives and History, Montgomery, Alabama (hereinafter cited as Randolph Papers.)
21. Birmingham *News*, November 3, December 15, 1946.
22. *Ibid.*, January 5, 1947; December 29, 1946. McGowin's tolerant and balanced conservatism did not sit well with those of more adamant stance. In 1942, Robin Swift had warned his friend Chauncey Sparks to beware of that "Judas with a *movie moustache* and an *Oxford accent.*" McGowin, a dapper man with a moustache, had been a Rhodes Scholar at Oxford. Swift to Sparks, April 17, 1942, Sparks Papers.
23. Birmingham *News*, January 22, 1947; December 15, 1946.
24. *Ibid.*, January 12, 1947.
25. *Ibid.*, January 14, 15, 1947.
26. Folsom's pledge to wage a "militant, unyielding battle against monopoly" and against "favoritism in government" did nothing to dispel conservative disquiet. Nor did his praise of Georgia's Ellis Arnall, or his pledge to lower the voting age to expand the electorate. *Ibid.*, February 22, January 26, February 16, 1947 and August 8, 1946; Grover Hall, Jr., "Hallmarks," August 2, 1946; John Temple Graves, Birmingham *Post*, August 29, 1946. Sparks

Scrapbook. Atlanta *Journal*, June 9, 1946, Montgomery *Advertiser*, August 25, 1946; Birmingham *Age-Herald*, January 23, 1947. BPL File.

27. In Alabama the governor and lieutenant governor are chosen entirely independently of each other, and clashes between the two are not uncommon. The lieutenant governor appoints the members of Senate committees and usually consults the governor as to his wishes.

28. Birmingham *News*, May 2, November 20, 30, January 26, 1947.

29. *Ibid.*, February 24, 1946; February 9, 1947.

30. Birmingham *News*, February 9, 1947. The Farm Bureau had opposed both Senator Hill and Senator Sparkman, and Folsom had their support in his efforts to remove the Extension Service from the control of the Farm Bureau.

31. *Ibid.*

32. *Ibid.*

33. *Ibid.*, November 23, 1941; February 9, March 3, 1947; Montgomery *Advertiser*, March 4, 1947, and Anniston *Star*, March 5, 1947, both in Folsom's *Legislative Scrapbook #1*.

34. Grover Hall, Jr., "Hallmarks," February 22, 1946, Sparks Scrapbook.

35. *Ibid.*; Leonard Dinnerstein, "The Senate's Rejection of Aubrey Williams as Rural Electric Administrator," *Alabama Review* Vol. XXI, No. 2 (April 1968), 133, 135, 138.

36. "Hallmarks," February 22, 1946, Sparks Scrapbook.

37. *Ibid.*

38. Sen. Lister Hill to Grover Hall, Jr., August 2, 1944. Hall Papers, Alabama Department of Archives and History, Montgomery, Alabama (hereinafter referred to as Hall Papers); Sparks to Beech, June 3, 1942, Sparks Papers; Birmingham *News*, March 5, 1947; Grover Hall, Jr., "Hallmarks," June 16, 1946, Sparks Scrapbook.

39. Birmingham *News*, February 9, 1947.

40. *Ibid.*, February 22, 1947.

41. *Ibid.* Farm cooperatives were of special interest to Beech. See Gov. Chauncey Sparks to Beech, June 3, 1942; Beech to Sparks, July 10, 1942. Sparks Papers.

42. Birmingham *News*, February 22, 1947.

43. See above, 50.

44. Birmingham *News*, February 23, 1947. See also, *ibid.*, February 2, 1947.

45. See above, 48.

46. Birmingham *News*, March 2, 1947.

47. *Ibid.* The action was unprecedented. It had evidently not occurred to the Bureau to challenge former Governor Sparks' interim appointees.

48. *Ibid.*

49. *Ibid.*, March 3, 1947.

50. *Ibid.*

51. *Ibid.*

52. *Ibid.*

53. *Ibid.*, March 4, 1947.

54. *Ibid.*

55. *Ibid.*

56. *Ibid.*

57. *Ibid.*, March 5, 1947.

58. Poole once commented to Grover Hall, Jr., that he did not "know much about this Beech. Isn't he sort of cockeyed in his politics?" "Yeah," a friend shot back, "he's cockeyed—he voted for the same man in the runoff that you

did." Poole roared with laughter. "Hallmarks," June 16, 1946, Sparks Scrapbook.

59. Birmingham *News,* March 6, 1947.

60. *Ibid.,* January 25, 1948; Hammond Interview, Arab, Alabama, May 17, 1968; Interview with Clifford and Virginia Durr, Montgomery, Alabama, July 8, 1968. For some indication of the impact of his ordeal upon Beech, see Aubrey W. Williams to Gould Beech, n. d. [1947?], Personal Files 1945–58, Box 35, "Civil Rights" folder; JPW [James P. Warburg] to Gould Beech, October 18, 1948, and Howard [Seitz] to Aubrey W. Williams, September 28, 1948, Personal Files 1945–58, Box 34, "Board of Directors" folder. Aubrey W. Williams Papers in the Franklin D. Roosevelt Library, Hyde Park, New York (hereinafter cited as Williams Papers).

61. Birmingham *News,* March 5, 1947.

62. *Ibid.*

63. *Ibid.,* March 18, 1947.

64. *Ibid.,* March 23, 1947.

65. *Ibid.,* July 13, August 3, October 5, 1947. Conservative forces were particularly eager to prevent passage of a forty million dollar road bond issue for fear that the administration could dominate the next session of the legislature by threatening to withhold road projects from the counties of recalcitrant legislators. Bruce Henderson, a conservative leader in the Senate, urged the president of the Alabama Farm Bureau to use the grassroots power of the Farm Bureau to pressure Senators on the Senate Committee on Finance and Taxation to kill the measure. "We have won a great many fights against the fantastic proposals of the administration," Henderson wrote, "but if we lose the last one and give them the 'Marbles,' they will turn about and lick us on everything on their entire program . . . . [T]he social, economic and political stability of the State is at stake." Henderson to Walter L. Randolph, September 1, 1947. Randolph Papers. See also Henderson to Randolph, September 6, 1947. *Ibid.* These two letters also provide insight into the use of parliamentary maneuver by conservative forces in the legislature to defeat Folsom's proposals. They also contain an account of the administration's moves to win support from individual legislators by promising what Henderson called "unbelievable rewards"—a bridge in one county, a road project in another, appointment to a probate judgeship in another.

66. Birmingham *News,* October 20, 30, 1947; Hammond Interview, Arab, Alabama, May 17, 1968.

67. Montgomery *Advertiser,* September 2, 1947, BPL File.

68. *Ibid.*

69. *Ibid.,* October 28, 1947, BPL File.

70. *Ibid.*

71. Birmingham *News,* November 2, 20, 1947.

72. *Ibid.,* March 16, 1947.

73. *Ibid.,* October 9, 1949.

74. *Ibid.,* July 27, August 10, September 7, 14, October 5, 1947.

75. Folsom's conception of executive supremacy, as well as his respect for Andrew Jackson, also colored his attitude toward civil service. He did not share the typical Progressive or reformer distaste for patronage. It was necessary, at least in part, he thought, if representative democracy were to function properly, if the executive were to implement his popular mandate. Civil service was fine for clerks and typists and for professional personnel hired by the state. But, as he had made plain during his campaign, civil service reform had gone too far and had intruded into policy-making positions. Thus an in-

coming administration, fresh from a popular mandate, might be thwarted in working the people's will by governmental employees immune from dismissal. Such an infringement upon the people's will as well as upon the governor's patronage was intolerable. Similarly, Folsom had little faith in non-partisan elections and even less in the supposedly apolitical commissions of experts that were the Progressives' delight. Politics was politics. It was the heart of democratic government, the way the people worked their will. Any attempt to "take politics out of politics" was not only futile but dangerous, for it removed those who made basic decisions of policy from direct responsibility to the voters. See, for example, Montgomery *Advertiser*, November 10, 1958, Folsom Scrapbook; Grover Hall, Jr., "Hallmarks," March 3, 1948, Sparks Scrapbook; Birmingham *News*, June 13, 1948.

76. Birmingham *News*, October 5, 1947.
77. *Ibid.*, November 1, 9, 1947.
78. *Ibid.*, November 2, 16, 20, December 28, 1947.
79. *Ibid.*, November 2, December 7, 14, 28, 1947.
80. *Ibid.*, January 4, 1948.
81. *Ibid.*
82. *Ibid.*
83. *Ibid.*, January 11, 1948. The vote on the self-starter again brought forth the traditional sectional cleavages within the state. See Illustration VI in the Appendix.

Chapter 6

1. Birmingham *News*, October 3, 1947.
2. *Ibid.*, October 5, 1947.
3. *Ibid.*, October 16, 1947.
4. Birmingham *Post*, August 27, 1946, BPL File.
5. Birmingham *News*, March 22, 28, April 25, 26, 1948. Marion Rushton, the conservative national committeeman from Alabama and a future Dixiecrat, also supported Truman. Gladys Burns, "The Alabama Dixiecrat Revolt of 1948" (Unpublished M.A. thesis, Auburn University, 1965), 44. (Hereinafter referred to as Burns, "Dixiecrat Revolt.")
6. See, for example, Dixon to A. G. Ewing, March 8, 1943; to Floyd Jefferson, March 29, 1943; To Lloyd Griscom, March 29, 1943; Sam M. Johnston to Dixon, September 6, 1944. Dixon Papers. Also, V. O. Key, *Southern Politics*, 329, 330, and J. B. Shannon, "Presidential Politics in the South," *Journal of Politics*, Vol. X (1948), 464–489. F.D.R. had tried to use the influence of Southern adherents of the New Deal to quell Southern dissidence. In 1943, Claude Pepper attended the Southern Governors' conference—uninvited—evidently as an emissary from F.D.R. to check the nature and extent of Southern dissatisfaction. Delores Ann Hobbs, "States' Rights Movement of 1948," (Unpublished M.A. thesis, Samford University, 1968), 7 (hereinafter referred to as Hobbs, "States' Rights Movement"). See Frank Dixon to Floyd Jefferson, March 29, 1943; to Lloyd C. Griscom, March 29, 1943, Dixon Papers, for a description of Pepper's appearance before the Conference.
7. Biographical Sketch of Frank Dixon, Dixon Papers (Departmental Reports—1942); McMillan, *Land Called Alabama*, 338–339, 376; Moore, *History of Alabama*, 799–801; for Dixon's speech, "Crossroads Democracy," see *Vital Speeches*, Vol. IX (February 1, 1943), 236–240; see also, Tindall, *Emergence of the New South*, 717, 724.
8. Dixon left no systematic statement of his general outlook, but his views

on politics and society can be pieced together from his correspondence. See
Dixon to A. G. Ewing, March 8, 1943; to Floyd Jefferson, March 29, 1943; to
Gov. Ellis G. Arnold [sic] of Georgia, August 16, 1943; to John Bankhead
[Jr.], March 8, 1944; to B. B. Gossett, August 2, 1944; to Gessner McCorvey,
October 12, 1944; to Sen. Walter F. George of Georgia, November 29, 1944;
to Frank Bane, April 9, 1945; to Gessner McCorvey, May 14, 1945; to Frank
R. Broadway, June 12, 1945; to Rep. Howard W. Smith of Virginia, June 12,
1945; to Rep. Carter Manasco of Alabama, January 14, 1946; to J. B. Ivey,
January 19, 1946; to Mrs. Mervyn Sterne, October 1, 1946; to Donald Comer,
August 13, 1948; to Editor, Richmond *Times-Dispatch,* August 14, 1948; to
Virginius Dabney, August 25, 1948; to Editor, Birmingham *News,* September
4, 1948; to John Temple Graves, July 8, 1948; to Charles J. Block, July 23,
1948; to Edward S. Hemphill, July 28, 1948; to Bruce W. Ball, August 3, 1948;
to Rep. Albert Rains of Alabama, January 19, 1949; to Stanley Rector, April
16, 1949; to Sen. John Sparkman of Alabama, June 21, 1949; to Grover Hall,
Jr., October 5, 1949; to "Chief Executive, State of Alabama—2050," July 25,
1950; to Paul Redmond, September 24, 1951; to Harry D. Linn, January 8,
1960. Dixon Papers.

9. These views are evident throughout the correspondence cited above,
ibid. One of Dixon's close friends and political associates expressed similar
sentiments in the late forties. W. C. Givhan, a power in state politics from the
rural Black Belt, thought in 1949 that "the trend in Alabama at the present
time is towards turning our government over to the masses, and in my opinion,
if we do not place restrictions and qualifications on a voter at this session of
the legislature, we will have seen our last election in Alabama where the people who carry the burden of taxation would have any voice in our State government. It is now time for the thinking people of Alabama to rally together
and get behind a movement that will protect the interest of the people who
have made Alabama great; and this is our last chance if we turn the ballot
box over to the uneducated masses in this State we can expect nothing but
chaos in the future [sic]." W. C. Givhan to Gessner McCorvey, February 24,
1949. Dixon Papers.

10. See above, 38, 47. Frank M. Dixon to Grover Hall, Jr., August 2, 1944,
Dixon Papers.

11. Dixon to Hall, November 11, 1944, Hall Papers.

12. McCorvey to Charles Wallace Collins, July 14, 1948; McCorvey to
Dixon, October 11, 1949. Dixon Papers. See also, the Preface to Thomas
Chalmers McCorvey, *Alabama Historical Sketches* (Charlottesville, Virginia,
1960), vii–ix.

13. Birmingham *News,* January 12, 1947.

14. Hammond Interview, Arab, Alabama, May 17, 1968.

15. See, for example, Birmingham *News,* April 25, November 21, 1948. For
background on the election of 1928 in Alabama, see Moore, *History of Alabama,* 777–780, 782, 785–786; Hugh D. Reagan, "Presidential Election of
1928 in Alabama" (Unpublished Ph.D. dissertation, University of Texas,
1961).

16. Birmingham *News,* April 4, 18, 25, 1948.

17. *Ibid.,* May 2, 1948; Burns, "Dixiecrat Revolt," 22; Hobbs, "States'
Rights Movement," 27, 38, 100.

18. Birmingham *News,* May 2, 1948; Mobile *Labor Journal,* July 13, 1948,
transcribed copy in legal brief prepared by Horace Wilkinson in Dixon Papers; Alsop quote in Hobbs, "States' Rights Movement," 65. Aubrey Williams,
the former New Dealer, viewed the Dixiecrats in a similar light. On a radio

program in late March, Williams charged that those opposed to Truman were the same men who had opposed F.D.R.—"the reactionary wing of the Democratic Party" in Alabama. The issues weren't new. They had been simmering under the surface for some time, but conservatives were unable to fight the liberal New Deal measures so long as F.D.R. lived. Montgomery *Advertiser,* March 26, 1948, quoted in Burns, "Dixiecrat Revolt," 102. See also the quote from the Hale County *News* in Key, *Southern Politics,* 329–330, fn. 13.

19. Birmingham *News,* April 25, 1948.

20. For an expression of Folsom's views on U. S. foreign policy in the years immediately following World War II, see Birmingham *Post,* July 9, 1946, and September 20, 1946; Birmingham *Age-Herald,* August 30, 1946; unidentified clipping containing a column by John Temple Graves [Birmingham *Post?*] September 3, 1946; Atlanta *Journal,* September 4, 1946; Montgomery *Advertiser,* October 30, 1947. BPL File. See also Birmingham *News,* February 8, April 4, 25, May 1, 1948. For Sparkman's views expressed during the 1948 campaign, see Birmingham *News,* April 25, 26, 1948. For an example of Hill's general orientation, see Birmingham *News,* March 7, 1948. See, also, Tindall, *Emergence of the New South,* 691–692, 729.

21. Birmingham *Age-Herald,* August 30, 1946; Atlanta *Journal,* September 4, 1946. BPL File.

22. Birmingham *News,* February 8, April 4, 25, 1948. In late April, Folsom accused "that crowd in Washington" of fomenting the cold war to ease their political troubles at home. The increasingly hard line taken toward the Soviet Union was a fundamental mistake. "If you'll just let old Stalin alone, the whole thing will crack on him under its own weight." *Ibid.,* May 1, 1948.

23. Folsom Interview, Cullman, Ala., July 1, 1968.

24. Birmingham *News,* March 21, 1948; see below, 106, 108.

25. Dixon to Earl L. Tucker, February 7, 1948, Dixon Papers; Birmingham *News,* March 28, April 4, 1948.

26. Birmingham *News,* March 28, April 4, 1948; Hobbs, "States' Rights Movement," 76.

27. Birmingham *News,* January 18, 1948.

28. *Ibid.,* February 1, 29, 1948.

29. In April, he remarked that he announced as a. favorite son candidate solely to aid his campaign for delegate-at-large. *Ibid.,* April 26, 1948.

30. *Ibid.,* February 1, 1948. The uses of the revived Red Scare, though less virulent in the South than elsewhere in the late forties and early fifties, were already apparent to some, and Connor advocated ʾoutlawing the Communist party and "putting the exterminator to them."

31. *Ibid.,* February 8, 1948.

32. Quoted in *ibid.*

33. *Ibid.,* February 22, April 11, 25, 1948; Dixon to Grover Hall, Jr., February 13, 1948, Dixon Papers. Dixon explained to Hall that "the Folsom group" hoped that "the Birmingham group" disliked the liberal Sparkman enough to support "our Jasper friend," Newton, thus defeating Sparkman while removing Newton "as a possibility in the next governor's race."

34. Birmingham *News,* April 25, 1948.

35. *Ibid.,* April 4, 25, 1948.

36. *Ibid.,* January 11, 18, 25, February 1, 1948.

37. See Birmingham *News,* March 3, 1948, BPL File, for the text of Mrs. Johnston's suit.

38. Reprinted in Montgomery *Advertiser,* March 9, 1948, BPL File.

39. *Ibid.;* Birmingham *News,* March 4, 1948.

40. Birmingham *News*, March 5, 7, May 8, 12, June 17, July 1, 1948. For a flamboyant but essentially accurate account of the paternity suit scandal see William Bradford Huie, "Draughts of Old Bourbon: Pregnancy and Politics in Alabama." *American Mercury*, Vol. 72 (June 1951), 748–766.

41. Folsom has never acknowledged that he was the father of Mrs. Johnston's child. After an unsuccessful courtship of Virginia Warren, daughter of Earl Warren, then governor of California, and the Johnston scandal, Folsom eloped with a young secretary who worked for the state, Jamelle Moore. (For a general comment on the sexuality of political figures, see T. Harry Williams, *Huey Long*, 318.)

42. Birmingham *News*, March 7, 1948.

43. *Ibid.*, March 7, 28, April 26, May 1, 1948. Folsom felt that someone other than Eisenhower, some "good Jacksonian Democrat," ought to be the Democratic nominee.

44. *Ibid.*, March 20, 28, April 25, June 26, July 4, 1948.

45. *Ibid.*, March 14, 1948.

46. Just as F.D.R. had sought to use Claude Pepper in the early forties to help quiet the dissidence among Southerners, so Democratic Party Chairman Howard McGrath evidently hoped to use Senator Hill in Alabama, Pepper in Florida, and Earl Long in Louisiana to quell the budding Southern revolt in 1948. *Ibid.*, March 7, 1948; Frank Dixon to Floyd Jefferson, March 29, 1943, and to Lloyd C. Griscom, March 29, 1943, Dixon Papers.

47. Birmingham *News*, April 11, 1948.

48. *Ibid.*, April 11, 18, 1948.

49. *Ibid.*, April 11, 25, May 1, 1948.

50. Since all ten of the candidates in the run-off for the five remaining positions as elector were States' Righters, an agreement was reached that the bottom five would withdraw and the top five would therefore be declared elected. *Ibid.*, May 16, 1948. See page 154 in the Appendix for a discussion of the difficulties in analyzing the 1948 returns in the contests for elector.

51. Figured from data provided by Burns, "Dixiecrat Revolt," 141, 153, 157. There was, evidently, some uncertainty among the States' Rights forces over the firmness of some of their delegates. See, for example, Dixon to Marion Rushton, June 22, 1948, Dixon Papers.

52. See below, 120–121, for an explanation of the Loyalists' failure to field their strongest slate in the race for elector.

53. Birmingham *News*, May 9, 1948.

54. Burns, "Dixiecrat Revolt," 142, 152–157; Dixon to Marion Rushton, June 22, 1948; Dixon to Gov. Ben Laney, June 24, 1948. Dixon Papers.

55. Burns, "Dixiecrat Revolt," 152–157; Birmingham *News*, July 11, 1948.

56. Burns, "Dixiecrat Revolt," 159–160.

57. *Ibid.*, 162; Hobbs, "States' Rights Movement," 31–32.

58. Burns, "Dixiecrat Revolt," 163; Hobbs, "States' Rights Movement," 32.

59. Burns, "Dixiecrat Revolt," 163; Hobbs, "States' Rights Movement," 32; Birmingham *News*, July 11, 1948.

60. Birmingham *News*, December 7, 1947.

61. There is no adequate history of the city of Birmingham. Other studies must suffice. See Martha Carolyn Mitchell, "Birmingham: Biography of a City of the New South" (Unpublished Ph.D. dissertation, University of Chicago, 1943); Ethel Armes, *The Story of Coal and Iron in Alabama* (Birmingham, 1910).

62. Hobbs, "States' Rights Movement," 38–39; Birmingham *News*, July 18, 1948.

63. Unless otherwise specified, this account of the proceedings in Birmingham is based on Hobbs, "States' Rights Movement," 37–60.

64. *Ibid.*, 168–169.

65. Mobile *Press-Register,* July 18, 1948.

66. *Ibid.*

67. There were others who were disturbed at the tenor of the morning session. Due to the "inflammatory" nature of the convention, the American Broadcasting Company ceased its coverage. The editor of the Montgomery *Advertiser* regretted the lack of "intelligent leadership" displayed at the Birmingham convention. The leaders of the States' Rights revolt could have made it clear to the nation that they would champion the Negro's cause as well as states' rights. Instead the meeting was contaminated with crude "nigger stories" that were "wild" and "lewd." "Hoarse blasphemies" and "unreasoning obstinacy," the editor warned, do not win national elections. Quoted in Birmingham *News,* July 22, 1948.

68. Dixon to Edward S. Hemphill, July 28, 1948, Dixon Papers. See also, Dixon to Charles J. Block, July 23, 1948, and to John Temple Graves, July 8, 1948, Dixon Papers.

69. It must be remembered that to a lawyer the police power of a state is broad and encompassing, not so narrow as the name might suggest.

70. Dixon to Editor, Richmond *Times-Dispatch,* August 14, 1948, Dixon Papers. See also Virginius Dabney to Dixon, August 23, 1948; Dixon to Dabney, August 25, 1948; John Temple Graves to Dixon, August 30, 1948. Dixon Papers.

71. Dixon to Editor, Birmingham *News,* September 4, 1948, Dixon Papers. See also, Dixon to Virginius Dabney, August 14, 1948; to Bruce W. Ball, August 3, 1948; to Robert R. Wason, August 3, 1948. Dixon Papers.

72. Dixon to Editor, Richmond *Times-Dispatch,* August 14, 1948; Dixon to Donald Comer, August 13, 1948. Dixon Papers. See also, Dixon to Edward S. Hemphill, July 28, 1948, Dixon Papers.

73. See, for example, Dixon to Judge E. E. Townes, May 19, 1948; to Rep. Laurie C. Battle, July 6, 1948; to Charles J. Block, July 23, 1948; to Gardner F. Goodwyn, Jr., July 30, 1948. Dixon Papers.

74. Dixon to Charles J. Block, July 23, 1948, Dixon Papers.

75. William H. Ivey to Dixon, July 24, 1948, Dixon Papers.

76. Dixon to Editor, Richmond *Times-Dispatch,* August 14, 1948, Dixon Papers.

77. Dixon to Judge Gardner F. Goodwyn, Jr., July 23, 1948, Dixon Papers.

78. McCorvey to Dixon, August 21, 1948, Dixon Papers.

79. *Ibid.*

80. Dixon to Thomas W. McGough, August 25, 1948, Dixon Papers. In November of 1946, despite the success of the Boswell amendment, Dixon had written to a friend that ". . . of course the fight is not over—the same group that wanted mass enfranchisement of the negro still want it! It will be necessary for us to be on the alert from this time on." Dixon to Samuel Fischer, November 13, 1946, Dixon Papers.

81. Birmingham *News,* September 26, 1948.

82. Burns, "Dixiecrat Revolt," 77.

83. *Ibid.*, 77, 79.

84. Hobbs, "States' Rights Movement," 76; Birmingham *News,* May 4, November 21, 1948.

85. Birmingham *News,* July 24, August 15, 1948. McCorvey to Albert Stapp, July 21, 1948; McCorvey to Editor, Roanoke *Leader,* July 23, 1948; McCorvey to Joseph N. Langan, August 13, 1948. Dixon Papers. To run in the Democratic primary, candidates were required to sign an affidavit pledging themselves to support the nominee of the party in the general election. A similar pledge was printed on the ballot, thus in theory also binding those who voted in the primary. The issue dividing Loyalist and States' Righter was once again entangled in the federal nature of our political system. Did that pledge of support extend only to the nominees chosen in that primary, that is, to the nominees of the Alabama Democratic Party, an organ separate from the national party? Or did it bind one to support the nominees of the Democratic party at all levels, local, state, and federal? What is the proper and legal relationship between state and national parties?

McCorvey's threat to bar the Loyalists from the 1950 primary was no idle indulgence, particularly to Senator Hill. Once before an incumbent Senator had been so barred: Tom Hefflin in 1930 for his support of Hoover against Al Smith in 1928. When the Loyalists regained control of the state committee in 1950 and rewrote the pledge specifically to include the national nominees as well as those at the state and local level, the States' Righters objected strenuously. Their protests rang somewhat hollow, however, for McCorvey had been willing to use the ambiguous wording of the pledge in effect in 1948 to threaten the Loyalists and thus force them in line.

86. See below, 123–124, for a discussion of some of the factors that influenced Hill and other Loyalist leaders in making this decision.

87. Birmingham *News,* July 24, August 15, 16, 1948; Gessner McCorvey to Albert Stapp, July 21, 1948, and to Joseph N. Langan, August 13 and August 16, 1948, Dixon Papers.

88. Birmingham *News,* August 16, 1948.

89. *Ibid.,* August 29, 1948. Langan pointed out that the Supreme Court decision in May in which the 1945 act requiring electors to vote for the nominees of their party was declared unconstitutional was an advisory opinion and was not legally binding.

90. *Ibid.* October 10, 17, 24, 1948. The eleven nominees for elector issued a statement that "neither the governor nor the courts are going to force us to vote for Truman," and one of them commented that he would "spend the rest of my life in jail" rather than obey a court order to vote for Truman. Folsom roundly criticized such statements. Folsom deviated from the usual Populist stance in his attitude toward the courts throughout his career. "That's where I draw the line. When a person says he won't abide by a decision of the Supreme Court of the land, that's where my patience ends," he said in 1948, and this was his attitude consistently throughout the 1950's and '60's, even at the height of racial turmoil and at great political cost.

91. Birmingham *News,* October 31, November 7, 1948.

92. *Ibid.,* August 22, 1948. Frank M. Dixon to W. D. Malone, October 1, 1948; Gessner T. McCorvey to Joseph N. Langan, August 16, 1948; McCorvey to C. M. Stanley, September 30, 1948. Dixon Papers. The eagerness with which the States' Righters ostensibly welcomed an independent Truman slate was made possible by their knowledge that, in the absence of a special session of the legislature, there was no legal way for an independent slate to secure ballot position at that late date. See, for example, Frank M. Dixon to Sibyl Pool (Secretary of State), August 3, 1948; Horace C. Wilkinson to Sibyl Pool, August 25, 1948; Dixon to R. R. Wallace, August 3, 1948. Dixon Papers.

93. Birmingham *News*, November 21, 1948.

94. *Ibid.*, September 5, 1948.

95. Montgomery *Advertiser*, October 15, 1948, quoted in Smith, "Loyalists and States' Righters," 10.

96. Birmingham *News*, November 7, 14, 21, 1948.

Chapter 7

1. Key, *Southern Politics*, 127–128; Samuel Lubell, *The Future of American Politics*, second revised edition (New York, 1956), 106–115.

2. Wilkinson to McCorvey, October 29, 1948, Dixon Papers.

3. *Davis v. Schnell*, 81 F. Sup., 872 (1949).

4. Birmingham *News*, January 9, 1949.

5. W. C. Givhan to Gessner McCorvey, January 29, 1949, Dixon Papers.

6. W. C. Givhan to McCorvey, February 24, 1949; see also, Givhan to Sid Smyer, August 4, 1948. Dixon Papers.

7. Birmingham *News*, March 28, 1949; *Davis v. Schnell*, 69 S. Ct. 749 (1949).

8. Birmingham *News*, March 28, 1949.

9. McCorvey to Dixon, January 12, 1949, Dixon Papers. See also, W. R. (Red) Withers to McCorvey, January 5, 1949, Dixon Papers.

10. Wilkinson to McCorvey, October 29, 1948, and January 31, 1949, Dixon Papers.

11. McCorvey to Dixon, January 28, 1949; Dixon to McCorvey, January 27, 1949; Wilkinson to McCorvey, January 31, 1949. Dixon Papers.

12. Wilkinson to McCorvey, January 31, 1949, Dixon Papers.

13. *Ibid.*

14. McCorvey to Dixon, January 28, 1949, Dixon Papers.

15. McCorvey to Dixon, December 14, 1948; Dixon to McCorvey, October 17, 1949. Dixon Papers.

16. See, for example, Dixon to Preston C. Clayton, January 19, 1949, Dixon Papers; see also, Birmingham *News*, January 9, 1949.

17. Birmingham *News*, February 27, March 6, 1949.

18. *Ibid.*, March 27, 1949.

19. *Ibid.*, January 2, March 27, April 10, 17, 1949.

20. *Ibid.*, March 27, 1949. The mention of a proposed "little TVA" created a measure of concern among those who had opposed the New Deal and the TVA, particularly those associated with the large utility interests. See, Memorandum from William Logan Martin to Dixon, January 6, 1949, and Martin to Dixon, January 7, 1949. Dixon Papers. Folsom had also proposed another boost in ad valorem tax assessments on utilities. Birmingham *News*, February 6, 1949.

21. Birmingham *News*, April 10, 1949.

22. *Ibid.*, November 21, 1948; April 24, May 15, April 17, 1949.

23. See W. D. Malone to Chauncey Sparks, June 23, 1936; Sparks to Jeff Beeland June 20, 1936; Sparks to A. B. Aldridge, June 25, 1936, all in Sparks Papers, for a discussion of the role of the "economy bloc" in the Graves administration.

24. Birmingham *News*, April 24, May 8, June 12, 1949. Some of these measures were genuinely needed reforms. Some were designed to prohibit abuses of executive power. Others were merely evidence of spite and displeasure with the incumbent governor. The sincerity of the "economy bloc's" interest in economy in government was questioned when several of its mem-

bers introduced a pork-barrel bridge-building bill which would have benefited their counties. *Ibid.*, June 19, 1949.

25. *Ibid.*, May 22, July 22, September 11, 1949. Anti-administration forces had votes enough to end the filibuster by changing the rules of the Senate. But they had used the tactic of delay in the past and might need to again and so were reluctant to make any rules changes. *Ibid.*, June 12, 1949.

26. *Ibid.*, May 8, 29, August 14, 1949.

27. *Ibid.*, May 8, 22, 29, June 5, 12, July 31, 1949. The final version of re-apportionment supported by the administration would have given each county one senator and based the House solely on population. While this measure would have decreased the power of the over-represented Black Belt in the Senate, it also would have decreased the relative strength of the major urban areas. For urban voters it was scarcely an improvement in the Senate. But the House would have been based on population, thus enhancing the strength of north Alabama, both rural and urban. Folsom's legislative supporters argued that this was a "foot-in-the-door" approach and would at least give the under-represented areas of the state a veto in the House. Full reapportionment in both House and Senate could be accomplished later. Opponents of the measure and of the administration pointed out its half-way character and argued that this was evidence of the administration efforts to drive a wedge between legis-lators in the economy bloc.

28. *Ibid.*, July 17, September 11, 1949.

29. An upsurge in Klan or Klan-like violence directed at Negroes, at "dis-reputable" whites, and attendent upon clashes between rival unions in the mineral district had created a public outcry. The Governor seized the initiative, forcefully backed an unmasking law with a "ringing message" to the legisla-ture, directed the Attorney General of Alabama to move against the hooded orders in the courts, and asked that their charters be revoked. *Ibid.*, June 19, 26, July 3, 17, 1949.

30. *Ibid.*, September 11, 25, 1949.

31. *Ibid.*; Folsom interview, Cullman, Alabama, July 30, 1968.

32. Birmingham *News*, April 24, 1949.

33. *Ibid.*, April 24, June 5, 1949.

34. See, for example, *ibid.*, June 12, July 3, 1949.

35. *Ibid.*, June 5, 1949.

36. *Democracy in America*, Vol. I, Chapter X.

37. Folsom Interview, Cullman, Alabama, July 30, 1968.

38. Birmingham *News*, November 19, 1949.

39. *Ibid.*, November 20, 1949; January 15, 22, 29, 1950.

40. *Ibid.*, December 18, 1949; *Speeches of James E. Folsom 1947–1950* (Wetumpka, Alabama, n.d.), 183–184. For further expressions of Folsom's concern for the inequities faced by black Alabamians, see *ibid.*, 130–132, 176–177. For the views of a member of the Folsom administration and close friend of the Governor, see the comments of Broughton Lamberth in the Birming-ham *News*, January 15, 1950.

41. See above, 130.

42. Folsom to McGrath, December 9, 1948, Folsom Executive Papers, State Department of Archives and History, Montgomery, Alabama (herein-after, Folsom Executive Papers).

43. Paul Maxwell Smith, Jr., "Loyalists and States' Righters in the Demo-cratic Party of Alabama 1949–1954" (Unpublished M.A. thesis, Auburn Uni-versity, 1966), 19.

44. Birmingham *News*, March 13, 1949. Charles W. Collins, a native of the

state, author of *Whither the Solid South?*, and an earnest States' Righter, equally disparaged Barkley's visit. Collins wanted a true Southern leader to "unmask the Vice-President," who was no friend of the South and who was trying to kill the States' Rights movement by masquerading as a Southern Democrat. Collins cited Barkley's stand on the poll tax, on federal anti-lynching legislation, and the F.E.P.C. to prove Barkley's anti-Southern animus. Yet, in the face of all this, Barkley "has the unmitigated gall to come into this State to make a brazen attempt at wedding the wooden handle to the silver spoon. He wants to overrule the decision the people of Alabama made at the polls last year. This goes to show what a low opinion he has of the character and integrity of the people of the South." Collins to Frank M. Dixon, April 6, 1949, Dixon Papers.

45. Birmingham *News*, April 3, March 6, 13, April 10, 1949; Smith, "Loyalists and States' Righters," 19–21.

46. Smith, "Loyalists and States' Righters," 22–24. Some Dixiecrats sought to embarrass the Loyalists by asking whether segregation would be maintained at the Birmingham dinner. The probate judge of Cullman County, a Loyalist, replied, "Yes, we'll have segregation. We're going to segregate the Democrats from the Dixiecrats." Birmingham *News*, April 3, 1949.

47. Dixon to E. H. Ramsey, November 6, 1948; to Gov. Fielding Wright (Mississippi), November 6, 1948; to Palmer Bradley, November 8, 1948. Dixon Papers.

48. Dixon to Charles W. Collins, November 19, 1948; to John C. Sheffield, December 29, 1948; to Wallace W. Wright, August 27, 1949. Dixon Papers.

49. See, for example, Wallace [D. Malone] to Dixon, September 18, 1949; Dixon to J. C. Weldon, April 29, 1950; Earl McGowin to Dixon, August 10, 1948; Dixon to Robert Albritton, May 25, 1950; to George Dixon, August 4, 1950; to Roy F. Parker, March 9, 1951. Dixon Papers.

50. Birmingham *News*, October 24, 1948; September 4, 1949; January 29, 1950. But see also the comments by Frank Dixon in the *News*, April 3, 1949. See also Dixon to Walter C. Givhan, January 9, 1950, Dixon Papers.

51. Smith, "Loyalists and States' Righters," 29; Wilkinson to Abernethy, March 14, 1950, Dixon Papers.

52. Montgomery *Advertiser*, October 15, 1948, quoted in Smith, "Loyalists and States' Righters," 10.

53. Hall to Dixon, September 30, 1949; Glenn Saunders to Dixon, October 19, 1949. Dixon Papers.

54. Smith, "Loyalists and States' Righters," 30.

55. *Ibid.*, 30, 32.

56. Quoted in *ibid.*, 33.

57. Quoted in *ibid.*, 38–39.

58. *Ibid.*, 41–44.

59. *Ibid.*, 45.

60. *Ibid.*, 50–52, 54. See page 157 and Illustration VII in the Appendix for an analysis of the 1950 returns.

61. *Ibid.*, 52, 58.

62. *Ibid.*, 62, 115.

63. See, for example, Charles Grayson Summersell, *Alabama History for Schools* (Birmingham, 1957), 347.

64. Smith, "Loyalists and States' Righters," 77, 85, 99–102, 110–112.

65. For a summary of Abernethy's political career, see Birmingham *News*, July 1, 1956. For comments on McCorvey's course, see Frank M. Dixon to E. H. Ramsey, December 9, 1954, Dixon Papers. For the intermittant hopes for

a conservative national party, see Albert W. Hawkes to Frank Dixon, September 29, 1951; J. Harvie Williamson to Dixon, September 26, 1951, and October 10, 1962. Dixon Papers. See also Sen. Karl E. Mundt to Dixon, December 3, 1956, Dixon Papers, and John Temple Graves' remarks in the Birmingham *News*, March 19, 1950. For Dixon's developing attitudes see Dixon to Thomas E. Coleman, September 10, 1952; to Palmer Bradley, May 24, 1957; to W. D. Malone, March 18, 1963; to E. H. Ramsey, August 19, 1963. Dixon Papers.

66. In October, 1949, Dixon wrote Grover Hall, Jr., that "I sincerely regard the future with distrust—primarily, I think, because I do not see how the political leader can prosper who does not appeal to those impulses in mankind that mean the death of initiative and originality, the spark of genius and the courage to depart from the level of the herd. I haven't much confidence that the mass will permit these deviations necessary for progress." Dixon to Hall, Jr., October 5, 1949. See also, Dixon to "Chief Executive, State of Alabama—2050," July 25, 1950. Dixon Papers.

67. Quoted in Smith, "Loyalists and States' Righters," 114–115.

68. Pardon and parole scandals were scarcely new in Alabama. They seemed to be a recurrent feature of administrations of all persuasions, appearing quadrennially as an administration prepared to depart. Many of the charges leveled by Folsom's critics proved unfounded. Still, there was enough evidence of wrong-doing to represent an indictment of the Governor's blindness or indifference to the character of some of those around him. (See Birmingham *News*, December 4, 1949, quoting the Atlanta *Journal* on the recurrent nature of parole scandals in Georgia and in Alabama.)

Folsom had long evinced an interest in Alabama's penal system. He was convinced that the state's judicial system dealt unequally with the poor and the black and that the fee system that prevailed in many areas (whereby an arresting officer or court was compensated only if a defendant were found guilty) had inflated Alabama's prison population. After he was out of office, in the midst of legislative and grand jury probes into the scandal, Folsom charged that Alabama jails were "filled with little whites and Negroes who should not be there." He was persuaded that "when you oppress the Negro you oppress the little white without influence," and recommended several steps to improve Alabama's penal system, the first of which was to "abolish oppression of the Negro race." Birmingham *News*, March 19, 1951.

Folsom's concern was genuine. Whether there were those who took advantage of that concern for their own private enrichment by securing pardons and paroles, or whether, given that genuine concern, Folsom found it easy to rationalize the loose practices of his Pardon and Parole Board—especially since this was a convenient and tempting way to repay political debts—is beyond determination. Even assuming the best about Folsom, however, his toleration of abuses in the pardon system did a grave disservice to those truly concerned about the inequities of Alabama's penal and judicial systems.

69. Birmingham *News*, May 7, 14, 1950; Birmingham *Post*, April 14, 1950, BPL File.

70. Montgomery *Advertiser*, October 24, 1954; Gadsden *Times*, January 18, 1955; Birmingham *News*, June 11, August 29, 1954. BPL File.

71. Montgomery *Advertiser*, May 12, 1954; Birmingham *Post-Herald*, September 8, 1953; Birmingham *News*, November 3, 4, 1954. BPL File. Birmingham *News*, September 26, 1954.

72. Birmingham *News*, May 5, 16, August 29, 1954; Montgomery *Advertiser*, May 9, 12, 1954. BPL File.

73. Anthony Lewis and the New York *Times, Portrait of a Decade: The Second American Revolution* (New York, 1965), 29–39.

74. Birmingham *News*, July 10, August 7, 1955; February 1, 2, 1956.

75. *Ibid.*, August 14, 1955. Birmingham *Post-Herald*, March 30, 1956; Montgomery *Advertiser*, May 11, 1956. BPL File. Powell had been scheduled to speak at Alabama State College for Negroes in Montgomery. He was met at the airport by the governor's limousine and taken to the mansion where he conferred with Folsom. He boasted of the meeting during his speech that evening, setting off a furor that brought down on Folsom a fury of segregationist sentiment. The dispute took on comic proportions. It was charged that Folsom had offered Powell a drink. Folsom's staff replied that Powell had asked Folsom's chauffeur for a drink as he was leaving and was served in the back kitchen. There was some dispute whether Powell entered the front door of the mansion as a guest or the back business door. The finer subtleties of Southern racial etiquette, for a time, became a matter of public debate in Alabama. Folsom sought to quiet the segregationist outcry by playing upon the humor inherent in the situation. To newsmen, he recounted the charge that he had entertained Powell in the mansion den over a glass of Scotch. He denied it. Those who followed him closely, the Governor said, knew the story was false. Why, he was a Bourbon man and never touched Scotch. Ultimately, Folsom maintained that he had not entertained Powell or any Negro socially—but in typical Folsom fashion he added that he reserved the right to do so should he choose. Birmingham *Post-Herald*, March 30, 1956; Montgomery *Advertiser*, May 11, 1956. BPL File.

76. Birmingham *Post-Herald*, March 30, 1956, BPL File; interview with Paul M. Gaston, Professor of History at the University of Virginia, Mobile, Alabama, April 19, 1971.

77. Birmingham *News*, April 10, May 1, July 17, 1955; February 4, 1956.

78. *Ibid.*, February 4–7, 1956.

79. *Ibid.*, February 4, 5, 1956.

80. *Ibid.*, November 11, 1956.

81. *Ibid.*, February 5, 1956; Montgomery *Advertiser*, July 22, 1956, BPL File; Limestone *Democrat*, August 22, 1961, BPL File; Montgomery *Advertiser*, May 8, 1958, BPL File; Birmingham *Post-Herald*, May 5, 1962, April 14, 1966, BPL File.

82. Birmingham *News*, March 27, 1970; Mobile *Register*, April 22, 1970.

83. The phrase is that of Clifford Durr, native Alabamian, Rhodes Scholar, and appointee of Franklin Roosevelt to the Federal Communication Commission in 1941. Durr Interview, Montgomery, Alabama, July 8, 1968. Birmingham *News*, October 14, 1941; September 1, 1946.

84. Deutschman, "Outsize Governor," 66.

85. Birmingham *Post-Herald*, May 5, 1962, BPL File.

86. Tindall, *The Emergence of the New South, 1913–1945*, 731.

BIBLIOGRAPHICAL ESSAY

The richest sources for this manuscript have been the collections of papers which have been deposited in recent years in the Alabama Department of Archives and History (hereinafter, ADAH) in Montgomery, Alabama. Especially valuable were the papers of Frank M. Dixon, governor of Alabama (1939–1943) and a leader of the Dixiecrats. Dixon's papers are as fine a representation of the mind and thought of a conservative political leader in the Deep South of the 1940's as are likely to become available. Useful also were the papers of Chauncey Sparks, governor of the state from 1943 to 1947. Sparks' Scrapbooks are a valuable part of this collection. They provide convenient access to a large collection of the newspaper columns of two talented journalists and political commentators, Grover Hall, Jr., whose "Hallmarks" appeared in the *Alabama Journal* and the Montgomery *Advertiser,* and John Temple Graves, whose column, "This Morning," appeared in the Birmingham *Post.*

Of lesser value are both the official Folsom Executive Papers and the personal papers of Governor Folsom in the ADAH. The papers of Walter L. Randolph, a long-time leader in the Alabama and American Farm Bureau, of Marion Rushton, a conservative Democratic leader who was the state's Democratic National Committeeman throughout much of the 1940's, and of Grover Hall, Jr. (a very small collection), also contained items of interest.

The papers of Ralph Hammond, press secretary and later, in the second administration, executive secretary to Governor Folsom, were useful for the insight they provided into Folsom as a man and as governor, but they were of limited value for this study since they concern Folsom's second administration (1955–1959) almost exclusively. These papers remain in the possession of Mr. Hammond, who was kind enough to permit me to use them.

Also of limited value for this study but fascinating for the glimpse they provide of a nationally known racial liberal who returned to Alabama after World War II and lived there until the late 1950's are the papers of Aubrey W. Williams in the Franklin D. Roosevelt Library in Hyde Park, N.Y. The files of the Democratic Party's National Committee (1928–1948), also in the Roosevelt Library, contain a few items of interest.

Although this work is not based to any great extent upon oral history, a number of interviews proved most helpful. James E. Folsom was kind enough to spend a considerable number of days in the summer of 1968 talking with me in Cullman, Alabama. So too did Ralph and Myra Hammond of Arab, both strong and long-time supporters of Folsom. Clifford and Virginia Durr, both natives of the state who were active in national Democratic politics of the 1930's and '40's, and who were among the foremost advocates of racial progress in the period, shared with me their reminiscences and assessments of the major figures in the book (July 8, 1968, Montgomery, Alabama). Two of Folsom's friends and campaign workers were interviewed in Cullman: John Stiefelmeyer (July 1, 1968) and Roland Johnson (July 30, 1968). Arthur Shores, a Negro lawyer long active in Democratic politics nationally and locally, related his assessment of Folsom and of the events of the 1940's in an interview in Birmingham, May 3, 1968. Federal Circuit Judge Richard Rives, a political leader in the 1940's, read the manuscript and shared his views of the personalities and events of the period in an interview in Montgomery, September 13, 1973.

For an historian of the recent past, the laborious and eyestraining process of turning slowly through the backfiles of newspapers is essential. Often the time consumed is disproportionate to the amount and quality of information gained. Nonetheless, it is a necessary task. The Birmingham *News,* available on microfilm in the Birmingham Public Library, gave relatively full coverage to political deveolpments in the state in the 1940's. The complete run from September 23, 1945, through December 31, 1950, was reviewed, in addition to the files from September 1, 1942, to May 5, 1943. The clipping files available in the Southern Collection of the Birmingham Public Library were useful in supplementing the coverage of the Birmingham *News* with that of newspapers throughout the state. Similar collections of newspaper clippings which were useful were the scrapbooks of Chauncey Sparks, cited above, and those of James E. Folsom, now in ADAH but in the possession of Mr. Folsom when used. The Elba *Clipper* and the Montgomery *Advertiser,* both available in the ADAH, were useful in the treatment of Folsom's races for the U. S. Congress in 1936 and 1938. The backfiles of a major Negro newspaper in the state, the Birmingham *World,* are available for the years 1948 and 1949 on microfilm in the Southern Collection of the Birmingham Public Library. *Alabama: The Newsmagazine of the Deep South,* reflecting the views of the conservative business and industrial interests of the state, is a valuable source for the period.

A number of works on the history of Alabama have been useful. A. B. Moore's *History of Alabama* (Tuscaloosa, 1934) remains the standard general history although it is badly dated. No recent, comprehensive, adult history of the state is available. Nonetheless, although intended as a high school text, Malcolm C. McMillan's *The Land Called Alabama* (Austin, Texas, 1968) is excellent. Another text, Charles Grayson Summersell's *Alabama History for Schools* (Birmingham, 1957) remains useful although its treatment of the period since 1900 is briefer than that of McMillan.

For the inquiring reader, a small group of monographs must serve as the fullest adequate introduction to the history of the state. Malcolm C. Mc-Millan, *Constitutional Development in Alabama, 1798–1901: A Study in Politics, the Negro, and Sectionalism* (Chapel Hill, 1955) is impressive in its detail and documentation. Thomas Perkins Abernethy, *The Formative Period in Alabama, 1815–1828* (University, Alabama, 1965, new edition); Theodore H. Jack, *Sectionalism in Party Politics in Alabama 1819–1842* (Menasha, Wis.,

1919); and Lewy Dorman, *Party Politics in Alabama from 1850 through 1860* (Wetumpka, Ala., 1935) are standard works on the pre-Civil War history of the state, all of which treat the development of persisting sectional patterns in the state's politics. Walter Lynwood Fleming's *Civil War and Reconstruction in Alabama* (New York, 1905) is a massive history of this period by one of the Dunning school. It has yet to be replaced by a more modern treatment, although a series of articles by Sarah Van V. Woolfolk in the Alabama Review, Vol. 15, 133–44 (1962); Vol. 17, 45–55 (1964); and Vol. 19, 41–52 (1966) and one in the *Alabama Historical Quarterly,* Vol. 26, 240–48 (1964) and the pioneering article by Horace Mann Bond, "Social and Economic Forces in Alabama Reconstruction," *Journal of Negro History,* Vol. 23, 290–348 (1928), offer revisionist perspectives. Allen J. Going, *Bourbon Democracy in Alabama 1874–1890* (University, Ala., 1951) takes the story up to the period of the Populist revolt.

John B. Clark, *Populism in Alabama* (Auburn, Ala., 1927) is the standard work on political developments in the 1890's. The story of agrarian discontent has been told much more fully in a recent work, William Warren Rogers, *One-Galloused Rebellion: Agrarianism in Alabama 1865–1896* (Baton Rouge, 1970). A more interpretive treatment and one that seeks to establish the degree of continuity between the Populist and Progressive movement in the state is that of Sheldon Hackney, *Populism to Progressivism in Alabama* (Princeton, 1969). Central to an understanding of this period is, of course, C. Vann Woodward, *Origins of the New South 1877–1913,* Vol. IX of Wendell Holmes Stephenson and E. Merton Coulter, eds., *A History of the South,* ([Baton Rouge], 1951).

Few published works of note have appeared on the history of the state since 1900. Perhaps the best introduction to this period are two books that treat the history and politics of the South as a whole: V. O. Key, Jr., *Southern Politics in State and Nation* (New York, 1949), and George B. Tindall, *The Emergence of the New South 1913–1945,* Vol. X in Wendell Holmes Stephenson and E. Merton Coulter, *A History of the South* ([Baton Rouge], 1967). Virginia Van der Veer Hamilton's *Hugo Black: The Alabama Years* (Baton Rouge, 1972) is an excellent introduction to the politics of Alabama in the 1920's and '30's as well as to an extraordinary man.

There has been relatively little published on the history of Alabama or of the South in the specific period under scrutiny in this work. Perhaps because Key's *Southern Politics* (1949) was so satisfactory a summing up and because the 1954 *Brown* decision seemed to inaugurate a new era, the period from the end of World War II through the early 'fifties has been relatively neglected. Even the literature on the Dixiecrat revolt is sparse and disappointing. Emile B. Adler, *The Dixiecrat Movement: Its Role in Third Party Politics* (Washington, 1955), is brief and lacking in depth. Samuel Lubell, *The Future of American Politics* (New York, 1956, second revised edition) contains an excellent analysis of the 1948 election but does not focus specifically upon the Southern revolt. Taylor Cole and J. H. Hallowell, eds., *The Southern Political Scene 1938–1948* (Gainesville, Fla., 1948) is a useful contemporary collection of articles on political developments in the South in the period covered. Jasper B. Shannon, *Toward a New Politics in the South* (Nashville,

1949) and Alexander Heard, *A Two-Party South?* (Chapel Hill, 1952) are similarly useful.

The following contemporary articles proved valuable: Emile B. Adler, "Why the Dixiecrats Failed," *Journal of Politics*, XV (August, 1953), 356–369; Ellis Arnall, "The Democrats Can Win," *Atlantic Monthly*, Vol. 182 (October, 1948), 33–38; William G. Carleton, "Dilemma of the Dixiecrats," *Virginia Quarterly Review*, XXIV (July, 1948), 336–353; Helen Fuller, "The New Confederacy," *New Republic*, CXIX (November 1, 1948), 10–14; John Temple Graves, "Revolution in the South," *Virginia Quarterly Review*, XXVI (April 1, 1950), 190–223; Fletcher M. Green, "Resurgent Southern Sectionalism, 1933–1955," *North Carolina Historical Review*, XXXIII (April, 1956), 222–240; Richard Hofstadter, "From Calhoun to the Dixiecrats," *Social Research*, XVI (June, 1949), 135–150; Sarah H. Lemmon, "Ideology of the Dixiecrat Movement," *Social Forces*, XXX (December, 1951), 162–171; A. G. Mezerik, "Dixie in Black and White," *Nation*, CLXIV (April 19, 1947), 449–456; Howard W. Odum, "Social Change in the South," *Journal of Politics*, X, No. 2 (May, 1948), 242–258; Eugene Peacock, "Why Are the Dixiecrats," *Christian Century*, Vol. 65 (September, 1948), 975–977; Thomas Sancton, "White Supremacy—Crisis or Plot?" *Nation*, CLXVI (July 24, 1948), 95–98; J. B. Shannon, "Political Philosophy for an Industrial South," *South Atlantic Quarterly*, Vol. 47 (October, 1948), 459–468; Mary H. Vorse, "The South Has Changed," *Harper's Magazine*, CXCIX (July, 1949); O. Douglas Weeks, "White Primary 1944–48," *American Political Science Review*, Vol. 42 (June, 1948), 500–510; Aubrey L. Williams, "There Is a Break," *Nation*, CLXIX (August 6, 1949), 128–130.

W. Bradley Twitty, *Y'All Come* (Nashville, 1962) is an uncritical and superficial biography of Folsom written almost as a campaign biography. James E. Folsom, *Speeches of Gov. James E. Folsom, 1947–1950* (Wetumpka, Ala., n. d.) is a useful compilation of speeches that captures much of the spirit and flavor of the man and time. Osmos Lanier, Jr., "The First Administration of James Elisha Folsom, Governor of Alabama," unpublished master's thesis, Alabama Polytechnic Institute (Auburn University), 1959, was useful. Marshall Frady, *Wallace* (New York, 1969) and the chapter on George C. Wallace in Robert Sherrill, *Gothic Politics in the Deep South: Stars of the New Confederacy*, revised edition (New York, 1969) contain popularized but essentially accurate descriptions of Folsom's administrations as background to the emergence of Wallace in the 1960's.

Two speeches by Frank M. Dixon, printed in *Vital Speeches of the Day* ("The Dangers of Centralization in Government," VIII, 621–624, and "Crossroads Democracy," IX, 236–240) provide insight into the political outlook of a leader of the Dixiecrats. Two unpublished master's theses were most helpful in the treatment of the Dixiecrat revolt in Alabama: Gladys King Burns, "The Alabama Dixiecrat Revolt of 1948," Auburn University, 1965, and Delores Anne Hobbs, "States' Rights Movement of 1948," Samford University, 1968. Paul Maxwell Smith, "Loyalists and States' Righters in the Democratic Party of Alabama, 1949–1954," unpublished master's thesis, Auburn University, 1966, was of great aid in understanding the aftermath of the Dixiecrat revolt in the state. J. Barton Starr, "Birmingham and the Dixiecrat Convention of

1948," *Alabama Historical Quarterly,* Vol. 32, Numbers 1 and 2 (Spring and Summer, 1970), 23–50, supplemented the treatment in Burns and Hobbs.

The dearth of literature in print on the Dixiecrats persists, but the gap is being filled, in other states as in Alabama, as theses and dissertations on the topic appear with increasing frequency. James A. Loveless, "The Dixiecrat Revolt of 1948," unpublished master's thesis, Stetson University, 1968, is useful. Robert Louis Pritchard, "Southern Politics and the Truman Administration: Georgia as a Test Case," unpublished doctoral dissertation, University of California at Los Angeles, 1970; James G. Banks, "Strom Thurmond and the Revolt Against Modernity," unpublished doctoral dissertation, Kent State University, 1970; Richard Calvin Ethridge, "Mississippi's Role in the Dixiecrat Movement," Mississippi State University, 1971; Peter Ros Henriques, "John S. Battle and Virginia Politics, 1948–1953," unpublished doctoral dissertation, University of Virginia, 1971; Ann Mathison McLaurin, "The Role of the Dixiecrats in the 1948 Election," unpublished doctoral dissertation, University of Oklahoma, 1972; Ann Celeste Hasting, "Interparty Struggle: Harry S. Truman, 1945–1948," unpublished doctoral dissertation, St. Louis University, 1972; and Gary Clifford Ness, "The States' Rights Democratic Movement of 1948," unpublished doctoral dissertation, Duke University, 1972, are all recent works which treat the Dixiecrat revolt.

An excellent brief essay by Richard S. Kirkendall, "Election of 1948," in Arthur M. Schlesinger, Jr., and Fred L. Israel, eds., *History of American Presidential Elections 1789–1968,* Vol. IV, 3099–3146, puts the 1948 presidential election in perspective. Also useful are Irwin Ross, *The Loneliest Campaign: The Truman Victory of 1948* (1968); Jules Abels, *Out of the Jaws of Victory* (1959); and Cabell Phillips, *The Truman Presidency: The History of a Triumphant Succession* (1966).

There are a number of books and articles on the period following 1950 in Alabama. Donald Strong's chapter on Alabama in William C. Harvard, ed., *The Changing Politics of the South* (Baton Rouge, 1972) is a comprehensive, brief treatment. Strong's *Urban Republicanism in the South* (University, Ala., 1960) should also be consulted. The Frady biography of Wallace, mentioned above, is a highly opinionated and colorful account of the career of the man who replaced Folsom as a dominant force in Alabama politics. Bill Jones, *The Wallace Story* (Northport, Ala., 1966), is a biography written by a former press secretary to Wallace. A more critical appraisal of Wallace and of events in the 1950's and '60's by an unabashed admirer of Folsom is Charles Morgan, *A Time to Speak* (New York, 1964).

The number of books and articles on political and social developments in the South since the 1954 Brown decision is already overwhelming. Two by Numan V. Bartley are particularly useful: *The Rise of Massive Resistance* (Baton Rouge, 1969) and *From Thurmond to Wallace* (Baltimore, 1970).

Finally, although the interpretations and conclusions in the text must rest on the evidence cited, there are two volumes, in addition to the works of Woodward and Key cited above, which have been important in shaping the larger perspective within which this topic was approached: Dewey W. Grantham, *The Democratic South* (Athens, Georgia, 1963) and T. Harry Williams, *Romance and Realism in Southern Politics* (Athens, Georgia, 1961).

INDEX